# POPULAR MUSIC, GENDER, AND POSTMODERNISM

# POPULAR MUSIC, GENDER, AND POSTMODERNISM

## Anger Is an Energy

## Neil Nehring

**SAGE** Publications
*International Educational and Professional Publisher*
Thousand Oaks   London   New Delhi

*For information:*

SAGE Publications, Inc.
2455 Teller Road
Thousand Oaks, California 91320
E-mail: order@sagepub.com

SAGE Publications Ltd.
6 Bonhill Street
London EC2A 4PU
United Kingdom

SAGE Publications India Pvt. Ltd.
M-32 Market
Greater Kailash I
New Delhi 110 048 India

Printed in the United States of America

*Library of Congress Cataloging-in-Publication Data*

Nehring, Neil, 1957-
   Popular music, gender, and postmodernism : Anger is an energy / Neil
Nehring.
      p.   cm.
   Includes bibliographical references and index.
   ISBN 0-7619-0835-8 (cloth). — ISBN 0-7619-0836-6 (pbk.)
   1. Punk rock music—History and criticism.  2. Feminism and music.
3. Anger in music.  4. Postmodernism.  I. Title.
   ML3534.N44  1997
   781.66—dc21                                      97-4590

This book is printed on acid-free paper.

97  98  99  00  01  02  03  10  9  8  7  6  5  4  3  2  1

| | |
|---|---|
| *Acquiring Editor:* | Margaret Seawell |
| *Editorial Assistant:* | Renée Piernot |
| *Production Editor:* | Astrid Virding |
| *Production Assistant:* | Denise Santoyo |
| *Copy Editor:* | Joyce Kuhn |
| *Typesetter/Designer:* | Danielle Dillahunt |
| *Cover Designer:* | Ravi Balasuriya |

# Contents

## PART 2

# Acknowledgments

This book is for my daughter Julia, who was born shortly after I came home from a Babes in Toyland/My Bloody Valentine show. After hearing her first musical composition, "I Want a Blue Guitar" (the only line), I'm confident she'll grow up to be a Riot Grrrl.

I owe a great deal to many of my students over the years, who have not only kept me up to date but also supplied crucial insights into all the issues in this book. I want to thank Chidsey Dickson, in particular, for his generosity in sharing useful material and for his general encouragement. The many bright young people I have known possess a decency—an honesty and hopefulness—sorely lacking in many older intellectuals. My conviction on this account animates the entirety of the book: It's why *I'm* angry, if you have to ask.

Further confirmation of my outrage appeared just as the book went to press, when the postmodern cynicism that I document went through still another recycling with regard to alternative rock: see Thomas (Tom) Frank's more-fatalistic-than-thou response ("Authenticity Crisis, Baby," *Nation*, 3 February 1997, p. 10) to Jon Pareles ("Alternatives to Alternative: What's Next?," *New York Times,* 15 September 1996, sec. H, p. 34).

Parts of this book have been published in another version, which the author gratefully acknowledges permission to reprint: "Rock Around the Academy," *American Literary History* 5 (1993). Reprinted by permission of Oxford University Press.

# Introduction

My favorite new song in 1992 was Bikini Kill's "Carnival." Among the first Riot Grrrl groups, BK delivers a visceral feminism through punk rock. At the time I was a 35-year-old SWM (straight white male) English professor, married and a new parent, and fortunate enough to live in the musical hotbed of Austin, Texas. The only changes since then are that I'm older, of course, have another child, and go out less than ever.

By the standard that "difference" in identity from SWMs determines authenticity, it may seem like sexploitation on my part to offer a testimonial to Riot Grrrls and to what feminism has to teach us about the political importance of anger. My previous work admittedly doesn't bode well for such a project. I've featured too many white males and expressed too confident a faith that humanity can cope with the "postmodern" world. That easy sort of generalization about humanity, in particular, is something I have since regretted. As black and feminist scholars have pointed out about invoking humanity in general, a white male speaking confidently for everyone else ignores the privilege that allows him to be so secure, so untroubled by the ambiguities and contradictions of individual and collective identity. In the worst instances, it's often implicit that only white males actually count. The chief culprit in either case, historically, has been the vision bequeathed to us by the Enlightenment of a society united through the free exercise of reason. That faith in reason developed over the century spanning John Locke's *Two Treatises on Government* (1690) and Thomas Jefferson's Declaration of Independence (1776). After or "post-" to the modern world's long, seemingly futile quest since the eighteenth century for a reasonable society, many postmodern theorists, including some feminists, would discard any conception of humanity as a whole.

But a number of feminists have argued that we can still express hope for something like the Enlightenment ideal as long as we are careful to stipulate that everyone must "participate in defining the terms of interaction." [1] I wish I'd taken greater care in the past to note that I was aware of all this. Thus I want to make it clear at the outset that along with my faith in people and hope for change, directed against theorists of postmodernism, I recognize the pitfalls in arriving at a truly just, egalitarian society. Among the potential pitfalls is being an SWM telling others, including non-SWMs, about the matter. This is especially true at a time when the "angry white male," even after an extreme case committed mass murder, enjoys a legitimacy denied other groups. I will certainly take pains to counteract this development by distinguishing his violent, reactionary anger in defense of the status quo from a humane anger at injustice.

I would have profited even more crucially, however, from investigating feminist philosophy focused on emotion, which offers the strongest possible support of my main purpose in earlier work, to validate and promote negation. The term *negation* refers to challenging conformist common sense about not only how to think but also how to feel. The anarchist Michael Bakunin took the concept from the philosopher Georg Hegel (who only had in mind the exercise of reason) in the middle of the nineteenth century. In close proximity to anarchism, the avant-garde subsequently pursued negation in art, most notably in Lautréamont's *Les Chants de Maldoror* (1869) and *Poésies* (1870), and the concept has been a constant in radical art right up through the Situationist International and its devotees in punk rock.

This new book about anger, the emotion at the heart of negation, atones for my neglect of feminism—but not out of guilt or servility, and not just because I missed some useful stuff. I want to atone especially because I made a crucial discovery, that feminism provides an antidote to a postmodern thesis I have been watching spread from purportedly radical academic work into the mass media. That thesis, the subject of Part 1, holds that any expression of rebellion in contemporary culture is inauthentic, merely a pose. It is supposedly impossible for any emotional appeal in a commercial medium like popular music to be anything but a prostituted imposture, whether Kurt Cobain's vitriol or Michael

Bolton's treacle. There are actually two closely related ideas here: All expression, even the most rebellious forms, is tamed and made completely inauthentic by its "incorporation" (sometimes "recuperation") into multinational corporate capitalism; and, more specifically, emotion is somehow detached from any meaning or significance in the process. Any performer's emotional commitment, as a result, is either transparently phony (like Bolton) or simply inarticulate and incoherent (like Cobain), making it impossible for anyone to take that emotion seriously and to make any commitment in return. This dual thesis is applied to alternative rock, hip-hop, and Riot Grrrls, and was most extensively and harrowingly employed to ridicule Cobain's group, Nirvana.

The ideas above aren't really postmodern at all, however. Since the eighteenth century and the birth of aesthetics (or the philosophy of art), academics and other intellectuals have held that meaningless emotional appeals are characteristic of the low or popular arts produced by the marketplace. The word *aesthetics,* ironically, derives from Greek terms, such as *aisthesis,* that refer to feelings. But Immanuel Kant, in his formative, highly influential treatise on aesthetics, *Critique of Judgment* (1790), announced that the taste for emotion fed by "mercenary" or commercial art is "always barbaric." [2] This loathing of emotion follows the general philosophical belief (until very recently) that emotion belongs to the body, and thus is no guide whatsoever to understanding. Emotion is inferior to reason, from this view, which is not to say that the passions are without power, for they presumably always threaten to overcome the mind. This fear of the disruptive power of emotion is as much political as philosophical, always bearing at some level a concern over subordinate groups getting out of control. The fields of aesthetics and philosophy have traditionally been self-contradictory in this regard, seeking to control the real danger posed by emotion by deriding it for its supposed weakness—often in terms of feminine weakness. (This is another good reason why some feminists aren't too wild about the legacy of the eighteenth century and its priority on reason.) The more specific argument that has come down to us, couched in terms of postmodernism, is that the mindlessness of emotional types means they can never adequately articulate the causes of their emotions, whether in art or in life. The ways in which an audience responds to the expression of anger and resentment in a form like popular music are supposedly always inarticulate, too, leading only to apathy and passivity.

Applying the traditional negative view of emotion to popular songs, recent postmodern critics find the expression of anger and resentment crippled by commercialization. Part 1 of this book details how academics and journalists, out of a variety of motives, have tried to will a hopeless postmodern condition into being. The result, says Andrew Goodwin, is "one of the most bizarre developments in the brief history of media and cultural studies, in which abstruse French theory has 'trickled down' into the popular consciousness, . . . so that the word 'postmodern' reached record stores, magazines and television programmes just a few years after it entered the academy." Postmodernists, he adds, "will no doubt feel that this phenomenon is itself hugely postmodern." [3] That the mass media have exploited academic postmodernism hardly reflects the accuracy of its insights, however, but instead indicates their usefulness in denying the authenticity of expressions of anger and discontent.

Knowing the historical context for this contempt is vital. As Peter Stearns argues in his history of intensifying instruction in emotional restraint, *American Cool* (1994), emotional standards have a long life, requiring that the study of "shorter-term variations" in them be presented in a "larger synthesis." [4] Seen in the larger context of traditional intellectual loathing for emotional appeals in popular art, recent judgments on angry music actually undercut rather than confirm claims for an unusually desperate, even apocalyptic postmodern age. And the specific thesis on emotion that passes for postmodern is hardly new, either. The "discovery" that rebellious anger, in particular, has lost any connection with commitment and action only reproduces a specific form the philosophical abuse of emotion has taken in the century since Friedrich Nietzsche: the demonizing of radical politics as disabling resentment, or *ressentiment*—an emotion of the weak, never acted upon. Nietzsche denigrated *ressentiment* for its supposed limitation to rationalized morality, first Christian and then socialist, which the powerless substituted for real action; postmodern critics actually go him one better by arguing that anger and defiance have become entirely disconnected from reason. In discounting resentful persons for lack of insight and action, theorists of postmodernism, even on the Left, consider them ill equipped by mass culture; establishment journalism seizes on this view to conclude that the resentful are simply unfit by nature.

My essential concern is with these forces at work above and beyond music, which at times work fairly directly on it. That direct work occurs not just when the press sufficiently alarms authority about contemporary music but especially when academics and journalists convince young people themselves that their efforts are inevitably futile, precisely what authority wants the young to believe. If young people often account for their anger as inarticulate or nihilistic, it is no wonder they do so, with so much instruction to that effect not only by the dominant culture but by "progressive" teachers as well. Even students with social consciences, as a result, repeatedly tell me that "you can't change anything." Broadcasting the postmodern belief in the futility and aimlessness of angry music, therefore, is far more insidious than the merely laughable denunciations of "aggressive and hostile rebellion"—lumped together with drug abuse and sexual perversion—by transparent idiots like the infamous Parents' Music Resource Center (PMRC).[5] Fortunately, much of the anger of young people is directed precisely against the establishment's discourse about youth, such as the marketing of futility in the form of Generation X, a label spawned by the proliferation of academic postmodernism into mass culture. Anger at the status quo has found the right shape when it brings "a renaissance of hope," as the editors of *Angry Women* put it, "stuck as we are in the midst of [a] culture of cynicism which has helped implant a widespread attitude of passivity." [6]

In terms of preserving the possibility of a rebirth of hope, perhaps the most successful radical politics at present are found in the angriest forms of popular music. With political institutions closed to all but the wealthy, that acerbic music has been the most conspicuous public voice of protest, almost singlehandedly keeping visions of humane social change alive in the mass media, where fissures in corporate dominance still exist. I do not mean that progressive change is going to grow directly out of the music but that the music has the potential to reawaken efforts in other areas, by offering instruction in the possibility of dissent at a time when it seems futile with respect to conventional politics.

I would question, though, whether apologies for attributing an important political function to popular music are really in order. Innumerable commentators have pointed out that no boundary exists any longer between entertainment and politics, especially after Ronald Reagan's presidency. Increasingly expensive, substanceless spectacles, posing as politics, have effectively disenfranchised the majority of the citizenry. And when the authoritarians have aestheticized and shut down politics, to paraphrase Walter Benjamin's conclusion to "The Work of Art in the Age of Mechanical Reproduction," dissidents out of necessity resort to politicizing the arts, where some access remains open.

Many on the Left, unfortunately, have failed to see "the popular and democratic elements in daily life because of the forms in which they are presently packaged," says Stuart Hall. A distaste for the products of mass culture creates a blind spot regarding the progressive "attitudes" that persist in many of the popular uses of those products. This is one reason why the Left has been so isolated, for no "popular political force" can emerge without being "a force in the popular cultures," a point the Right has long grasped and always been in a better financial position to exploit.[7] It's not that intellectuals and politicos on the Left don't know that any successful collective politics must have a basis in collective feeling; the problem is their contempt for less articulate or less explicitly political forms of anger.

A typically dismissive view of youth culture appears in the complaint of historian and political scientist Adolph Reed that the field of cultural studies "willfully inflates . . . youth fads . . . into the status of political movements," or even considers "youth culture's strategic importance . . . more vital than political work focused on government and public policy." The result, in his view, is a "don't worry, be-angry politics of posture," a label I can imagine being stuck on my book. But I fully agree with Reed, in fact, that "anger and self-definition are potential precursors to political action, but they don't constitute political action in themselves." The problem is his lack of interest in that anger, based on his belief that youthful alienation "is by definition resignation and quiescence," [8] a quite traditional association of emotion with intellectual passivity. Bereft of interest in the emotional "precursors" to political action, Reed sets aside the problem of just how young people are supposed to become radicalized in an authoritarian world—and to be as untroubled as he is over the origins of political action is just as facile as the position he attacks. (If my side's motto is "Don't worry, be angry," Reed's seems to be "Just do it!")

To approve only of those youths who somehow manage to become registered lobbyists denies the obvious fact that young people, as Simon Frith observed some time ago, necessarily "focus their politics on leisure . . . because they *lack* power" or any sort of access to political institutions. In the authoritarian climate of the 1990s, Henry Giroux points out, their situation has worsened considerably: "Once lauded as a symbol of hope for the future, youth are now scorned as a threat to the existing social order," particularly in exaggerations of the extent of violent crime committed by the young. As is the case for other groups without power, the victims get "blamed for the problems they experience in a society marked by escalating poverty, unemployment, and diminished opportunities." At the same time, though, indictments of the young take a self-contradictory, trivializing form, as in the condescending postmodern view that "coming-of-age rebellion" on the part of young people at every level of society is merely a "pathology or stylized narcissism" preyed upon by the marketplace. But considering that the young "get the lowest pay, have fewer rights, and suffer more structural regulation than anyone" not in prison, Donna Gaines argues, those problems necessarily have to be "examined and resisted through cultural processes, expressed in cultural products—music, style, dance." I see no reason why young people would want to enlist in traditional activism, moreover, when a politico like Reed considers them twerps for feeling strongly about their leisure pastimes. Gaines, in contrast, rejects the assumption "that youth culture is prefabricated and mass, that kids consume and participate in garbage culture without a critical eye." [9]

Perhaps the most relentless promoter of that assumption has been Tom Frank, editor of a much vaunted popularizer of postmodern ideas called *The Baffler.* Much like Reed, indicating the critical mass building up among "serious" intellectuals, he chides more positive academic work on popular culture for "its fetishization of the angry, alienated subaltern." Such celebration presumably serves only to acquaint "the children of the well-to-do with their proper roles [as] 'good' fans and consumers, [finding] pleasure in the masscult text and ourselves in our subcultures. The most revolutionary thing we can do, it seems, is to lie back and enjoy it." *The Baffler,* by the way, is funded by a noted cultural conservative, the novelist and literary scholar Saul Bellow, who is understandably happy to sponsor divisiveness on the left over academic attention to mass and popular culture (or to producers and consumers, respectively).

Frank's views accord more specifically with an increasingly frequent attack on "cultural populism," a vice attributed to cultural studies by scholars concerned with political economy. To use Frank's terms, political economy concerns "the operations of the advertising, film, or broadcasting industries" at the production end of culture, as well as those of governmental policy (Reed's concern), which are presumably "not a valid subject of study" as far as the populists are concerned.[10] Uncritical populists in academia are actually few and far between (leaving John Fiske the usual suspect for several years now); the real target of political economy is any and all scholarship focused on popular artists and their audiences, as if the entirety of aesthetic and sociological work had somehow ceased to hold any utility. With repetition, therefore, the accusation of populism has started to seem like a stalking horse for a pessimistic repudiation of continuing creative possibilities in mass culture. Virtually everyone is aware that mass communication is dominated by corporate conglomerates—daily news reports celebrate each new merger within the media monopoly—and to insist that we focus on that fact alone is merely in keeping with more fatalistic versions of postmodernism, with which political economy must now be considered synonymous.

Cultural studies, moreover, has always considered work on production essential to its efforts to construct a fuller, more adequate picture of the dynamics of mass and popular culture. By conjuring up cultural populism and divorcing themselves from cultural studies, political-economy types have actually been the ones openly expressing the belief that only their work holds any validity. Their positivist insistence that only empirical science is serious, coupled with postmodern pessimism, leads Jim McGuigan to assert with complete confidence in *Cultural Populism* (1992) that the "youthful consumer is a . . . construct of consumer capitalism" whose power is overstated in cultural studies. Cultural populists supposedly rely on little more than sheer assertion to the contrary. But the political-economy perspective, as expressed by the otherwise estimable Herbert Schiller, offers only elitist counterassertion emboldened simply by its longer tradition, which dates to romantic disdain for the arts of the marketplace (a history I elaborate in Chapter 2). Cultural studies, he claims, is misbegotten because the various audiences for mass culture "are all subject to the rule of market forces and the domination of capital," and thus their capacities are routinely "overwhelmed [by] the commanders of the social order." [11] The obvious objection to this view is that political economy does not stand like a colossus over completely helpless individuals and groups but has its products subjected to a variety of idiosyncratic, sometimes even iconoclastic interpretations and uses.

The best work in cultural studies is not a simple populist reversal of an older misanthropic aloofness, however, but instead makes a virtue of the often ridiculed distance of scholars from popular life. If not overly detached, that distance provides a vantage point from which to observe larger patterns not evident to those heavily involved in a particular subculture. As Raymond Williams puts it, "It is with the discovery of patterns . . . that any useful cultural analysis begins." The goal of reconstructing a pattern should be to "reveal unexpected identities and correspondences in hitherto separately considered activities," such as the ostensibly distinct activities of journalists and scholarly theorists. Dick Hebdige, a well-known sociologist of youth subcultures, adds that "by pursuing a limited number of themes . . . across a fairly wide range of discourses it may be possible . . . to modify the received wisdom" [12]—such as the fatalism fostered by the cynical strains of postmodernism.

The primary "theme" I pursue is the dismissal of angry music and its audience by postmodernists on the Left, due in particular to their blind spot regarding emotion, and by journalists exploiting academic ideas. When I see music I love dismissed this way—and knowing from my own experience that there's nothing inarticulate or irrational about the music or many of its fans—I want to help fight back, and the best ally I have found in this cause is feminism. Feminist arguments in defense of emotions like anger usefully support music, like that of the Riot Grrrls, that in turn embodies and verifies those intellectual propositions. The synthesis of those two subjects in Part 2 serves to refute the establishment journalists and postmodern academics drawn together in Part 1 and their pattern of contempt for angry music. Part 1 is my indictment, Part 2 my advocacy; Part 1, not coincidentally, largely concerns men, whereas Part 2 features women.

Among those women, feminist philosophers, in particular, have extended the case of "cognitivism" (in philosophy) and "social constructionism" (in psychology) for the interdependence of emotion and reason. These scholars argue persuasively that emotion always results from appraising or judging a social situation and thus contributes significantly to reason. The further argument of feminist philosophy is that emotions are indivisibly a matter of the body and the mind, of physical responses and articulated judgment. Male cognitivists and social constructionists may take emotion seriously, but they leave rationality supreme in construing emotion as a matter purely of judgment, distinct from its manifestation in physical feelings.

The causes of emotion do eventually need to be fairly fully articulated or rationalized, I should stress, although such evaluation should always be considered an intrinsic part of emotional experience, not a means to some therapeutic removal of ostensibly negative feelings. Especially at a time when "unchecked greed runs rampant and the distance between the haves and the have-nots becomes wider," says Andrea Juno, "anger can be a sane, creative" force, but only if it becomes "conscious enough." [13] Otherwise, emotions like anger can wind up directed at the wrong objects, as is the case when the perfectly reasonable resentment of less privileged white males, after the ravages of the class war being waged by corporate capitalism, is channeled into hatred of government—not entirely without reason, considering the dominance of public institutions by hirelings of big business.

In accounting for the whole person, as opposed to various cognitivist schemes dividing terms like *affect, emotion, feeling,* and *passion* between reason and the body, feminist work on emotion also provides an antidote to the explosion of postmodern work on the body. The abstraction and gloom of postmodern theory leads it to treat the body as either an inarticulate instrument of power or, at best, a potentially unruly "desiring machine." When the subject of emotion does come up in postmodern theory, another division in terminology occurs: *Affect* designates the range of emotional possibilities organized by power—as part of its orchestration of bodily desire—and presumably dictates any particular *emotion* as subjects of power experience, leaving emotion of little interest. A proper understanding of emotion offers a way out of the trap posed by the choices aesthetics has given us for 200 years now, culminating in postmodernism, between either the mind alone or its polar opposite, a purely sensory body, essentially mindless and even emotionless, however disorderly it may be. Part 2 is intended not only as a counterargument to postmodern theory but also as an indication of how this dichotomy might be surmounted in thinking and writing about popular music, by understanding emotion as a mediator between the body and the mind, and biology and society.

Given the inherent rationality of emotions, there's nothing odd at all about a book called *Anger Is an Energy* beginning with reference to the Enlightenment and hope for a more just, reasonable world. Anger is in fact precisely what needs to be factored into that quest, says Ellen Willis: "The problem with the Enlightenment . . . was not its belief in understanding, but its failure to understand a culture whose civilized veneer concealed mass . . . frustration and rage." [14] The mean-spirited plutocracy in which we now live makes little pretense of being civilized, apart from vapid talk about "values," but that simply makes the importance of anger to political change all the more apparent. Political ideas and programs alone, that is, will be powerless to effect change unless they have an unmistakable basis in anger at injustice. That indignation must be equally as strong as the anger that demagogues—who are quite attuned to the politics of emotion—encourage in defenders of the status quo like the angry white male. At a time when politicians and media hucksters "have no commitment to what intellectuals recognize as legitimate and rational exchange," as Michael Bérubé observes, some blunt response in kind is necessary. (Again, the Left knows this but too often has a very limited conception of what kind of responses count.)

But "neither can we simply abandon discursive models of social contestation," Bérubé points out,[15] or we will indeed sink in the morass of anger that mainstream media already construct out of the Left and Right alike, as they like to put it. Their distortions typically require turning all the way back to the 1960s and the Weathermen to suggest that everyone on the Left is a potential bomber, a scenario supposedly confirmed by the Unabomber, or that the counterculture in general spawned a somehow identical antigovernment stance in the current right-wing militia movement, although the latter has no interest in democracy. Thus one important "discursive" task is to distinguish insubordinate anger from reactionary anger, defensive of the status quo. Such a distinction would counteract not only establishment journalists who denounce all anger but also their opponents who celebrate "anger's potential for aggression as anti-social" or antiauthoritarian, a view that overlooks anger's "conservative possibilities," notes Peter Lyman. Anger often takes the form, for example, of the "moral outrage by which society defends its mores and sacred values." Anger at injustice argues from moral grounds, too, but its difference from conformist "moral outrage" is clear: the latter "is trained, not learned; and is intolerant, not flexible." [16]

Reactionary anger is particularly widespread and approved at present, as is evident in the behavior of the mass media: At the same time they demonize and ridicule anger on the part of subordinate groups, reactionary anger, in contrast, is tolerated if not actively encouraged because it reinforces existing conditions. Anger defensive of privilege, like Rush Limbaugh's, is broadcast to a far greater extent and with little or no similar instruction about its dementia. There are few large commercial sponsors, unsurprisingly, for someone on the Left who would challenge Limbaugh's orgy of hate and lies. (With organized labor prohibited from advertising, Jim Hightower's radio show was cancelled in 1995 for lack of business sponsorship—although not, the public was assured, because the ABC radio network had just been taken over by the conservative Disney conglomerate.) The Right, as a result, has been more successful in exploiting resentment in the recent past, to the extent that anger became synonymous with the white male after the 1994 elections. This is unfortunate, and one reason I want to emphasize feminist arguments for the importance of anger articulated by other groups (including the many white males who aren't "Limbaughnazis").

The anger of both progressives and reactionaries, however, may actually result from a similar cause: namely, the current widespread social and economic anxiety. Resentments with essentially the same origin, in other words, can find very different, more and less accurate directions to take in choosing objects on which to fixate. What continuing interest there is in Max Scheler's *Ressentiment* (1915), for example, is due to his apparent diagnosis of the roots of fascism, yet Scheler himself assumed he was dissecting its complete opposite, socialism. The choices we ought to prefer in judging the direction a person's or group's anger takes are those that reflect concern, empathy, and tolerance for the greatest number of people as well as a sense of humor directed at oneself and at one's targets (so much for Limbaugh on every count). This pluralism, however, is precisely what the mouthpieces of the ruling class, following Friedrich Nietzsche, wish to denigrate as the weak-minded humanitarianism produced by resentment of injustice.

However differently people focus their anger—on the powerful or on the powerless—it shares something else besides the same fundamental basis in economic anxiety: Virtually everyone agrees that anger in the face of injustice is not only justifiable but imperative. But here again, what should be our common cause is split by the corporate and political sponsorship of a divisive anger pitting those with some power against those with less—the anger of men against women and of whites against nonwhites. Usually, the anger of privileged groups needs some self-justification, and because anger at injustice is generally felt to be justifiable, the privileged habitually claim to be victimized by the underprivileged. Thus we have the spectacle of the relatively affluent claiming that the country is being bled dry by welfare recipients, who are popularly believed to consist entirely of unmarried black teenage mothers also posing a threat to the nation's morality (and in more extreme arguments, to its gene pool); of whites battling affirmative action as reverse discrimination; of male-dominated antiabortion groups out to end reproductive choice in the guise of saving fetuses from their mothers; of the men's movement trying to preserve the family by restoring women to domestic roles; and of popular entertainment about women sexually harassing men. When those with at least some power or social advantage express anger at supposed injustice *against themselves,* committed by those challenging that advantage, anger serves to maintain the status quo. Nietzsche and all of his successors who denigrate resentment are themselves full of resentment toward those perceived as threats.

When the motive is the preservation of privilege, moreover, we typically find the most violent anger, such as that directed by white heterosexual males toward gays, minorities, and women. Given the actual physical violence that men commit against women and the injustice that the criminal justice system commits against blacks and Latinos, the pose of victimization by white males is a pretty thin veneer. More naked assertions of power, therefore, especially by "respectable" individuals such as corporate CEOs and politicians, are justified in terms of another kind of anger widely deemed appropriate and valid: not anger "involved with a sense of injustice or unfairness in an abstract or [social] sense, but in a more personal sense of having one's own rights, property, or authority challenged or limited in some way." [17]

The recent "property rights" movement, for example, has been crafted by big farming, mining, and real estate interests to appeal to this sense of appropriate outrage at personal deprivation, in this case the supposed injustice against private property committed by governmental efforts to protect the common good, particularly the environment. The property-rights types, revealingly, often employ a rhetoric of violence that reflects their actual privilege—a wealthy, macho-ridden real estate developer in my hometown publicly threatens environmentalists with beatings. Consistent with the blaming of victims noted earlier, our culture applauds these bullies in business. With the exception of the brief-lived attention to corporate downsizing prompted by Pat Buchanan's ersatz populist presidential campaign, the news media chortle over CEOs vituperating nuns, of all people, for daring to write letters protesting corporate policies, while mass entertainment, as many critics have noted, celebrates violence committed by the agents of property in law enforcement.

The primary reason why feminism has defended anger, despite the misbegotten forms it has taken, actually involves the one exception to the traditional association of women with emotionality. In both academia and the culture at large, anger has been the only emotion approved of in men and "exempted in everyday discourse from the expectation that women feel and express more emotion than men." [18] Anxiety is certainly expressed over the need for men to control their anger (except in approved outlets such as sports, as Stearns indicates in *American Cool*), but in women, anger is simply considered an abnormality that must be suppressed. Casting anger as incoherent "rage" has thus been a staple in efforts to reverse the gains of the women's movement, with the result evident in young women who say "I'm not a feminist, but . . ." and proceed to express a perfectly feminist position. They issue the opening disclaimer because they have learned that feminists are angry fanatics as well as bitter unattractive women. Condemning anger has also become, more recently, a means of indicting young people disenchanted with a society in which opportunity continually diminishes for everyone outside the small minority in the ruling class.

No matter how socially inclusive my work becomes, though, by catching up with feminist advocacy of insubordinate emotion, as an SWM I am still stuck with the most banal of identities, considering the unprecedented exploration of ethnicity, gender, race, and sexuality going on in popular music. A direct correspondence between taste and identity, however, has hardly been characteristic of the reception (or use) of popular music. A large part of the audience for popular music gets left out, as a result, in any argument claiming that only a direct equivalence between lived experience and a particular musical genre allows a correct understanding of the music. The distinction of insiders and outsiders doesn't hold up when some affluent white kids enjoy hardcore rap for relatively genuine, legitimate reasons, such as sharing the performers' anger at injustice, and nearly middle-aged college professors enjoy feminist punk groups for similar reasons. Hip-hop artists and Riot Grrrl bands, among many others, certainly operate from conscious identity politics, but the people who consume their music are quite diverse, and thus the meanings made of any particular music are, too. Of course, that diversity includes such regrettable cases as the "fratboys" at a Rage Against the Machine show described by Valerie Agnew of 7 Year Bitch, who "were just singing along with rebellion" and "did *not* get the message at all."[19]

The most interesting thing about popular music, in fact, is precisely "its blurring of insider/outsider boundaries." The "best studies of popular music," says Simon Frith, recognize the blurring and "don't try to pin down sounds according to existing social maps, but rather allow the music to make its own political argument." [20] In keeping with this admonition, I will simply stress the legitimacy of the anger shared by contemporary forms of music made by men and women of different races, especially in light of the effort of establishment media to demonize that anger, which makes the political import of those musics quite evident.

I have more to say about gender in music, though, especially in Chapters 6 and 7, than I do about hip-hop and race, which appear throughout but are less extensively developed. I hope it's obvious that I concentrate on the Riot Grrrls and other women in rock because the crux of this book, advancing a better understanding of emotion, derives from feminist philosophy. To transfer its work on anger too far within the context of hip-hop would pose a serious contradiction, moreover, as the anger of many male hip-hop artists is directed precisely at women, to the extent that a number of female critics have indicted the genre for misogyny. Whatever the merits of that view, I couldn't add much in any case to Tricia Rose's well-known *Black Noise* (1994), which has already surveyed not only the more and less sensible objects of "rage" in hip-hop but also the considerable number of female performers. Comparable critical studies of the Riot Grrrls and their aftermath, on the other hand, have yet to appear—the most extensive surveys have been the collections of interviews in Andrea Juno's *Angry Women in Rock* (1996) and Amy Raphael's *Grrrls: Viva Rock Divas* (1995)—so I feel more confident that I have something to contribute in that area.

Another concern with respect to identity involves the feminist point that because the personal is part of the political I need to be explicit about the link between the areas I have chosen to study and my own identity, or my personal experience, interests, and tastes. Because I am not at first glance, as an SWM, a poster boy for identity politics resisting the new fascism, I want to emphasize that loving punk in 1977 required a genuine bent for difference, if difference largely among white male voices. After a very young infatuation with the Rolling Stones when they still seemed to epitomize rebellion and decadence, with the beginning of their endless decline in 1973 I really cut my teeth on sexually ambiguous glitter rockers like David Bowie, the New York Dolls, Lou Reed (formerly of the Velvet Underground), and Roxy Music, some of whom dressed in drag. I remember using Halloween as an excuse for dressing up as a New York Doll and being laughed at in school just for wearing a piece of paste jewelry on a string around my neck, à la Bowie, although a Stones pendant based on their tongue logo had been much admired. (Years later I was startled to learn that David Johansen of the Dolls had wondered in an interview if the group would reach a "kid in Kansas"—yes, David, you did.) The sexual implications were easily sloughed off; at a time well before homophobia arose to fill the vacuum left by the demise of Communism, when Alice Cooper and Elton John could easily take glitter mainstream, simply being bored with the state of rock music was an acceptable explanation for liking "fruity" performers like Bryan "The"

Ferry (as one Dan Fogelberg fan put it without too much rancor). Only with punk did the Velvet Underground's influence on everything deviant in the 1970s become fully apparent to me and, much later still, thanks to other aging academic music fans, the influence through the Velvets of gay culture, specifically the 1960s camp of Andy Warhol's Factory.

I still remember the subsequent emergence of punk rock around 1976-1977, the prehistory of Bikini Kill, as the most exciting time in my life. I visited the record store every day, always finding something new to fuel my complete disgust at the insanely unjust, plutocratic world we live in. Raving nihilism, as I heard it at the time, punk stoked my alienation; particularly appealing to my personal unhappiness was the loathing of romance by punks (not of women, mind you, except in cases like the Stranglers). Yet at the same time the music made me feel less alone by confirming that sane people did indeed still exist. As Greil Marcus says of the Mekons (who began their long, glorious career in the first punk era), "In a world ruled by a language one refuses to speak, they are a reminder there are still people one might want to meet." Although I only met a few of the performers (including, years later, the Mekons, and they were indeed fun to talk to), I met plenty of others in their audience who felt the same way I did, all of us, near and far, real and imagined, linked by knowing we were not alone in our outrage and refusal to conform and accept the status quo. Gina Birch of the Raincoats describes a feeling "so intense" in the late 1970s "that I really thought something profound was going to happen. Not only in music but in the world." [21]

I continue to this day to get emotional sustenance from music conveying both discontent and a concern with renewing common feeling. Coupling anger at authorities and conformists with goodwill toward everyone who resists them, that solidarity includes empathy for those who are suffering, however distant one's own experience. Contrary to postmodern ideas about affective dysfunction, says Hebdige, there remains a widespread belief that there is indeed "a reality 'out there,' that something real and something terrible . . . is happening somewhere else and that . . . all the rest of us" share responsibility for it. [22] Negation has a *positive* outcome, in other words, in keeping with its origin in Hegel's dialectical thought (which speaks of a negation of the real negation represented by conformity), here recast as a matter of emotion as well as logic. But I should also add that a few years after punk I arrived at full ideological as well as emotional deviance, embracing leftist politics. I will not let postmodern scoffers deny my experience and that of many others: I am here to attest that it is possible to be steered fairly directly, by popular music, toward fully conscious radicalization.

This is not to say that an avant-garde working in the popular arts should somehow fuel revolutionary change but, to reiterate, that its critical function is simply to hold open the possibility of refusing to go along, always a potential first step toward political renewal. As one eulogy for Kurt Cobain put it, "he believed in the communicative powers of popular music, [and] showed what was possible, even in this ugly and demoralized culture."[23] I am angry at postmodernists writing on rock music, academics and journalists alike, for claiming that we all should have moved beyond such an unhip expectation of music.

I cannot end my account of my enthusiasms with that impassioned climax, unfortunately, because now that I've relived the glory days, I need to address how personal taste affects my coverage of contemporary music. Apart from the considerations mentioned earlier regarding feminism and the state of current scholarship, the primary reason why I haven't written more on hip-hop involves the unpredictability of taste: As much as I like bitter punk and continue to gratuitously condemn hippies just as I did twenty years ago, my favorite hip-hop groups are ones that hardcore rap has derided precisely as laid-back hippies, such as De La Soul and P.M. Dawn. The hip-hop I listen to most, in other words, doesn't represent the part of the genre that suits a book on anger.

The best explanation I can offer for this anomaly occurred to me in reading Tricia Rose's description of a combination of flow, layering, and rupture in all the practices of hip-hop culture: breakdancing and graffiti as well as music. In music, rupture involves break beats, or the sort of abrupt rhythmic changes pioneered by James Brown. Punk, in contrast, is all flow, sometimes densely layered, depending on the recording budget, but seldom if ever marked by rupture—a song like Bikini Kill's "Carnival" is unvarying in its forward momentum. My taste isn't subtle, in other words, and has something to do with being uncomfortable about dancing: I like repetition of a few melodic hooks, a pop taste due no doubt to my age. Especially when combined with some punk speed, that's what gets me riled up to the bursting point and thus where I locate my musical politics. This is true even in the case of some less politicized and hyperaccelerated but equally unyielding songs such as the Fall's "Kurious Oranj" and My Bloody Valentine's "I Only Said." If that taste seems narrow, I would point out that my favorite recording of 1995 was Cornershop's *Woman's Gotta Have It,* on which self-styled "Western Orientals" cross the raga with the Velvet Underground.

I have different expectations of the break beats in hip-hop, which are just as visceral and often support voices just as strident as those in punk but are nonetheless something of a luxury or relief given the unrelenting music I like best. (Even in James Brown's case, in keeping with my taste for unbroken flow, my favorite song is one of his most stripped down and unvarying, "Brother Rapp.") If I want that luxury of "merely" enjoying music, the harder strains of Dr. Dre actually suit me as much as De La Soul—why would gangsta rap threaten me in my living room?—but if I can't have constant forward movement, due to hip-hop's characteristic rhythmic rupture, I admittedly find in De La Soul more of the repetition of melodic hooks that suits the pop side of my taste. (There are worse forms of old-fogeyism, I should think, such as the unexamined complaint that hip-hop as a whole is all beats and lacks melody, which often serves up racism in the guise of aesthetics.) The one thing I will concede, with respect to identity and taste, is that the difference between music that supplies motivation and music that is enjoyed with less fervor does have something to do with tastes one developed while coming of age. But if the music of my youth, such as glam-rock and punk, still influences the core of my tastes, the way new tastes keep accreting to it has been one of the pleasant surprises of growing older.

The final personal point I want to emphasize is that whatever you think of this book, don't think it's some calculated effort to "get with" identity politics via feminism. Don't think I don't, in the immortal words of Johnny Rotten in 1977, *mean it, maaan*—and *grrrl*. (Although the line signals the irony in "God Save the Queen," it also resonates more broadly as a declaration of seriousness.) My first book took its title from a line he wrote while in the Sex Pistols ("We're the flowers in the dustbin"); as John Lydon in Public Image Limited, he wrote the line that supplies this book's subtitle (in the 1986 song "Rise"). It's not that I admire him all that much, although both are good lines (assuming that he wrote them). It's just one way of keeping faith with the promise of 1977, now routinely dismissed by academic postmodernists and journalists alike—and redeemed by women, from feminist philosophers to Riot Grrrls. The voices from "the first year of punk," says Greil Marcus, have "hardly been answered, let alone superseded." [24]

After the late 1970s, conformist common sense only moved further away from punk negation, when to "feel good" or be "positive" became watchwords of the hysterical authoritarianism that prevailed after Reagan came to power. In retrospect, punk clearly sensed what was coming, especially in Britain just prior to Thatcher. It's also worth remembering that Jimmy Carter was at the same time setting into motion many policies now associated with Reagan (just as Bill Clinton scarcely differs from a Republican), such as the military buildup and the assault on organized labor; Iggy Pop's satiric "I'm a Conservative," an exhilarating tune backed by an all-star band of punk musicians, appeared just *before* Reagan's election in 1980. Thus my fixation on 1977 is hardly sheer nostalgia:

Latter-day punks such as the Riot Grrrls still battle with that authoritarianism, now a virtual fascism bashing any choices besides domesticity for women (whether Hillary Rodham Clinton or pregnant teenagers), any resistance against big business (whether environmentalism or organized labor), every nonwhite person guilty of poverty (whether black or Latino), and any trace of deviance (whether in ideology or sexual orientation). The various cultural conflicts of the 1990s might be summed up under one "general heading: the culture of self-satisfaction versus the culture of the dissatisfied." [25]

From the postmodern view, however, punk was the last hurrah for any faith that popular music could have a genuinely radical impact on even a small portion of its audience. In essence, presumably, postmodernism fully arrived in rock and roll when punk lost its momentum around 1981, with the advent of New Pop posers (e.g., "haircut bands" such as Duran Duran) and a new cable channel reliant on their videos, MTV. If punk achieved mass popularity a decade later, it did so under very different circumstances, when "alternative" music was well incorporated into the music industry. The second coming of punk could only amount to a trivial shift in poses for those with more outrageous tastes. Someone like me (or Greil Marcus or Jon Savage) who continues to dwell on the possibilities I felt in 1977, therefore, is guilty of bringing "pop history [to] a halt" and ducking the demise of "authenticity" in music in the 1980s, claims Steve Redhead. (As Dominic Strinati points out, though, musical authenticity has never really existed, except in mythologies about past innocence and in marketing strategies exploiting that nostalgia.[26]) The terms *rebellion* and *resistance* have supposedly become irrelevant since punk's heyday, making postpunk synonymous with postmodern (the view of a number of the academics discussed in Chapter 3).

But the long life of punk, I argue, simply reflects the fact that punk has been the persistent nemesis of the authoritarianism that emerged in the 1970s and expanded and intensified throughout the 1980s and 1990s. (That the authoritarians still bash around the 1960s, while the 1970s are popularly associated with *The Brady Bunch,* indicates how long they've held the upper hand.) The large amount of angry music at present reflects the steadily worsening situation since the original moment of punk, which followed shortly on the beginning of Western capitalism's all-out assault on its domestic adversaries in 1973, with the shock of the Arab oil embargo and the realization that the postwar economic expansion would not go on forever. David Harvey's *The Condition of Postmodernity* (1989) provides a good summary account of the transition in 1973 to the insecure world of "flexible accumulation," in which the financial system has become increasingly detached from real production (and his point is to give a more concrete explanation of recent cultural and social changes than talismanic invocation of postmodernism). With the deliberate contraction of economic opportunity on the part of the plutocratic class—resulting in such lunatic viciousness as the Federal Reserve Board keeping at least eight million people unemployed at all times while politicians seek to starve them for not working—there has understandably been an expansion of anger in the music of the increasingly large number of economically obsolete young people. Although I argue that they can be overly preoccupied with the commercial incorporation of their music, the many fans who express outrage at corporate power in the music business are quite conscious of the association of conglomeration in the mass media with the direction of the economy in general, as any issue of *Maximum Rock 'n' Roll* will attest.

Along with hip-hop (christened the "new punk" when it first exploded), punk antagonism is the most widespread cultural form concertedly repudiating the combination of feel-good banality and blame-the-victims meanness—think Ronald Reagan—promoted by the plutocrats and their mass media. This has been true of much of hip-hop and punk even when they have worked *within* those media, the result being the continuing furor over the inability of business to keep a lid on the market for youth music. Even from the view that ideology refers strictly to express meaning (setting aside emotion), perhaps the most exciting explicitly political rock songs ever recorded, such as the Clash's "This is England" and the Minutemen's "The Price of Paradise," were produced smack in the middle of the 1980s, when cynics claimed the music scene was "like punk never happened" (the subtitle of a book on Culture Club). The best-selling punk groups in the 1990s, Green Day and Offspring, clearly belie this notion in building on Bad Religion, a group that emerged precisely when punk was written off—and thus critics have been anxious to write off those newer groups as well. The view that there were no mid-decade outbreaks in rock music like Elvis in the 1950s, the Beatles in the 1960s, or punk in the 1970s, moreover, depends on trivializing hip-hop music's breakthrough in the 1980s as just another postmodern corporate fraud. In fact, hip-hop's origin dates to the late 1970s, too, and the concerns it shares with punk have been acknowledged in a number of forms, including another great political song of the mid-1980s, Time Zone's "World Destruction," recorded by Afrika Bambaataa and John Lydon.

As opposed to the view that some hopeless postmodern condition has taken hold of music—the eternal rule of multinational corporations—the fact is that punk has matched its authoritarian nemesis in persistence. Punk circa 1977 left a continuing legacy that has broken out again with Nirvana and the Riot Grrrls. It may be the case that "the very notion of a cultural politics implies a unity of focus and a direction which it is difficult to find in youth culture." But especially from a feminist point of view stressing the importance of feelings in themselves, "perhaps [politics] is not what we should be looking for in any case." What it may be more realistic to look for, suggests Angela McRobbie, "are cultural forms and expressions which seem to suggest new or emergent 'structures of feeling,' " especially among young women. In exploring "a greater degree of fluidity about what femininity means," [27] the Riot Grrrls, for example, are significant for trying to change how feeling itself is valued, especially anger—no longer something to be ashamed of and repressed but to celebrate.

If punk at its origins was still primarily for males, straight or not, Riot Grrrls do punk in the 1990s because that genre was also opening up rock music to strong female voices, though they only fully arrived fifteen years after Patti Smith, Deborah Harry, Poly Styrene of X-Ray Spex, Siouxsee and the Banshees, and Chrissie Hynde of the Pretenders, to cite the usual list of the original punk women. At the same time the Riot Grrrls appeared in 1991, punk finally broke for a mass audience, of course, with Nirvana. Nirvana's album *Nevermind* "forced the pop world to accommodate the long-resisted punk aesthetic at both its harshest and smartest and did so at a time when many pundits had declared that rock & roll was effectively finished." [28]

Yet as soon as possible, after a year of fairly dreary music in 1995, music journalism ranging from my local paper to *The Village Voice* Pazz & Jop Poll was quick to announce once again the death throes of rock, in every instance invoking postmodernism. One critic held in 1996 that "rock really *is* dead" because it "lacks a temperament or sensibility" like that of earlier "unique and individual geniuses" such as John Lennon, offering instead only "manufactured pathologies." [29] This seems fairly damning evidence of the continuity between romanticism—extolling the individual artistic genius while loathing the manufactured—and postmodern diagnoses of a widespread dysfunctional (or pathological) sensibility. Although postmodern theorists often tell us that the possibility of artistic distance (or autonomy) has now been eliminated by mass culture, the romantic aversion to commerce persists *within* mass culture, absorbed (sans the theorists' nostalgia) by many music fans.

In my own case, in contrast, I've been delighted by the commercial breakthrough of punk. For one thing, obviously, my musical tastes formed two decades ago remain current. For another, the mass popularity of punk in the mid-1990s ought to put in question the incessant, ostensibly populist concern, dating to 1977, about alternative groups on independent (or "indie") record labels selling out to corporate (or "major") labels. I don't mean that since punk has irreversibly become a commercial success, such concerns are unfounded or irrelevant. I fully agree that the more the media promote punk, the greater the need for suspicion, and that "there is no sadder sight than [a] thirty-something ex-Punk" who has come to consider quantity of sales evidence of quality, as in some cases of cultural populism. I would never insist on "uncritical acceptance of an agenda set by market forces." [30] Followers of alternative music do need to realize, though, the influence that postmodern ideas have had on their anxiety that their favorite groups either have sold out or will sell out.

The refusal of some fans and journalists to consider if worthwhile music might actually be getting released, when someone such as Nirvana or Green Day emerges, is in fact residual romanticism, not populism, a residue quite prominent in postmodernism, as we have already seen. After two centuries, we are still plagued by the reflexive, absolutist division drawn by romanticism and, later, modernism, between art and the marketplace, or creativity and commerce—or, put in more formal terms discussed in Chapter 3, authenticity (or spontaneity) and reflexivity (or self-conscious calculation). An astonishing number of people still consider starving in a lonely garret a sign of artistic legitimacy.

The division between art and the market doesn't hold up, though, when independent record labels continue to serve up provocative, scurrilous, yet often surprisingly profitable music, even if most now depend on distribution by major labels. Deserving performers have been ruined, admittedly, and a lot of dreck has resulted from indies evolving into subsidiaries of major labels. Nonetheless, I argue that the terms *alternative* and *independent* ought to be distinguished: Significant musical alternatives do manage to emerge from the current regime; the achievement and preservation of economic independence is a whole other issue. We need a more flexible view, in any case, than the conventional one pitting corporate rock, "fundamentally about the open and blunt exercise of power," as a *Spin* writer constructs matters, against "indie rockers [who] have always favored exclusivity and an aesthete's sense of reserve." This romantic (not to mention elitist) division is a dead end, a permanent stasis of the sort that defines postmodernism for many analysts. But the "whole martyr thing"—staying "chaste, poor, and suffering"—is "a bunch of bullshit," as Kathleen Hanna of Bikini Kill puts it, because the romantic idea that "the only way you can create authentic art is if you're suffering [just] helps people stay in the same place." [31] That paralysis hardly confirms postmodern theorists, I would add, because it only reflects the circulation of their own ideas about commercial incorporation, to the extent that *Maximum Rock 'n' Roll* takes essentially the same editorial stance that the *New York Times* does (as Chapter 4 indicates).

One of the main purposes of this book is to document this perverse closed loop or circularity in academic and journalistic postmodernism, in which the common wisdom—a willful fatalism—takes its own repetition as proof of its claims. That circulation dates from the mid-1980s and the work of academics such as Fredric Jameson and Lawrence Grossberg and music critics such as Simon Reynolds. A large amount of postmodern academic work on rock music was written just before the pivotal year of 1991, in fact, and much of Part 1 focuses on the perverse result: Just as that outpouring of academic cynicism was immediately debunked and rendered obsolete by Nirvana, the Riot Grrrls, and others, its postmodern themes were seized on and widely broadcast by hostile journalistic responses to that reemergence of punk.

It's important to see the sheer repetitiveness of postmodern theory so as to understand that postmodern academics and journalists never offer any justification for their claims. Instead, like other ideologues, they expect familiarity and fashionability, or the repetition itself, to legitimate their ideas. Part 1 may seem lengthy, but perhaps the most effective way to put paid to the wrongheadedness of postmodernism lies in documenting the sheer absurdity of its repetitiveness (including its reproduction of earlier romantic and modernist travesties) as it circulates back and forth through academia and the mass media. The endless recycling of postmodern theory, moreover, as Dana Polan observes, seems the only actual embodiment of the predicament assigned to the rest of the culture: "These writings cannot say anything non-repetitive. The postmodernist effect [is] a kind of mechanistic *combinatoire* in which everything is given in advance, in which there can be no practice but the endless recombination of fixed pieces from the generative machine." What seems an "inflationary spiral of contemporary critical theorizing," marking in itself the onset of some new condition or crisis, is in reality more like "stagflation," in John Clarke's view.[32]

When any ideology proliferates to the extent that postmodernism has, reaching the consensus we will see, it can certainly seem to correspond to reality regardless of its validity. Theorists of postmodernism have done so much to underwrite perceptions of the current situation, however, that the actual existence of an apocalyptic postmodern era remains highly questionable. The intellectual's millenarianism, academic postmodernism has offered little besides sophistry, or a smokescreen of seemingly subtle argument, typically involving a few dizzying theoretical abstractions leavened with a smidgen of highly selective evidence. This myopia is especially evident in theorists of postmodernism issuing judgments on affect in mass culture, who have clearly read nothing written about emotion by other scholars.

In trying to translate and make lucid what those theorists are saying, or "to imagine nonacademic readers who ask only that the languages of academic criticism be translated into their languages," [33] there is never any guarantee, of course, that the best intentions in writing will make any difference. But I know a lot of smart young people who won't find what follows all that difficult. This book is for them; I'm thoroughly disgusted with academics after writing it. In seeing postmodernism fully at work, hopefully, younger, nonacademic readers will develop a bullshit detector for it. Then we can return to the business of history, which many postmodernists insist is over. With more self-consciousness than the original Enlightenment about including everyone in the process, we can renew our faith that liberty and justice for all is not an embarrassing piety nor hopelessly and forever out of reach.

# PART 1

# CHAPTER 1

# No Respect for Suffering
## *An Introduction to Postmodernism*

Before launching into problems related to emotion and popular music, I begin with some initial assertions about postmodernism in general; ample evidence for them appears throughout the remainder of Part 1. My arguments are based on a compound of leftist politics that I am reluctant to pin down as any single -ism (as was the Situationist International), except in terms of a cultural anarchism encouraging a critical, democratic attitude toward conformist common sense. As Noam Chomsky has recently observed, anarchism in terms of loathing the state makes little sense at a time when the anarchs wishing to eliminate government come from the Right and seek to unleash the discipline of an even worse authority, that of the ostensibly "free" market.

The new wave of authoritarians, ripping away at any shred of security possessed by those outside the plutocracy, have actually been abetted by postmodern theorists, whose cynicism leads them to supply their nominal opponents with the means to condemn insubordinate cultural forms such as angry popular music. Where postmodernism has done a great deal of damage by fixating on what people *cannot* do because of the power of corporate capitalism, I prefer to dwell on what they *can* do in spite of it. I would prefer, ideally, to be dialectical about the matter, but the merchants of the postmodern are so widespread and so incapable of dialectical thought that they need to have as much counterweight as possible thrown at them.

Another thing I want to make clear at the outset is that I do not mean to attack the various forms of identity politics concerned with gender, race, ethnicity, and sexual orientation, which are often associated with postmodernism by both opponents and proponents. It makes perfectly good sense to question and revise modernity, or the period since the Enlightenment, given its oppressive drive for authoritative, unitary interpretations and judgments—by supposedly disinterested, rational white men, of course—regarding everything from the political sphere to literary texts. Closer scrutiny of the actual complexity and contradictions that different social identities pose in social life and in artistic forms is hardly objectionable, in light of the white male's traditional certainties about his perspective's rectitude (placing an "e" before that last word would be a cliché by this point). I have no interest, therefore, in joining the recent jeremiads by leftists critical of identity politics, a genre including Todd Gitlin's *The Twilight of Common Dreams* (1995), Michael Lind's *The Next American Nation* (1995), and Michael Tomasky's *Left for Dead* (1996).

What I consider objectionable about postmodernism, instead, originates in more exclusively theoretical work that has rebelled against modernity by portraying identity as unstable, even completely in flux or chaotic. This picture is often crossed with a loathing of mass culture not at all postmodern but a direct inheritance from romanticism and modernism. Some postmodern theory, particularly that emanating from France, goes even further, actually advocating the dissolution of any identity and, by extension, the abandonment of any social goals claiming a rational basis. The rationalist notion of testing ideas and interpretations through examination of material experience, one's own and that of others, and arriving at a legitimate claim to the truth is presumably inherently repressive. A project with such a large scope can only be totalitarian, in theory, because it inculcates false notions of individual and collective agency in people when the "power" of the discourses we try to master, instead, inescapably controls and directs our efforts. The result of this view, a reluctance to promote any large-scale politics, hardly helps matters when the master narratives of neoconservative politicians and pundits, who are uninhibited by such com[tions], already go unchallenged in the mass media.

Because some versions of identity politics do follow postmodern theory, I am under no illusion that my characterization of postmodernism will offend only the epigones of theorists of more dubious value, such as Jean Baudrillard. But I will argue nonetheless—with a good deal of feminist theory, in particular, to back me up—that we need, in various forms depending on the person or groups in question, some relatively stable sense of individual and collective identity to assert against the status quo. Multiculturalism and pluralism are vital; theories of the fictionality, fragmentation, and nonexistence of identity are another matter. Identity politics ought to be uncoupled from the rubric of postmodernism—although not from a concerted questioning, revision, and improvement of the legacy of modernity—and they certainly are in my own thinking in what follows. Identities, however diverse, ought to be a matter of assertion, not dissolution, and Part 2 argues that the fundamental basis for a reasonably authentic assertive identity lies in emotion.

Postmodernism can be perplexing, even for the initiated, because there are many versions of it, ranging from the positive and celebratory to the negative and apocalyptic. Virtually all those versions share a common basis, however, belying the seemingly opposed extremes of enthusiasm and despair: the attribution of an enormous passivity to nonintellectuals. The postmodern perspective on the general populace differs very little from the views of romantics and modernists (from about 1790 to 1940), except in its extremity. Intellectual passivity, or distraction, is now considered either a radically subversive force or the dismal endpoint of history—yet both sides, revealingly, employ a similar rhetoric in diagnosing a universal "schizophrenia," or delusional detachment. One prominent variation on this theme is to treat schizophrenia as insufficiently developed and to issue prescriptions for its cultivation.

In general, postmodernism involves developments in three areas:

- The individual fields of architecture, art, and literature, plagued by a sense of exhaustion after the achievements of modernists like Frank Lloyd Wright, Pablo Picasso, and James Joyce
- Philosophies such as antifoundationalism, denying any grounds for "truth," but especially French poststructuralist theory concerned with the frailty of the individual, now the "subject" in the sense of being ruled (or dispersed or dispossessed, etc.) by the "structure" of language, and through it the structures of ideology and power
- Either sweeping criticism or uncritical celebration of mass culture (or the consumer-information-postindustrial-services society)[1]

These three areas do have a common denominator—a crippling loss of faith in human agents, both individuals and groups. Modernism had already grappled with alienation, or a sense of separation from others and from the possibility of fulfillment through everyday experience. Thus, modernist works of art are largely monuments to the internal processes of their individual creators, deliberately refusing any political engagement.

"Post-" modernism basically means pushing modernism over the edge by giving up on the lonely individual as well as possibilities for political action: The problem is no longer alienation but sheer fragmentation. The difference, however, is not all that clear-cut when anxiety, bewilderment, and panic have been staples of "cultural and artistic expression over the last 150 years," as Angela McRobbie points out. The self-consciousness of contemporary artists about following modernism hardly merits description as postmodernism: artistic practices often held to typify the postmodern—such as self-reflexiveness, pastiche (a degraded form of montage), and indeterminacy, all reflecting a preoccupation with the weakness of the individual—occur throughout modernism. The only difference from modernism in what passes for postmodern, therefore, lies merely in the increasing extremity of descriptions of fragmentation. Thus the "category of fragmentation," says McRobbie, has "become either too technical to be of general use (i.e. in [the psychoanalyst Jacques] Lacan's work) or too vague to mean anything more than torn apart." [2]

In the case of popular music, Sara Cohen finds it "rather naive" that an academic postmodernist such as Lawrence Grossberg describes rock and roll in terms of discontinuity and fragmentation and that a postmodern critic such as Simon Reynolds celebrates schizoid music that takes listeners nowhere. Such assertions about "a blurring of levels and categories, of places, spaces, times and identities [are] based upon little information about the ways in which people actually use and value" music. Holly Kruse agrees that the examination of actual lived experience in any music scene inevitably calls into question the claims of postmodern theorists, such as Grossberg and Steve Redhead, that "rock culture allows youths to enact ever-changing sexual and gendered identities in a space of radically conflicting social messages," as opposed to more straightforwardly "oppositional musical identities." [3]

For the theorists of fragmentation, the only material entities left—that is, the only real actors in the world—seem to be language and the ideologies expressed through it. As in postmodernism's relation to modernism, the "post-" in poststructuralism essentially means moving beyond the already pessimistic identification of such structures by structuralism. The structuralist linguist Ferdinand de Saussure had assigned the individual a subordinate status in relation to the language-system (or *langue*), essentially in keeping with the modernist sense of the difficulty the beleaguered artist faced in forging poetry out of ordinary language. Sometimes described as the persistence of literary modernism in academic theory, poststructuralism does take a further, more desperate step, depicting a subject whose very existence depends on language. The actual interdependence or dialectic between structure and subject, or language and its users, is often reduced to a one-dimensional world with minimal possibilities for action. Any sense that the structures of language might be enabling as well as constraining is lost.

Some versions of poststructuralism crossed with identity politics, especially in feminist, queer, and postcolonial studies, have usefully exposed the division of the world into superiors and inferiors by structures such as gender and Orientalism. Although there ought to be some distinction possible between undermining those specific constructs and altogether repudiating language—the structure overarching them—academic and creative responses to the cultural construction of gender and race often share the fatalism about language at the core of poststructuralism. Whether in *écriture féminine,* queer theory on troubling gender, or postcolonial fiction (e.g., Wilson Harris's *Palace of the Peacock* [1960], an early, more original variant)—not to mention French postmodern equations of schizophrenia with anarchism, as in Gilles Deleuze and Felix Guattari's *Anti-Oedipus*—postmodernists on the attack often counsel not just the exposure and critique of the destructive, inhumane forms of identity offered by the dominant culture. The further quest becomes the undermining of any and all identities through a dissolution of language, meaning, or both.

The resulting quandary is inadvertently summed up very well by Bruce Robbins in a statement intended to justify, to the layperson, postmodern theories concerning the instability of identity. Compelled to speak plainly, he maintains that such theory "gathers people and groups who are trying to deconstruct the same identities they also rely on." [4] A juggling act of this sort is plausible, although the deconstruction of identity typically becomes an end in itself at the expense of actual politics, by requiring a disabling acknowledgment of a free-floating power that supplies identities. But the circularity of Robbins's description strikes me as entailing futility rather than empowerment in the first place. That the activity he describes could easily be considered an alarming stasis seems confirmed, for example, in the case of feminist theory. Feminist intellectuals have been negotiating for some time now an intractable deadlock between an academic, "ludic," or playful postmodern quest for dissolution, on the one hand, and cultural or radical feminist calls for assertion, on the other, which requires the stable basis of an identity. A feminist rock musician, Nina Gordon of Veruca Salt, deplores a situation in which feminism "seems to be more about criticising other people's visions of feminism than supporting each other." [5]

In reviewing Mas'ud Zavarzadeh and Donald Morton's *Theory as Resistance* (1994), which advocates a revival of systemic (or holistic) social criticism, Rob Wilkie points out that the various ludic postmodern theories not only have no special claim to stymieing the system, but may actually serve it very well (a charge of complicity that we will see launched against postmodernism in general).[6] Theory emphasizing the slipperiness of meaning and identity, due to their construction through language, may only serve in higher education to produce the kind of employees needed by postindustrial capitalism: Students accustomed to considering identity something multiple and even indefinable will adapt better to the insecurity of "downsizing," of being routinely shuffled between jobs. Many others, of course, have noted the alacrity with which buttoned-down college administrators have embraced a sanitized, business-oriented version of multiculturalism.

The postmodern reduction of all experience to matters of language amounts to a "materialization of the sign," as John Clarke puts it in *New Times and Old Enemies* (1990), or a preoccupation with discourses and ideologies transmitted through it, "and the dematerialization of everything else." [7] His view was amply borne out in 1996, in an incident that became notorious in the press as well as in academia, when physicist Alan Sokal hoaxed the determinedly cutting-edge journal *Social Text* with a fairly impenetrable article replete with ludicrous scientific claims. The journal's editors (including Bruce Robbins) published Sokal nonetheless because his text is laced with postmodern clichés, first and foremost the bald-faced argument that "an external world" does not exist because "physical 'reality,' no less than social 'reality,' is at bottom a social and linguistic construct." [8]

A similar though perfectly serious insistence on dematerializing social life—a withdrawal from "sociality by problematising language" in abstract arguments—characterizes many of the varieties of postmodernism. Some postmodernists find a modest sort of freedom in fragmentation, but that instability in identity, in their systems, always remains subject to control by discourse. Chantal Mouffe, one of the founders of a "post-Marxism" abandoning the structures of social class and identities based on them, says in a revealing oxymoron that the subject "is always precariously and *provisionally fixed . . .* at the intersection of various discourses" (emphasis added). The variety of discourses forming the subject are active and volatile, that is, but the "fixed" subject appears quite passive. An exponent of queer theory, Judith Butler (who shares with Mouffe a basis in Nietzsche and Foucault that I elaborate in Chapter 2), even has it that no subject exists to house the "converging relations of power" and its discourses. There is "no site at which such relations converge," which is essentially what Mouffe is saying—that discourse is everything.[9] Even the physical body, according to Butler, is nothing more than a discursive construction, the sort of claim parodied in Alan Sokal's hoax in *Social Text*.

It is certainly the case that identity, whether individual or collective, must be "achieved, negotiated, invented" through discourses not entirely authentic to oneself. But to speak of the subject as a "fixed essence" produced by "abstract forces or technologies," says Sara Cohen—and especially to erase the subject altogether—effectively obliterates the efforts of real persons to define themselves. In light of such abstractions concerning social experience, Kwame Anthony Appiah suggests that postmodernism needs to be countered by "a certain simple respect for human suffering."[10] If people are indeed in distress to anything like the extent portrayed by postmodern academics and journalists, a simple respect for misery would seem to be in order, instead of fatalism or even ridicule. Yet I now have graduate students well versed in postmodern theory telling me that the experience of physical pain depends on how a culture constructs it—that suffering is a relative, subjective matter and somehow no cause for alarm.

The more dire views of postmodernism, centered on discourse and power, have been heavily influenced by Michel Foucault, by now a celebrity whose books are featured in Tower Records. His descriptions of power operating virtually untouchably have been highly influential on the fatalistic strain of postmodernism. (I have in mind the "middle" period in Foucault's career, work of the mid-1970s like *Discipline and Punish* and *Power/Knowledge*, which by all accounts has had the most widespread influence.) Through their control of specialized discourses, Foucault found, various institutions such as medicine, psychiatry, and the penal system control language itself. Foucault emphasized at the same time that power is not exercised by any person or any intentional actor. Those "subject" to power, therefore, could hardly intervene in specialist discourse so as to confer their own meanings because there is no human opponent to fight. If power was exercised by other human agents, that would mean it could be resisted. Instead, supposedly, power exists as an unknowable or "sublime" abstraction, exercised not only through discourse but through ethereal entities like "surfaces, lights, gazes," which the subject passively absorbs as a voluntary discipline or self-policing. This dehumanized (or antihumanist) abstraction allows Foucault to claim in *Discipline and Punish* that we don't exist as functional selves any more than some persons exercise power: The whole notion of individuality, whether our own or that of the powerful, is actually "carefully fabricated" by power.[11]

In his late work on ethics, or the subject of techniques of self-formation and -conduct in which some resistance of power may occur, Foucault does readmit the fact that power is exercised by some persons over others—a point cited by followers as if it were a major insight. Alan Schrift, for example, concludes that "Foucault left to us the task of thinking a notion of the subject that is both autonomous and disciplined." But as Kate Soper points out, numerous theorists in the Marxist tradition, such as Mikhail Bakhtin, Antonio Gramsci, and Raymond Williams, had already noticed that dialectic. The Foucault "in quest of the lost subject," furthermore, "seems curiously ready to present modes of self-regulation," or relatively independent personal development, "which his earlier work had problematised as being the internalized policing effects of 'panoptical' power." His work in sum total leaves an "ambiguous and unresolved dialectic" between the libertarian and the oppressive, or between "his activist critique of power and his pessimist emphasis on the inevitability of domination." [12]

Whatever one believes about Foucault, I don't think I'm wrong to be troubled when advanced students, trained by Foucault scholars, consider statements like "Opposition to power only reinforces it" a radical insight. The logic of this formulation also owes a good deal to another French theorist of postmodernism, Jean-François Lyotard, who is best known for condemning any "grand narrative" of history. One of his particular targets, Marxism's account of the historical stages of class struggle leading inevitably to the fall of capitalism, is hardly immune to criticism. But Lyotard also helped establish, more importantly, the general postmodern revulsion at any vestige of the Enlightenment, at any belief that people can act coherently to bring about some progress in the human condition. Judith Butler, for example, simply declares "that Emancipation and the Good have proven their unrealizability." Such dismissals of any grand narrative (historical or theoretical) concerning political change, argues Steven Connor, have the sad effect of "high-mindedly evaporat[ing] the legitimacy . . . of emancipatory struggles, which may depend on . . . shopsoiled ideals of universal freedom and justice" dating from the Enlightenment. [13] Even many postmodern opponents of the Enlightenment legacy, moreover, continue to echo its concern with human liberation, as Jürgen Habermas points out in *Between Facts and Norms* (1996). Lyotard is more consistent, at least, in dismissing any theory regarding social change as inherently totalitarian. Such a large-scale narrative, literally "totalizing," is in his view a form of violence against the postmodern force he extols, the supposed anarchy of the numerous incommensurate language games that dissolve (or fragment) subjectivity. Systemic change is considered not only impossible but undesirable in the first place, effectively detaching the local from the global.

Many feminists find anti-Enlightenment philosophy attractive for its rejection of the self-assured individual, an entity tainted throughout modernity by a masculine (or phallocentric) perspective. But feminists such as Nancy Hartstock ask why it is

> that just at the moment when so many of us who have been silenced begin to demand the right to name ourselves, to act as subjects rather than the objects of history, that just then the concept of subjecthood becomes problematic. . . . Just when we are talking about the changes we want, ideas of progress and the possibility of systematically and rationally organizing human society become dubious and suspect.

Dick Hebdige speculates that male postmodernists promulgating pessimistic views, such as the general "line that we are living at the end of everything," have responded to the increasing presence of women (as well as racial minorities) in academia by resolving to "take it all—judgment, history, politics, aesthetics, value—out of the window with them." [14]

Belying its rejection of "totalizing" philosophies or grand narratives characteristic of the Enlightenment and its aftermath, moreover, French postmodernism features holistic accounts of totalities (like power) that can be just as disabling. In the closed, seamless, circular systems of power, radical politics can only serve a preordained subordinate role, as a phony foil to power. Because power operates through every form of language or discourse, "it is not possible to say or do anything which undermines power," as Sadie Plant characterizes the argument: "Political opposition is integrated within the structures it thinks it is opposing." (I have been chided in exactly these terms for talking about cultural anarchism.) Any resistance that individuals (or subjects) express is actually built into them by power itself to perpetuate itself. To identify a fundamental contradiction between power and people opposing it, therefore, only reinforces the subordinate status of the opponents, according to postmodernism. No negation or genuine criticism of authority, no political resistance can exist, except to serve a convenient drama preserving the illusion of democracy. But this postmodern notion is merely the unfortunate consequence of taking a *part* of society, "power" however one explains it, as absolutely determining or governing the *whole* of society. The lamentable results are evident in Jacques Derrida's conclusion that the only "just" politics is an unarticulated politics of silence. (The occasion for this observation, incredibly, was an essay on apartheid in South Africa; no one there, fortunately, paid any attention.) To resist openly and explicitly "the present state of force and law" would supposedly only allow resistance to "be reappropriated" into the closed loop organized by power. Derrida had long since said of language in general, in "Structure, Sign, and Play in the Discourse of the Human Sciences," that "we cannot utter a single destructive proposition which has not already slipped into the form, the logic, and the implicit postulations of precisely what it seeks to contest." Lyotard's blunt derivation from Derrida holds that "to criticize is to remain in the field of the thing criticized." [15]

Postmodern views of popular music follow logically from the conviction that resistance to the status quo is contained within the closed loop of power, finding only a terrible fragmentation and passivity in its intended audience. Simply put, no one really cares about the social world, presumably, or at least everyone is convinced of the impossibility of understanding and influencing it. So any expression of conviction in music is a pretense, a fraud, and emotions expressed in music, especially anger, aren't potential dynamite—they're just good for business. There are no individuals or collective groups out there who care enough or are functional enough to act on those emotions.

The postmodern circular model of power is only a very reductive treatment of the real problem, however. Anger at authority, for example, does sometimes set up a circular relationship by "mythologiz[ing] the object of antagonism" as an " 'opposite,' the negation of one's self." The problem, observes Peter Lyman, lies in making authority something abstract or symbolic—"explained in terms of its essence, not as a social relation"—and thus beyond reach.[16] For this precise reason, therefore, the best writers on anger all stress the importance of discovering and articulating its social basis. As will be seen throughout Part 1, postmodern theorists are actually the ones most guilty of the flaws they diagnose, in this case in "mythologizing" or "essentializing" power, and thereby suppressing the real volatility of social relations.

In Great Britain and the United States (the purview of this book), scholars influenced by French postmodernists seem actually to believe that "power" and "authority" are invisible and untouchable (or sublime) in their complex institutional forms. The operations of society, says one postmodernist, have become "mysterious, omniscient, and omnipotent, capricious, pervasive, and seemingly beyond the control of any single individual or group." Feminist theorist Donna Haraway believes that "none of 'us' have any longer the symbolic or material capability of dictating the shape of reality to any of 'them.' . . . Abstraction and illusion rule in knowledge, domination rules in practice." [17]

The influence of French postmodernists on advanced scholars and their students is not hard to understand: The sense of futility conveyed by some French theorists has enormous appeal to leftist academics frustrated at their inability to affect the world. Left-leaning journalists like it, too, as the example of Leslie Savan's work on advertising indicates: "The new hipsters who control the boardrooms of advertising have a vision: the triumph of technopopulism, . . . affectless and wired back in upon itself as an *endless loop* of global marketing" (emphasis added), actually providing anger and conflict as an antidote for boredom.[18] A cultural form like angry music, therefore, similarly only feeds delusions of rebelliousness, and the PMRC's complaints about rebellion in music are merely part of the charade.

Both the gloominess of French intellectuals and the extraordinary popularity of their work in Great Britain and the United States need a little more historical context, however. They do not in and of themselves, I want to stress, confirm the existence of the "postmodern condition," as many tend to assume. A number of commentators have instead explained the French postmodern gloom as an outgrowth of the May Revolution of 1968, led by students and workers, which raised radical political hopes only to dash them all the more traumatically when it failed. The failure in May 1968, says Sadie Plant, has a great deal to do with the French "postmodern insistence that criticism is impossible, subversion futile, and revolution a childish and reactionary dream." (Personally, I find the fact that the May Revolution happened within my lifetime quite encouraging, and as I finished this book in late 1995, an alliance of students and workers much like that in 1968 arose to challenge draconian economic policies intended to integrate France into the new world order of international capitalism—an event that some leftist journalists in the United States reflexively reported in terms of postmodern aimlessness.) Chagrin after 1968 even led to the view that any effort to radically alter social relations, if successful, would only substitute one oppressive "totality" for another—to some extent an opportunistic equation of May 1968 with an earlier object of intellectual scorn, the Stalinism of the French Communist party. By this logic, *any* traditional concept of revolution becomes reactionary, an "anti-Marxist" stance that Foucault declared vindicated by 1968. But the postmodern insistence on political futility may actually have as much to do with a defeated chauvinism: "The emergence of France as the world capital of theory," Laura Kipnis suggests, can "be read as the sequel of its loss of mastery—in the war, in Indochina, in North Africa." [19]

The result in any case was not postmodern at all but actually a sensibility like that of modernist artists—both revolutionary and reactionary, as Bertrand Russell says of the romantics in *A History of Western Philosophy* (1945), in the sense of being anticapitalist but also disdainful of mass politics. (Loathing of the masses and mass culture, of course, led many modernists to enthuse about fascism, accepting a rigid social order as the price for preserving cultural order—the autonomous realm of art had to be preserved against the material world.) Hostility toward the bourgeoisie and proletariat alike has bred in postmodern theory as well, says Kipnis, an "aesthetics of defeat compounded by a gravitation toward the hermetic." Critics such as Andreas Huyssen, in *After the Great Divide* (1986), have even described French poststructuralism as a direct migration of literary modernism into academic theory. While the postmoderns hardly share the frequent modernist enthrallment with fascism, the "chasmal distance between left intellectuals and popular consciousness," as Kipnis puts it, is no improvement.[20]

Out of this left-wing elitism—frequently compared with the Marxist modernists in the Frankfurt School—postmodern theory on the frailty of the individual and the fragmentation of social life seems either unable or unwilling to "constitute [a] political object" that could fill the supposed "gap left by the absence of a [collective] historical subject" acting for change. Thus postmodernism may retain an anticapitalist, essentially "Marxist desire for freedom from domination," says John McGowan, but it seems only "an implicit norm that intellectuals find hard to justify and even harder to imagine achieving." (French postmodernism has also been compared to liberal thought, as a result, and its fear of excessive social change.) The post-Marxist Mouffe (writing with Ernesto Laclau), for example, describes the working class as a "space left vacant," [21] if not the primary barrier to radical politics, as Ellen Meiksins Wood reads post-Marxism in *The Retreat from Class* (1986). (It is hardly surprising that post-Marxism proves scarcely Marxist at all, of course, for Marxism depends on rational analyses, grand narratives, etc.) The appeal that psychoanalytic stress on unconscious motivation holds for post-Marxists and others reflects this loss of faith in political agency, which Kipnis reads into one of Lacan's key terms, "lack." That sense of an absence when there should be opposition is also apparent in the "Gothic" Marxism of Derrida's recent work on the "specters" of Marx and other revolutionaries of the past, the best Derrida can detect due to his fatalism over the impact of electronic media.

The postmodern advocacy of "micropolitics," in the place of class politics, illustrates about the best that can be derived from Foucault and Lyotard. One should be satisfied, as McGowan sums up the argument, if "the play of resistance at particular [or local or micro] sites of confrontation with power" offers merely theoretical consolation "that 'practices of freedom' are possible." But if the possibility of something different can be identified, it presumably remains impossible under present conditions to articulate and promote that difference without placing it back into the closed circuit controlled by power. Even

Foucault's late, less dismal work in *The History of Sexuality* (published during 1978 to 1988) and elsewhere, based in Nietzsche's aesthetic of self-creation, offers little more than the "strategy of personal transformation in isolation that was chosen by so many modernist radicals," McGowan points out. Ian Hunter (a literary scholar promoted in the field of cultural studies by Lawrence Grossberg) approvingly reads Foucault's "ethic of care for the self" even further back, to romanticism and the origin of the artistic desire for autonomy from society. Foucault's ethics likewise feeds only "an individualist and elitist approach to liberation," as Kay Soper says of Foucauldian feminism, which theorizes a subversive "gender self-styling" that is simply not an option for most women.[22]

As opposed to their successors in Britain and the United States, though, French intellectuals at least had a taste of revolution, if it only convinced them of the ultimate impossibility of radical social change, even its undesirability. Their pessimism is all the greater for their actual proximity to a mass social revolt and to the continuing existence of the large political left in France (which some celebrity postmoderns, such as Derrida, did support during the uprising in 1995). The wildly enthusiastic reception of French postmodernism in the United States, in contrast, reflects a sense of the utter absence of progressive political possibilities. Intellectuals and others in the United States understandably share the French disillusionment over the failures of the 1960s and the subsequent success of hyperconsumerism in buying off the segments of the populace able to participate, a frustration compounded by dismay at the near total defeat of labor in the United States. The apparently irreparable lack of a mass movement for genuine social change, says Laura Kipnis, has postmodernists on the Left overwhelmed by a sense of "political catastrophe and defeat." [23]

The ludicrous political climate of the United States, moreover, in which establishment culture (e.g., *Time* magazine and Robin MacNeil) can explicitly deny the very existence of the Left, has bred a sense of futility that understandably makes the fatalism of French postmodern theory attractive. Many in the United States have certainly been persuaded that any political alternative from the Left is unthinkable, and the old cold war accusation of "socialism" continues to tar scarcely revolutionary proposals as well (such as a single-payer national health plan like that in other developed nations). With the domination of political institutions and mass communications by corporate America and the resulting absence of progressives in public discourse, the far Right has become the status quo, Bill Clinton can be denounced as a left-wing radical, and the absurd meanness of making war on the poor, not poverty, is the national sport. Postmodern theory has been appealing to intellectuals of various ideological stripes, though; as in France throughout the postwar era, apparently, the decline of the United States over the last two decades (outside of the ruling class) has led a wide spectrum of its intellectuals to adopt fatalistic theory.

With direct political action a frustrating proposition for disenfranchised persons across the political spectrum, the academic concentration on vivisecting identity is understandable. That the problem of actual politics remains postponed in theorizing about identity makes postmodernists no worse than music fans, of course—although no better, either. A great deal of academic postmodernism has hardly been merely paralyzed or static, however, but has actively reinforced the general sense of futility at present.

I am inclined to agree, as a result, with the response of the leftist periodical *In These Times* to academic readers who criticized its hostility toward postmodern theory: "The only poststructuralist contribution we can think of is an enhancement of the particularist tendencies inherent in identity politics. And that has had a negative impact on an already disoriented left." [24] But if *In These Times* eschews poststructuralism, it also frequently features Tom Frank, whose dire views on the enfeeblement of young people by consumerism derive directly from other areas of postmodern theory concerned with mass culture. Frank, in fact, wrote the reports on the foolishness of poststructuralists that provoked their ire at *In These Times,* but the concreteness of his rhetoric and subject matter in other articles on mass culture is the only respect in which his own gloom over the possibility of authentic identities differs from that of academics. (Thus the real problem his editors have with postmodern theory would seem to amount to the common complaint about its abstraction and difficulty.)

Despite these differences over the political significance of theorizing about identity and despite variations in the amount of explicit attention paid to mass culture, postmodern commentators continually arrive on common ground with regard to the harm done by mass culture. Postmodernism, as John McGowan argues in *Postmodernism and Its Critics* (1991), is perfectly in keeping with the romantic tradition, dating to the eighteenth century, of intellectuals defining the arts (including academic theory, an essentially literary practice) against commercial society. The postmodern reduction of cultural consumers to a homogenized mass—whether a passive or a subversive one—simply perpetuates a long-standing resentment at the erosion "mass culture and mass democracy" have inflicted on the role of intellectuals "as cultural educators and arbiters of taste," as Dominic Strinati puts it.[25] The extremity of postmodern theory, however, would seem to mark a conviction that that role has been eclipsed once and for all, which accounts in some part for the general postmodern claims regarding the end of history.

I stress the centrality of mass culture in postmodern thought because even sympathetic readers will feel that I speak too broadly in indicting virtually the whole of academic postmodernism and its reproduction in the mass media rather than a more cautious rubric such as "certain narratives and theories of postmodernism." I am frequently told that the varieties of postmodernism are too numerous to allow sweeping repudiation of the very term itself. One reason why I will spend a considerable amount of time tracing the migration of postmodernism, therefore, is to make an irrefutable case that there is really very little variation in it. (There is no way very many academic readers will agree with me; as one might expect, I think that's because they suffer from denial.) African American scholar Cornel West, for example, champions poststructuralism as a corrective to the Enlightenment legacy and thus would seem to present a complete contrast with the likes of Tom Frank. But we will see in Chapter 2 that West condemns hip-hop music on exactly the same grounds that lead Frank to ridicule youth culture in general—the supposedly universal commercial falsification of expressions of dissent.

Across the board, postmodern theory that seems more exclusively concerned with the problem of identity invariably turns out to be about mass culture. In this chapter I have surveyed criticism of the abandonment of "mass" politics by French postmodern theory; in Chapter 5, I cite feminist critics who link the elusive, heavily theorized literary style of *écriture féminine* with modernism, in particular the Frankfurt School's antagonism toward mass culture. At the same time, postmodern analyses of mass culture invariably express doubts about identity, as Fredric Jameson does in importing French notions of mass schizophrenia. Even the most celebratory, quasi-populist accounts of mass culture share in the common postmodern conviction of the disintegration of identity. The same holds true for architecture, art, and literature identified with postmodernism, in which the author, character, history, and so forth are treated as fictions just as they are in academic theory—with which creative work frequently overlaps nowadays, of course (e.g., Umberto Eco's *The Name of the Rose*).

Cornel West at least recognizes that the source of the widespread postmodern picture of misdirected, unenacted dissent (including the populist celebration of a sort of dumb anarchism) lies in Friedrich Nietzsche's theory of *ressentiment*. (The role of the later modernists in the Frankfurt School, especially Theodor Adorno, lies in broadcasting the theory of *ressentiment* in the guise of a Marxist critique of mass culture.) That theory was the linchpin of Nietzsche's elitist effort to reinforce existing social rank, and its incongruous popularity among contemporary intellectuals on the Left is a sad indication of the nasty turn their political despair has taken. This is just as true of nominally cutting-edge work on identity influenced by Michel Foucault, such as that of Judith Butler, as it is of Fredric Jameson's neo-Marxist account of mass culture. Foucault, Butler, Jameson (in his literary criticism), and countless others continually invoke Nietzsche's account of *ressentiment* in what is undeniably the urtext of postmodernism, *On the Genealogy of Morality* (1887). Virtually anyone who speaks incautiously of postmodernism, therefore, participates in the reproduction of Nietzsche.

That reproduction is especially evident in postmodern theorists who clearly suffer from little or no doubt about their own powers, while writing so confidently about everyone else's lack of effective agency. The persisting elitism in postmodern theory lies in the division implicitly drawn between people sophisticated enough to dwell on identity—those who *know better*—and yahoos who take it for granted. John M. Ellis describes the appeal of poststructuralist theory as "the sense of belonging to an intellectual elite, of having left behind the naiveté of the crowd [by] operating on a more sophisticated intellectual plane." Sometimes this division between the elite and the crowd is quite explicit: The "man who has fallen is somewhat wiser than the fool who walks around oblivious of the crack in the pavement about to trip him up," writes one of the leading lights of poststructuralism, Paul De Man.[26] This is, in fact, a synopsis of Nietzsche's comments on *ressentiment* and subjectivity in *On the Genealogy of Morality,* which De Man discusses at length in *Allegories of Reading* (1979). (The sensational discovery of De Man's intellectual collaboration with the Nazi occupation of Belgium during World War II, as a number of commentators have pointed out, was not really inconsistent with his known work.)

The logical result of transmitting Nietzsche is the inadvertent, although perfectly culpable, complicity of academic postmodernism with cultural and political authorities. That complicity lies not only in providing mainstream media with specific ideas with which to ridicule expressions of dissent but also in the general tendency of postmodern theory to promote its correspondence to objective conditions. "By conflating postmodernism as *theory* and as [actual] *condition,*" Andrew Goodwin argues, "the former finds itself with a vested interest in promoting the latter, if not morally and/or politically, then as a cultural form of far greater significance than the evidence often suggests." [27] The result of the persistent slippage that Goodwin describes, from theory to insisting on an objective condition, is that innocent reference to either postmodernism (referring to the arts, including mass culture) or postmodernity (referring to our general condition) is simply no longer possible, except to describe their promoters. Neither would be known to us were it not for people with the "cultural capital" to make them exist, to use Pierre Bourdieu's term for institutionally sanctioned cultural authority, such as that of scholars (including leftist ones). Thus the study of mass culture must necessarily include a history of the cultural arbiters who shape the judgment of popular art and its reception, as Andrew Ross argues in *No Respect* (1989). The remainder of Part 1 supplies that history in the case of postmodernism.

Because the correspondence of postmodern theory to actual experience is highly questionable, the core of that theory is understandably an effort, licensed by Nietzsche, to supersede any notion of an objective reality. (Descriptions of the postmodern condition, however, comprise just as much a grand, holistic narrative as repudiated versions of reality.) The denial of an objective reality, or truth, relieves academics not only of any need for veracity in their accounts of the spectacle, of the state of knowledge, and so on but also of social responsibility for the results of their efforts. While some will concede that postmodernism, as a paradigm generated by academics, is open to debate as to its exact relevance to actual historical conditions, few if any scholars have not subscribed to it to some extent, placing it effectively beyond institutional reconsideration—until the next paradigm shift, of course. The ludicrous result is that postmodern theory denies the objective or natural status of all concepts *except* that of postmodernity (much as Nietzsche seems quite serene regarding his assumptions and terminology).

It's a sign of the current stasis that a relatively conscientious academic such as David Simpson feels compelled to remind readers, in *The Academic Postmodern and the Rule of Literature: A Report on Half-Knowledge* (1995), that what has occurred inside academia is hardly identical with what is occurring outside it. Simpson expresses less certainty than I do concerning just what postmodernism in sum total might be, but he is confident nonetheless that he understands what *academic* postmodernism has been: an insistence "that it is impossible to authenticate any form of knowledge as truth" that risks not only becoming "familiar to the point of being banal," but especially mistaking "priorities among the disciplines inside the academy for a radical redescription of the world outside the academy." Such a mistake makes it "very tempting to propose that the world has indeed changed." Thus the theorizing of postmodernity typically slips into promotion of an actual death of the subject and of the social and an actual end of history.

Simpson argues instead that "the subject never really died, but was merely put on hold for a while as an attempted corrective to an entrenched version of liberal expressivity" dating from the Enlightenment.[28] Given the thorough interrogation of identity that has gone on for some time now, I suggest in Chapter 6 that we ought to move on to a post-postmodern effort to restore a belief in agency, although a more examined belief, alive to contradictions, than that of the Enlightenment. (I use *post-postmodern* only as a provisional expedience, I should stress, because I loath reproducing the sense of belatedness, of being "after" the possibilities in modernity, in the original use of "post.") The key to restoring some confidence in our identities lies in overthrowing the long history of intellectual contempt for emotion, which means taking on the postmodern school of Nietzsche, one of the primary subjects of Chapter 2.

CHAPTER 2

# The Vicious History of Aesthetics
*Romanticism, Modernism, and Postmodernism*
*on Mass Culture and Ressentiment*

I began to notice academic accounts of postmodernism—Marxist critiques of postmodern culture, in fact—creeping into mainstream music criticism in 1991 and in the *New York Times* of all places. The appearance of nominally Marxist theories in that venue, first of all, partially belies the claim of writers like Russell Jacoby, in *The Last Intellectuals* (1987), that leftist academics preoccupied with dense theory have no influence on the culture at large. I say "partially" because he had in mind a positive influence; in the case of postmodern theory, the influence has been pernicious, if unintentionally so. But even if the academic Left was involuntarily exploited, that the *Times* would find supposedly radical ideas useful in trashing dissent ought to alert us immediately to the liabilities and irresponsibility of those ideas. They represent a classic instance of postmodern theory that "masquerades as critique," as George Lipsitz puts it, but is "so one-dimensional that it ultimately serves as a form of collaboration with the oppressors." [1]

In its pessimism about the power of multinational corporations to absorb or co-opt any expression of dissent, much of postmodern theory only reinforces a sense of hopelessness, a conviction of the inevitability of the status quo. Thus "postmodernism ultimately manages to install and reinforce as much as subvert the conventions . . . it appears to challenge," says Linda Hutcheon, and its apparent criticism belies "its own complicity with power and domination." The unexamined nature of postmodern views, which will be quite clear, indicates that the ways we might transform society are "not to be found in the study of power" as an abstract theoretical matter, as Greil Marcus argues. What we need instead is "a long, clear look at the seemingly trivial gestures and accounts of ordinary experience" like those found in popular music and its audiences.[2]

What has particularly concerned me, therefore, since the events of 1991 that I recount in Chapter 4—the establishment reaction to Nirvana's breakthrough and to the appearance of the Riot Grrrls—is writing on alternative music by younger journalists and scholars that features favorable references to postmodernism. In trying to enhance both the timeliness (the hipness, that is) and the intellectual prestige of their work, those younger critics have been citing postmodern theorists who, in point of fact, doubt that any real cultural alternatives even exist, whether within or without corporate-produced culture.

For the problem with invoking postmodern ideas while celebrating alternative music to be clear, one first needs to know what the academics who are cited—always superficially—actually have to say. Perhaps the most influential of those academic analysts of postmodernism is Fredric Jameson, the elder statesman of Marxist scholars in the United States, who by 1994 had become the subject of academic panels on his "legacy." Some might expect I would start with Jean Baudrillard, but I have seen Jameson cited more often in the recent U.S. work I have in mind; Baudrillard's stock seems to have dropped since *Rolling Stone* touted him a few years ago. But the idea of Jameson's I wish to criticize—that the expression of strong emotion in mass culture only reinforces a jaded, apathetic audience—is considerably indebted to Baudrillard, I believe, so he is present in much of what follows.

Although Jameson writes in essence as a Marxist critic of the postmodern condition, he casts it as an irresistible theoretical construct: It is "not possible intellectually or politically simply to celebrate postmodernism *or* to 'disavow' it" (emphasis added).[3] In this insistence that we are stuck with the postmodern, and in light of the many commentators convinced of the postmodern condition who cite Jameson as an authority, he offers a classic example of the ironic complicity that Hutcheon and Lipsitz observe in theorists of postmodernism. It comes as no surprise, therefore, that his suggestions for counteracting postmodernity, such as "cognitive mapping," are rather slight.

What I want to stress in Jameson is one of his central theses in his often cited 1984 essay "Postmodernism, or the Cultural Logic of Late Capitalism" (an essay which was unchanged in his similarly titled 1991 book). That thesis proposes that a general "waning of affect" has occurred in postmodern life, most evident in a diminished emotional engagement with the arts. There is no distinction of "high" and "popular" arts here; distinctions in quality no longer exist, supposedly, in a postmodern world filled with incoherent pastiche. The speciousness of this notion, in light of the actual experience of the widely varied audiences for mass culture, makes clear that Jameson participates in the long tradition of "critical arbitration of taste," as Dominic Strinati puts it, that only sees a homogeneous mass audience. Recent efforts to correct that distance through "a sociology of culture," in contrast, demonstrate that audiences continue to make discriminations, sometimes according to the traditional high-popular divide, sometimes based on a consciously populist defense of their tastes, and sometimes even along political lines of conformity and nonconformity, especially in the case of popular music.[4] Given Jameson's complete lack of reference to any kind of sociology, it is no surprise that his evidence for the waning of affect is a largely irrelevant demonstration of his breadth and erudition regarding artistic texts (typical of the cases made for all the theses in his article): a contrast between Vincent Van Gogh's highly suggestive depiction of peasant shoes and Andy Warhol's blank *Diamond Dust Shoes*.

The preference for Van Gogh, moreover, indicates Jameson's general nostalgia for modern art, and he acknowledges that his theory is far from "post" modernist; it is in fact perfectly modernist. (Thus "cognitive mapping" merely recycles a common motif in modern art, a quest to reorient oneself to urban areas.) We will eventually see, however, that music critics, among many others, nonetheless misconstrue him as an oracle of postmodernism, a misunderstanding invited by the slippage between critique and complicity that he shares with all postmodern theory. That Jameson does not seem to have experienced a waning of affect himself but observes it from on high also makes him (and other postmodern theorists such as Baudrillard) hard to distinguish from a long chain of elite modernist critics lamenting mass culture. The postmodern world dominated by multinational corporations, he finds, poses an "impossible totality"—impossible for us to understand, in other words, and thus sublime or unknowable—yet he has no problem in describing it comprehensively.

In the case of mass culture, Jameson does not mean by waning of affect that emotions are not available, but that their impact lacks any "depth." On the face of it, he seems to argue that through sheer inundation by mass entertainment, we've become jaded as our visceral responses have waned. We don't shock easily, if at all, anymore, although we may go through the charade of claiming we are still roused from time to time. What the loss of depth really implies, however, is an absence of intellectual reflection on the part of the mass audience, hence the call for the "cognitive" as a corrective for affective dysfunction.

The disappearance of depth has resulted in a distinctly political loss, Jameson claims at the outset of "Postmodernism," in a passage that has since been echoed repeatedly: "Overt expressions of social and political defiance no longer scandalize anyone, and are not only received with the greatest complacency but have themselves become institutionalized." Accustomed to "the frantic economic urgency of producing fresh waves of ever more novel-seeming goods," everyone knows, presumably, that nothing really matters amid the ceaseless, furious circulation of commodities. Defiant music is just another consumer choice out of that chaotic whirlwind, meeting just another submarket taste in the same way that OK Cola provides a phony alternative to Coca-Cola. (When it comes to music, in reality, it is hard to argue that Green Day and even R.E.M., whatever their record labels and sales, are not a genuine "alternative" to Michael Bolton.) By 1995, Jameson's thesis on the commercialization of defiance had spread to the editorial page of my hometown newspaper: "Almost any kind of defiance, . . . every outrage, seems to quickly become a trend—from body piercing to grunge." [5]

Jameson actually detected the loss of depth in consumer society as early as 1971, in *Marxism and Form*: "The products with which we are furnished are utterly without depth [and thus] totally incapable of serving as a conductor of psychic energy." [6] It took him a while to declare the phenomenon postmodern, in other words. I note the long shelf life of his thesis first because it reflects the fact that he's not saying anything new at all: Like so many theorists of the postmodern, he's simply rehashing modernism. He seems, moreover, to have been forced to modify his 1971 assertion that the products of our culture have no depth, for in 1984 he concedes that some do still exhibit defiance; hence, the fault (the complacency) lies in ourselves. As in modernist criticism, the producers of mass culture are all powerful and the consumers merely passive receptacles who don't merit any close scrutiny of how they actually behave. And if Jameson did indeed relent over time on the lack of depth or power in the products of mass culture, one ought to suspect that his view of their audience could stand reconsideration as well.

His fallacy here has its roots in the refusal of modern aesthetics to separate those responsible for commerce, including cultural commerce, from those without power—a failure to distinguish producers from consumers, that is, or mass culture from popular culture. The result in cultural analysis is *productivism,* or assuming that the commercial process that makes available something like punk rock completely determines (or limits) the possibilities of both the artistic product itself and the ways people respond to it. What actually happens in "consumption" is of no interest, just as what ordinary people (or "the masses") were actually up to was of no interest to modernism, except as a subject of uninformed derision. This is precisely the approach of many postmodern theorists, who, as a result, don't look so "post" after all.

What really confuses the definition of postmodernism is the diametric opposition of productivism by cultural populism, which emerged from cultural studies and its attention to audiences (or consumers) like youth subcultures. Although scholars practicing political economy are often productivist in outlook and use cultural populism as a strawman to attack cultural studies, some academics and critics, such as the "New Times" group in Great Britain, do indeed go to an equally insupportable extreme in arguing that virtually all consumer behavior is somehow subversive. The reputation of cultural populists for over-optimism is misleading, though. John Fiske, for example, and other adherents of Michel de Certeau's *The Practice of Everyday Life* (trans. 1984)—which celebrates the arts of "making do" in popular culture but also describes it as an uncoordinated, reflexive "anthill"—actually seem indistinguishable from Baudrillard, who simply reproduces the traditional modernist view of the passive, herdlike mass audience ("dumb like beasts") but purports to find intellectual passivity a revolutionary virtue. Because the masses accept everything, they are actually subversive—or beyond manipulation, anyway—a "black hole" swallowing up all efforts to influence it. Fiske attributes plenty of physical exuberance to consumers in *Understanding Popular Culture* (1989) but likewise rules out any conscious critical reflection on society on their part, let alone any counterproduction of meaning. In Baudrillard's case, moreover, his description of the muteness and intellectual passivity of the masses in explicit terms of femininity makes it clear that the extremists among the populists represent no break at all with aesthetics since the eighteenth century.[7]

Given Baudrillard's own residue of romanticism and modernism, it should come as no surprise that he had some influence on Jameson's adjustment (between 1971 and 1984) in his description of the waning of depth, although Jameson is a more straightforward productivist. Baudrillard's first book, *Le système des objets* (1968), describes the circulation of commodities as a frantic world of apparent motion and transformation in which nothing actually changes. (Like Jameson, he owes a considerable debt to the Situationist International, especially Guy Debord's *Society of the Spectacle,* which completely differs in considering negation of the system a continuing possibility.) Baudrillard later coined the term *hyperreality* to describe this world of illusory change, or a world without real depth, that is. Hyperreality results from simulations—of change, of emotion, and so on—abolishing the real. Thanks to the technologies of entertainment and information, everything is a copy or a *simulacrum,* to use the Platonic term he popularized. Nothing is original, so to speak, or authentic; a facsimile or simulation in this sense has no depth. Even raw violence, including violent emotion, "no longer has any meaning," for we live through "a completely imaginary contact-world of sensorial mimetics and tactile mysticism." What we experience as feelings is in reality just an imitation of feeling, and we all know it. His conclusion on the resulting complacency—"radical disenchantment" has entered a "cool and cybernetic phase"—seems quite similar to Jameson's thesis on defiance only feeding complacency.[8]

Other academics have applied the postmodern picture of the frenetic, depthless world of commodities directly to popular music. In 1990, Steve Redhead described a "rapidly changing velocity of Pop Time [in the] speed at which things come around again in the circular time scales of fashionability." The "velocity of the process of change" has established, presumably, the " 'absolute power of the instant.' " But pop music has always been disposable, leading some academics to declare that rock and roll and postmodernism, in retrospect, have always been synonymous. The limited time frame in which a popular song seems immediate and vital, however, is so intense that its brevity is not something to sneer at or lament as postmodern, if one considers rock music "news, not art." Popular music, argues Simon Frith, "works as commentary, commentary that can, at best, seize, articulate, change the moment, but always pass[es] with it." [9] Mass-reproduced objects (or simulacra) actually possess considerable depth, even if their impact doesn't have longevity.

I would add, though, that the historical example of such moments—the Velvet Underground, James Brown, Big Star, George Clinton, the Sex Pistols—always remains useful for those who would like to create more. Many musicians, fortunately, continue to exploit that history, even if postmodern theorists convinced we've reached the end of history are no longer interested in it. Rock music will not die just because it has reached a stage at which self-consciousness about its history has become a necessary part of wringing new life out of its techniques—what art form hasn't repeatedly faced this task? The self-styled postmoderns ridiculing rock for being played out, such as Simon Reynolds writing on "The Perils of Loving Old Records Too Much," are in fact only clinging to specious romantic and modernist notions of authenticity and spontaneity—of constantly "making it new," as Ezra Pound put it—which rock absorbed in the 1960s. Reynolds is essentially nostalgic for a purportedly lost creativity, yet indicts others for looking backward. Kathleen Hanna of Bikini Kill, in contrast, says she doesn't "care about creating a new sound—everything's been done anyway. I want to use the tools that are here right now and make something that works." Sometimes told she sounds like Poly Styrene of X-Ray Spex, the comparison is fine with her: "I think Poly Styrene is great! I'm not into the *novelty of the new.*" [10]

Neither will rock "die just because it is not alone," as Johann Fornäs puts it—not alone in the sense that rock has fragmented into a number of subgenres reflecting the influence of new technologies and other musics. The resulting appearance of accelerated velocity in Pop Time is hardly a matter of sheer chaos but, instead, reflects the fairly comprehensible competition for attention among a wide variety of sounds. "A more optimistic interpretation," says Fornäs, might find that rock music's "sucking in of various new and non-orthodox tendencies is indeed what might be able to keep it alive." [11]

Oblivious to these historical considerations, a pretty shameful failing in a Marxist, Jameson actually includes punk rock in his thesis concerning deadened complacency, in the shorter original version of his essay on postmodernism (in Hal Foster's 1983 collection *The Anti-Aesthetic*). Punk, he believes, is a primary example of the way offensive expression can be "commercially successful" and merely "taken in stride by society." In the completed essay of 1984, Jameson detaches punk rock from his thesis to save it for his conclusion on the same dismal point, punk serving as a knowing example of his hipness:

> We all, in one way or another, dimly feel that not only . . . local countercultural forms of cultural resistance and guerilla warfare, but also even overtly political interventions like those of *The Clash* [his emphasis], are all somehow secretly disarmed and reabsorbed by a system of which they themselves might well be considered a part, since they can achieve no distance from it. [12]

The postmodern wand simply waves away the experience of anyone who was and still is inspired by the Clash, among others, to seek further radical insight and maybe even action on it.

This "peculiar depopulation" of the postmodern world, as Howard Hampton puts it in a review contrasting Jameson with the Mekons, arbitrarily ignores many dissidents: "those stubbornly uneuphoric citizens of the multinational, multimedia economy [who find] in images of free-market abundance and democratized apathy a stunning poverty of the imagination." There is no good reason, therefore, to accept his belief that the possibility of refusal has been foreclosed in the recent past as a result of "aesthetic production today [being] integrated into commodity production generally." [13] For one thing, this lament has been around for at least two centuries: The desire for "distance" or autonomy from commercial culture is precisely where postmodern theory only reproduces romantic and modernist aesthetics.

Before I get into that historical background, I want simply to object to the incorporation thesis on art and commerce, which is subscribed to almost universally by leftist academics. Incorporation in this sense refers to the ability of capitalism to co-opt and sell any expression of dissent, no matter how unpalatable at first, and thereby eviscerate it. The result is emotion bereft of commitment and meaning, specifically the poses of defiance or anger that Jameson claims are met only with a corresponding complacency. I encounter the blithe citation of incorporation all the time, both in personal responses and in academic books and articles.

Pessimism over the presumably disastrous influence of commerce has become commonplace among hip journalists and alternative music fans, too, and in no small part thanks to postmodern academics. Leslie Savan, for example, repeatedly despairs in *The Village Voice* at "how easily any idea, deed, or image can become part of the corporate sponsored world, . . . a culture that sponsors rebellion, that provides the conflict that our society . . . would grow bored without." (This is undiluted Jameson: Defiance meets with complacency as a result.) Thanks to the "corporate powers bark[ing] instructions at you to be rebellious," apparently, the only way left to do so is symbolic—"in what you buy and parade as your identity." [14] Thus the followers of cutting-edge musicians worry that a group has "sold out" when it signs with a major (or corporate) label or even simply when it sells an increasing number of units through an independent label. There's also been considerable fatalism over the decline of the most prominent indies, like Rough Trade, in the early 1990s.

But the result has been more grassroots petit (or small-scale) entrepreneurship than ever, judging from my students. Some get a little money together, call themselves a record company, and press a single for a group they know; others organize performing spaces open to all ages, as an alternative to clubs dependent on liquor sales to adults. If critics and scholars would relent on their anticommercial absolutism, in fact, they would find young people in every subculture, from grunge to hip-hop to Riot Grrrls, "learning and sharing skills, practising them [while] making a small amount of money," and creating alternative job opportunities that can also be quite empowering. In the process of making music, clothes, and fanzines, says Angela McRobbie, attempting to earn a living "directly expresses the character of its producers in a way which is frequently in opposition to those available, received or encouraged images or identities" offered by the dominant culture. What is too often seen as the "commercial, low ebb of [a] subculture"—hastening the process of its incorporation, that is— ought to be considered central to it, instead, and a potential vehicle of change and social transformation.[15]

Candice Pedersen, co-owner of the indie label K Records, defines working in the punk subculture as involving "a choice whereby, perhaps financially my world's going to suck, but it's *what I want to do*." In this sense, the punk subculture is "not about style" at all, just as McRobbie suggests, but about independence, which explains in large part why punk continues to hold so much appeal for the young. That independence, Pedersen adds, should not be confused with the romantic ideal: Rejecting the martyrdom associated with indie music by many of its fans, she stresses that sometimes one "*can* be really successful," at least in terms of personal satisfaction.[16]

Petit entrepreneurs have long provided the basis for radical political organizations; why are young people working through various music cultures any different, except for conventional assumptions about the callowness and ignorance of youth? Andrea Juno points out that rock audiences since the 1960s have always had a do-it-yourself element broadcasting ideas. But where the "seeds of change" could once only be spread through "ritual social gatherings in small clubs," now computer technology has facilitated "a *samizdat*-like network of fanzines, tapes and records, . . . an alternative from mainstream ideas [that] helped birth the Riot Grrrl movement and groups like Homocore." [17]

The postmoderns insist nonetheless on the highly abstracted observation that since the counterculture of the 1960s "youth rebellion" has only been a marketing tool. Tom Frank of *The Baffler* has conducted a steady rant on the matter:

> Youth culture means just one thing: a perpetual revolution of tastes, values, and styles; a living symbol for advertising's manufacture of endless consumer discontent. . . . And so we will have new generations of youth rebellion as certainly as we will have new generations of mufflers or toothpaste or footwear.

Echoing Savan, he describes "counterculture-style liberationism [as] the ideological stock-in-trade of the American culture industry, coloring everything with its simple catechism of rebellion and individual fulfillment through products." In keeping with the general postmodern view that every aspect of life is directed from above by multinational corporations, Frank insists that irreverence and "sneering disdain" for restraint and conformity can no longer be anything but marketing tools. The picture is very different, however, if we attend to what young people are doing on the fringes of corporate capitalism—and I'm deliberately not saying *outside* it. The whole problem with mass-culture critics, for two centuries now, is their impossible desire that art be "authentic" or exist outside commerce, which turns into despair when that impossibility becomes apparent. The romantic agenda simply no longer makes sense, argues Andrew Goodwin, as "the supposed contradiction between art and commerce" has become "increasingly artificial." [18]

In contrast with the incorporation thesis, an avant-garde group well known for its influence on punk rock, the Situationist International, argued continually that attempting to prostitute cultural forms that expressed a genuine dissatisfaction was a dangerous business for capitalism. (This is a subtler version of the old Marxist maxim that a capitalist would sell you the rope to hang him or her with.) Sooner or later, people might take those forms seriously again, in a backlash of resurgent outrage. Punk provides a good example of such a renewed vehemence: Declared dead in the early 1980s, a decade later it returned with a vengeance. By 1994, of course, journalists well-versed in the incorporation thesis were decrying the commercial success of Green Day and Offspring.

Postmodern arguments about the domination of popular music by commerce obliterate the fact that the music, whatever the changes in production and consumption (including our increasingly cynical self-consciousness about both), continues to be meaningful the same way it always has—emotionally, in its best forms as anger laced with humor (however acid). The complexity and fragmentation of the contemporary soundscape, the varieties of music serving narrow market niches, does not alter the impact of music either.

But the main point I want to make is that Jameson's work is not postmodern at all but residual modernism. In the essay in *The Anti-Aesthetic,* in fact, he directly contrasts punk's easy incorporation with the supposedly disturbing "productions of the older high modernism," or the work of Joyce and Picasso. Setting aside the question of whether Joyce or Picasso ever produced any more genuinely radical a scandal than the Sex Pistols did, I want simply to note once again that Jameson's nostalgia for modernism is quite explicit. In the subsequent version of his essay, his contrast of modernism and recent "defiant" expression expands into a nostalgic regret that "the younger generation of the 1960s will now confront the formerly oppositional modern movement as a set of dead classics." That nostalgia culminates in his conclusion that there is "no distance" anymore for art, or no possibility of existing autonomously—as if there ever was. When modernism is treated as the supposed terminus of aesthetic possi-

bilities, Raymond Williams points out, "everything afterwards is counted out of development. It is *after*; stuck in the post." [19] The fraud of postmodernism is its perpetuation of modernist values, its stoppage of history.

Elsewhere, Jameson has said that modernist scholars in the Frankfurt School, Theodor Adorno and Herbert Marcuse, represent the only critical perspective on mass culture of any value. They are silent partners in much of Jameson's "Postmodernism" essay as well, even in his thesis on the "waning of affect," or complacency in the face of defiance. (Many other postmodern academics think very highly of Adorno, too.) The fact that Jameson's influential argument for this new postmodern condition dates to the 1930s indicates its highly suspect nature. Consumerism as a strategy for social control, furthermore, equated by Jameson and many others with the postwar period, dates at least to the 1920s, as documented by Stuart Ewen in *Captains of Consciousness* (1976). And if one examines, finally, the history of loathing for emotion in aesthetics dating to the eighteenth century, the postmodern description of a radically new epoch really looks dubious.

The traditional disparagement of emotion in aesthetics provides a prominent basis for an essay Adorno wrote in 1938, "The Culture Industry: Enlightenment as Mass Deception" (published in *Dialectic of Enlightenment* in 1944). He was trying in particular to refute Walter Benjamin's hopeful essay "The Work of Art in the Age of Mechanical Reproduction" (1936), and their exchange essentially initiated serious theoretical discussion of mass culture, laying down battle lines that persist in the postmodern period. Benjamin believed that the "shock effect" possible in new forms of cultural technology, like film and recorded music, could bring about "a heightened presence of mind." His argument in this respect is very amenable to more recent feminist claims for the rationality inherent in the expression of anger: Benjamin clearly retains the sense of the original coinage of "shock-effect" by Sergei Eisenstein in "Montage of Attractions" (1923), which was preceded by the word *emotional.*

Benjamin's belief in the mutual dependence of the emotional and the rational was influenced by the playwright Bertolt Brecht. Although Brecht by all accounts treated women abysmally, he argued much like contemporary feminism that avant-garde artists should encourage audiences, through disruptive techniques and attitudes, to take a critical approach to emotions as well as ideas. (In the poem "To Posterity," he singles out "anger over injustice" as his primary motivation.) Both emotions and ideas had to be altered in the interest of social change; thus to divide emotion and reason was a sin in his view. [20] (It would be interesting to know if Brecht's female collaborators impressed this upon him.)

In the traditional manner, in contrast, Adorno quite readily disparages mass culture for its emotional appeal. Thanks to the "standardization" or repetitiveness of its techniques, he finds, mass entertainment allows emotions to be "reliably controlled," turning "genuine personal emotion" into "mere twaddle." It isn't that he's really all that concerned about emotion; the loss of "inwardness" he decries has more to do with the decline of "mental effort," or intellect. Adorno was not alone in these views. The art critic Clement Greenberg, in his 1939 essay "Avant-Garde and Kitsch," similarly criticizes formulaic mass culture (or kitsch) for its reliance on "faked sensations." As a result of emotional experience becoming an "open lie," says Adorno, forms of entertainment like popular songs are only "a straitjacket for longing" and other feelings. Because mass culture "prescribes every reaction," all pleasure, including emotional identification, "hardens into boredom." Language becomes "devoid of quality," as a result, or disconnected from meaning.[21] All expression of emotion lacks *depth,* in other words, to use Jameson's term, and the possibility of negation disappears. (Another opponent of mass culture, George Orwell, wrote in his 1946 essay "The Decline of the English Murder" that the influence of U.S. mass culture had resulted in real-life English murders having "no depth of feeling," yet another instance of Jameson's postmodern discovery actually being rather hackneyed.)

Thus the "emotional types" among music fans "are taken in by the musical expression of frustration" in particular, Adorno says in his 1941 essay "On Popular Music." (He does provide some unintentional comic relief in his description of "rhythmically obedient" types or jazz dancers whose slavishness to "machine music . . . expresses their desire to obey"—so much for dance music, disco, hip-hop, house, industrial, and rock.) Because unhappiness and rebellion come "pre-digested," or in stereotypical form, the "so-called releasing element of music is simply the opportunity to feel something."[22] A listener gets his or her fix of anger and frustration and never acts on it. This would be Jameson's claim four decades later, that expressions of defiance only serve as fodder for complacency.

An important conduit for this view was Herbert Marcuse's later work. In his 1964 study *One-Dimensional Man,* a highly influential text for the counterculture, Marcuse describes the "absorbent power" of contemporary culture, which easily incorporates even the most antagonistic forms of expression. This "new totalitarianism," he finds, "manifests itself precisely in a harmonizing pluralism, where the most contradictory works and truths peacefully coexist in indifference."[23] This is the incorporation thesis, of course, which in this light is indisputably modernist in origin, not unique at all to the postmodern period.

When Jameson paraphrased Marcuse two decades later, postmodernism was merely born out of modernism's ashes.

Besides indicating how little is new in postmodern theory, I have traced out the influence of the Frankfurt School to address a frequent source of puzzlement for my students and others, the fact that these scholars are all Marxists. Why do intellectuals presumably on the side of the "masses" express so much contempt for them, and the same hostility to mass culture as conservatives who like to rail about cultural decline to emphasize their own superiority?

The judgments are indeed essentially identical, and thus Adorno had no difficulty getting published in the United States during the Cold War (in Bernard Rosenberg and David Manning White's 1957 collection *Mass Culture*). The bases of those judgments are different, however. From the origin of aesthetics in the eighteenth century, as Martha Woodmansee documents in *The Author, Art, and the Market* (1994), conservatives have condemned mass culture for feeding disorder and revolt, whereas leftists believe that the very possibility of rebellion is stifled by mass cultural pacification. Western Marxism in this century has generally been pessimistic, typically retreating into academic philosophy—now postmodernism—because a socialist revolution failed to occur outside the Soviet Union, which itself presented a travesty of Marxism. To the Left, "mass" culture has been a particular villain in the failure of revolutionary hope: supposedly it makes "masses" by pacifying people, and thereby preserves the status quo. Only the high arts seem to have resisted commercialization, and if they did so at the expense of having a popular audience, that was a necessary price to pay.

To the Right, mass culture undermines the authority of the classics, both by raiding high culture and by encouraging disinterest in it or even active disrespect for it. The hierarchy of "high" and "low" culture must be maintained because, in essence, the supposedly natural basis for such judgments helps make conservative ideas about society in general seem more natural as well. Chief among them is the idea that social classes, or wealth and poverty, merely reflect the stratification of society into superior and inferior persons. If distinguishing high and low culture helps teach us to distinguish exceptional and ordinary people, in other words, then the undermining of high culture by mass culture threatens a significant support of the status quo. To the Left, in contrast, the loss of a distinct realm of high culture would be the loss of the only space posing an alternative to capitalism.

The problem here is the Left's failure to break with conventional aesthetics, a failure that continues to undermine claims that postmodern critics have abandoned modernist elitism. As we have seen in the case of Jameson, postmodern academics continue to participate in the romantic tradition of pitting the arts against commercialism. The only change has been an increasing despair about the inability of intellectuals to influence a world that seems ever increasingly hostile to their values. Thus, I want to discuss the history of aesthetics briefly to bring out its long-standing contempt for mass and popular culture in general and for emotion in particular.

What we call "art," first of all, has from the origin of the concept been defined against mass culture: Aesthetics was born v. hen the novel arose to worry intellectuals in the eighteenth century. Unnerved by the rapidly increasing bourgeois—and feminine—audience for commercial literature such as Gothic fiction, philosophers of art for the first time grouped together the fine arts, including painting and poetry, as a separate discipline. (That the novel is now considered one of the fine arts indicates just how arbitrary aesthetic discrimination has always been.) This new consolidated field of aesthetics defined proper art in opposition to mercenary art, as Kant constructs matters in *Critique of Judgment.* His further denunciation of commercial art as "mechanical," although he had in mind the audience's response to popular literature, indicates as well the antitechnologism in aesthetics, fueled by the specter of the Industrial Revolution.[24] Subsequent inventions, starting with photography, only further inflamed the view that pure art is "free" art, free of contamination by commerciality and industry—a view reproduced in Jameson's despair over achieving any "distance" from capitalist culture in his passage on the Clash. Charles Baudelaire, in "The Salon of 1859," disparaged photography for giving the "mob" access to both the viewing and the making of art, a moment that marks the origin of modernist contempt for mechanically and electronically reproduced culture.

Good art from the start of the field of aesthetics, whether one points to Kant or as far back as Joseph Addison, was held to appeal to intellect and erudition and bad art to emotions and pleasure. Kant, of course, specifically stipulated that a pure judgment upon art (or a pure taste) was one free of the "barbaric" influence of emotion. So when theorists of postmodernism like Jameson tell us about the fatal disjunction between emotion and intellect in mass culture, they are not telling us something new or "post" but only reproducing two hundred years of condescension toward popular taste for its supposedly mindless emotional component. Aesthetics was founded on such principles in large part due to the decline of aristocratic patronage of the arts, with the rise of the urban industrial bourgeoisie. Thrown into the terrible freedom of the marketplace and its uncertainty—free to do what one wanted but also to starve if one didn't sell the results—artists deplored the general values of commerce, as a result, as much as the perceived vulgarity of bourgeois philistines. Chief among those despised

values was use value, or utility: Increasingly, from romanticism through modernism, high art was defined as essentially *useless* (a purposive activity without
a purpose, in Kant's terms). Vulgar art (or mass culture), in contrast, was art that
people found useful for its stimulation of emotion, of sensual pleasure, and of
thought concerning social matters like politics. (This last sin, of course, is still
castigated under the rubric of political correctness.)

In revising his preface to the *Lyrical Ballads,* for example, the romantic
poet William Wordsworth decried the "gross and violent stimulants" of "sickly
and stupid" popular entertainment. Poetry is a matter of "emotion recollected in
tranquility," or emotion brought under control by the intellect. In actual practice,
for Wordsworth and a number of other male romantics, this is often a matter
specifically of reducing and thereby mastering feminine voices embodied in
song, which are felt to be "ecstatic, dangerous, seductive, and mysterious," Sarah
Webster Goodwin points out. In this respect, the romantics wound up on the
same ground as Kant, whose *Critique of Judgment* was extensively plagiarized
by Samuel Taylor Coleridge; although they were no enthusiasts for the Age of
Reason, the romantics could agree with a rationalist such as Kant that the arts
should be judged by an intellectual standard. Thus Coleridge set the mind against
passion and the "music of savage tribes," and Wordsworth's description of
tranquilized emotion echoes Kant's belief (in *Anthropology From a Pragmatic
Point of View*, 1798) that emotion is acceptable if properly rationalized, as in the
transformation of anger and vengeance into a morally constructive concept of
justice.[25]

Since the romantics, the fundamental value of art has been the *originality*
or uniqueness of the individual artist, whom Baudelaire, Nietzsche, and other
modernists elevated into a superior being. Originality for its own sake, or the
proper uselessness, lies in being incomprehensible, a virtue declared early on by
the German romantic Johann Goethe. The works of art of the subsequent two
centuries that have become canonical among intellectuals and scholars (of
all political stripes) are those that pursued, increasingly intensely, the imperative to be impenetrable to all but an intellectual aristocracy. That new aristocracy,
based on taste rather than title, was defined by Baudelaire in his essay on the
dandy in *The Painter of Modern Life* (1863)—a concept beloved of postmoderns
writing on rock music, we will see, even though Baudelaire stipulated that the
dandy was an enemy of democracy. For all the furor over political correctness
in academia, the contemporary institutional version of who and what has
counted in aesthetics and literature remains much the same, built upon that
self-styled aristocracy. Much of postmodern theory represents little change from
earlier elitism but just another stage in the long, repetitive, vicious history of

aesthetics; hence the continuing irrelevance of intellectuals, as "ordinary" people make hopeful use of popular forms regardless of pessimistic academic pronouncements.

Among the aesthetes whom scholars have deemed significant (or "canonized"), by the end of the nineteenth century the desire to detach one's art from a mercenary world became openly and irremediably elitist. The worst case was the Symbolist movement headed by Stéphane Mallarmé (and founded on Baudelaire), which, not coincidentally, has also been the primary fixation of academic work on modern literature. In contrast with poetry and its purported spirituality, Mallarmé, in "Crisis of Poetry," described everyday language in "the hands of the mob" not only as journalism—or vulgar by virtue of communicating with others—but also as "a commercial approach to reality, [with] the same facility and directness as . . . money." This seems an odd thing to say unless one understands that Mallarmé is after any cultural form contaminated by commerce, which in his mind is inevitably a facile or *easy* art. Through sheer intellectual *difficulty*, in contrast, or deliberate abstraction and vagueness that blinds the common eye by demanding close study, the modernist achieved freedom (or "autonomy") from commerce by making art inaccessible to popular taste. The only "ecstasy" that counts involves appreciation of the resulting "obscurity." [26] Impenetrable language floating free of meaning into a supposedly spiritual realm of pure form and feeling produces a "silent music," to use terms Baudelaire borrowed from Edgar Allan Poe. It's not a very material music or feeling that's at issue, in other words: The invocation of music belies its basis in a primarily cerebral if also antirational effect, the deliberate vagueness, hardly as spiritual as it pretends to be. Thus critics denounce "incomprehensibility"—a virtue according to Goethe—when it involves popular song lyrics like Kurt Cobain's because the effect results from their emotional performance instead of their intellectual demands.

That disdain for emotion, fundamental to aesthetics, is simply an elitist (as well as sexist) double standard—and a self-contradictory one at that. Professing to transcend base utilitarian reason, the Symbolists, other modernists, and many postmodern theorists aspire to empty meaning out of language in art and criticism. But an absence of reason and meaning, lauded in high culture, is condemned in mass culture. The difference, supposedly, is that mass culture has emotional and utilitarian rather than intellectual effects. None of this makes the slightest sense, however, in the face of the fact that all expression possesses a tactile emotive force based in judgments on social experience. Neither high art nor mass culture can be detached from either feeling or reason—and the high never exists apart from the mass, however negative the relation. By resisting contemporaries in modernism along these lines, Benjamin and Brecht (along with Mikhail Bakhtin, as will be seen in Chapter 6) inadvertently became precursors to feminist philosophy.

Modernist work in history, philosophy, psychology, and sociology shares the aestheticist loathing of the mob, as Patrick Brantlinger amply demonstrates in *Bread and Circuses* (1983). Through "negative classicism," or comparison of modern civilization with the decline and fall of Rome, modernists—and now many postmodernists—cast a highly developed mass culture as the major cause of all manner of crises, ranging from revolution (more a nineteenth-century concern) to totalitarianism. (The contradiction in these perceived possibilities is much like the very different readings of the effect of mass culture by aestheticians at opposite ends of the political spectrum.) Negative classicism is a frequent theme in modernist treatises such as Gustav Le Bon's *The Crowd: A Study of the Popular Mind* (1895), Oswald Spengler's *The Decline of the West* (1918), Sigmund Freud's *Group Psychology and the Analysis of the Ego* (trans. 1922), and José Ortega y Gasset's *Revolt of the Masses* (1930).

But the greatest modernist influence on postmodernism, especially French theory, has been that of Friedrich Nietzsche. Like other negative classicists posing the seeming paradox that democracy brings about totalitarianism, thanks in particular to mass culture, he considers the idea of progress in modern society utterly false—a considerable source of the appeal that he holds for postmoderns. In reality, though, there is no paradox: The wealthy masters of the mass media understandably work to undermine the possibility of genuine democracy by suppressing significant political alternatives, the kind of concrete social problem in which the grand theorists of negative classicism have always been uninterested. They prefer instead, like Nietzsche, to blame the victims—somehow the masses are responsible for mass culture, although they have little or no hand in its production. (*Mass culture* properly refers simply to mass-*reproduced* culture.) Negative classicism typically insists on the dubious homogenizing proposition, as Brantlinger sums up, that the "ruling classes and the ruled develop between them forms of mass entertainment rooted in shared tastes and interests." [27]

In Nietzsche's view, sharing the values of the weak—compassion, justice, pity, and so forth—has corrupted the strongest in society, who should exercise their "will to power" unfettered by any moral inhibitions. As opposed to the social Darwinists of his day, however, Nietzsche doesn't directly sing the praises of industrialists but takes a simultaneously revolutionary and reactionary position much like that of Baudelaire and other modernists who hated the tools of capitalism, including the machine and its rationalized application, but despised the masses even more. Although Nietzsche is sometimes deemed the first modernist, his "overman" is essentially a logical extension of the natural intellectual aristocrat Baudelaire called the dandy. But Baudelaire, interestingly, includes a quasi-social Darwinist piece, "Beat Up the Poor," in *Paris Spleen* (1869). Nietzsche likewise gets the same results as the social Darwinists by viewing intellectuals and the best of aristocratic barbarians as naturally superior persons, or masters, who should trample on the weak; *The Anti-Christ* (1894) actually cites the evolutionary "law of selection." [28] And although he professed to find the acquisitive age in which he lived a weak one, this observation apparently pertains only to the masses, or "herd": *On the Genealogy of Morality* (1887) extols the lust for possessions on the part of the masters as a properly active emotion. Nietzsche encourages them, in particular, to ignore the demand of slave morality that they feel the paralyzing emotion of guilt over the incongruity of luxury and misery—an argument that would certainly find sympathetic ears in the contemporary corporate boardroom.

How in the world, then, could Nietzsche be the hero of postmodern Left intellectuals in the midst of our own era's resurgent social Darwinism? (Modernism, too, only reinforced prevailing conditions, in its cultivation of alienation, but at least it was a disapproving mirror.) The primary reason is the "Camille Paglia syndrome": Nietzsche's break with rationalism and his celebration of Dionysian energies allow his philosophy to be construed as profoundly radical dissent—even as anarchism, according to Peter Marshall in *Demanding the Impossible* (1992), though Nietzsche despised anarchists. But if Nietzsche is in this respect the first modernist, in some scholarly appraisals, others consider him quite radical for being the first postmodernist. His denunciation of progress as a false idea appeals to the disenchantment of many postmodern theorists with the Enlightenment faith in reason. And his emphasis on the exercise of power underlying life has also been popular among postmodern theorists, especially Foucault and his followers, who particularly admire Nietzsche's "genealogy" of the struggle between masters and slaves, which treats history as discontinuous or "contingent," a random, unpredictable matter—hence falsified by grand narratives of the sort deplored by Lyotard. (Nietzsche's postmodern popularity is also due to a minor, unoriginal essay popularized by Jacques Derrida, "Truth and Morality in an Extra-Moral Sense," in which Nietzsche points out the arbitrary relationship of language to concepts and objects; I will return to the subject of his views on language and agency.) The fact that a negative classicist such as Nietzsche can be identified with both modernism and postmodernism indicates how much they have in common in their elitism.

His views on emotion can also be identified with both modernism, or an evolution beyond romanticism, and postmodern repudiation of the Enlightenment: The rational refinement of emotion advocated by both the romantic Wordsworth and the rationalist Kant, for example, is exactly what Nietzsche excoriates in *ressentiment,* the passive anger of the weak, which he considers a rationalization of the slave's vengeance in the form of Christian and socialist morality. His specific achievement, in fact, lies in supplying negative classicism with a theory of emotion. His influence in this regard has steadily expanded until, in the postmodern epoch, virtually everything academics and music journalists have been writing about young people echoes Nietzsche's description of *ressentiment* in *On the Genealogy of Morality.*

Nietzsche does not entirely discount emotion in *On the Genealogy of Morality,* however, just the subjection of emotion to reason. In his view, *ressentiment* is confined to internalized, unenacted emotion, but this limitation actually leads him to commend the slave. To be consistent in making a virtue of *ressentiment* all by itself, Nietzsche notes, the slave must claim that all feelings are significant in themselves: In "sanctify[ing] *revenge* with the term *justice,*" *ressentiment* makes justice "simply a further development of the feeling of having been wronged—and belatedly legitimize[s] with revenge emotional reactions in general." This is "something with which I take least issue," says Nietzsche: "I even view it as an accomplishment [because] the value of . . . emotions has been underestimated up till now."

But if Nietzsche wishes to revalue emotion, in simply reversing the traditional priority on reason he leaves emotion detached as a "biological problem," no improvement on the rationalist treatment of emotion as a bodily force distinct from the mind. What he actually revalues is not the whole subject of emotion but simply "a different set of emotions," still a matter of biology or the body, than those associated with *ressentiment.* Of "much greater biological value [are] the actual *active* emotions such as lust for power and possessions and the like" on the part of the active master, as opposed to the passive slave. This is not to say that the emotions associated with *ressentiment*—envy, hatred, resentment, suspicion, vengefulness—are passive by nature; they are rendered passive by being internalized as morality in both political and theological forms. In its motivation by pain and suffering, *ressentiment* is as much a biological or physiological matter as more active emotions but, unlike them, is confined to a calculated (or rationalized) form of revenge. Any expression motivated by *ressentiment,* as a result, is only a pitiful attempt "to *anesthetize pain through emotion,*" far from real action, or the physical brutality prized by Nietzsche. In a sense, he registers here the interchange in emotion between body and mind. But to consign the process to *ressentiment* as something despicable while deploring the subjection of physical feelings to reason is hardly to posit the general dialectic between emotion and reason argued by recent cognitive philosophy. Nietzsche was an open misogynist, moreover, and his execration of *ressentiment* for its passivity unquestionably reproduces the quite traditional sexist linkage of emotion with feminine weakness.

In its unenacted moral judgments on the powerful, in Nietzsche's view, *ressentiment* expresses itself not through self-creation but through the creation of an opposing external world, that of the masters. The slave only reacts to life, that is, rather than taking real action, with one's self-definition based solely on the contrast drawn with the master, the contrast of "good" with "evil." *Ressentiment* designates and condemns oppressors simply to suffer all the more exquisitely. *On the Genealogy of Morality* says that "the slaves's revolt in morality occurs when *ressentiment* itself turns creative and gives birth to values: the *ressentiment* of those beings who, being denied the proper response of action [by their unfit nature], compensate for it only with imaginary revenge." Putting the words "it is good to do nothing *for which we are not strong enough*" in the mouths of "weak people," Nietzsche finds that those supposedly unable to take revenge on their masters turn "impotence which doesn't retaliate into 'goodness' " (thus an earlier book's title emphasizes getting "beyond good and evil").[29]

When it is released, presumably, *ressentiment* cannot lead to any genuine relief, let alone action. Unable to act, says Max Scheler in his book titled *Ressentiment* (1915), persons filled with *ressentiment* prefer the false, "negative opposites"—or negation—of the positive feelings of "joy, splendor, power, happiness, fortune, and strength." Nietzsche's description of the kind of emotional release entailed by *ressentiment*, interestingly, sounds a lot like traditional descriptions of the audience for mass culture: "the attempt is made to anesthetize a tormenting, secret pain which is becoming unbearable with a more violent emotion of any sort, and at least rid the consciousness of it for a moment—for this one needs . . . the wildest possible emotion." [30] Such momentary escapes from consciousness through wild emotion, in order to anesthetize one's pain, are exactly what postmodern journalists attribute to young people who listen to angry music.

In both cases, Nietzsche and postmodern journalism, the denunciation of purely creative, imaginary acts of revenge is an effort to shut down one of the primary avenues of self-assertion available to people with less power: expression in creative forms, which the powerful can never entirely contain. Nietzsche's and postmodern efforts to condemn imaginative expression, fortunately, rely not on any remotely convincing or valid line of argument but on sheer ridicule alone. As feminists such as Catherine Lutz have pointed out concerning the specific subject of emotion, the ridicule of weakness is always "double sided"—the emotion of dominated groups is also feared as a danger to the prevailing order. In Nietzsche and Scheler, emotion is quite clearly "both a sign of weakness and a powerful force" to be kept under control. Rather than a source of embarrassment at our limitations, therefore, our creative, imaginative activities ought to be understood as expressions not only of our continuing hope to change an insanely unjust, plutocratic world but even as an indication of our potential power to do so. If that potential seems far from being realized, instead of becoming complicit with social Darwinists past and present looking for innate dysfunctions, we need to acknowledge the actual external barriers to action posed by social class (or lack of economic power), racial and sexual oppression, and exclusion from political institutions and processes and from mass communications. Such impediments make it "quite rational for subordinates to fear expressing their anger," says Elizabeth Spelman, "because those who have power over them may be threatened by such expressions and take steps to stifle them." [31]

Nietzsche's portrayal of the supposedly passive person full of *ressentiment* becomes even more repugnant when we consider the contrast he draws with the "Active Type." The "active" person he has in mind is the creditor who properly inflicts direct physical pain on his debtors—the sort of pain that reactionaries continue to prescribe for the poor and the unemployed. This physical assault would mark a return to ancient societies existing before indebtedness became a largely internal matter of moral guilt or "bad conscience" rather than actual suffering for financial failure. A similar move is afoot, as I write, to supplant the "pathology" or moral failure of poverty by returning the poor to an earlier historial epoch when the physical hardships of homelessness and hunger were rampant. There isn't much in postmodern social Darwinism that isn't in Nietzsche, as evidenced by Richard Herrnstein and Charles Murray's *The Bell Curve* (1994), intended to "end *ressentiment*," Adolph Reed notes (in an astute choice of terms), on the part of those who "aspire beyond their natural capacities." [32] For Nietzsche as for many postmoderns, a renewed viciousness in transactions between creditors and debtors would be the primary form of a renewed "affirmation." If this is affirmation, give me its resistance—or its opposite term, negation, synonymous with *ressentiment*—which seems all the more appealing in contrast. In supplying the powerful with an intellectual rationale for contemptuously inflicting misery on the less fortunate, Nietzsche, like many postmodern pundits, obviously feared and hoped to squelch the possibility of negation taking an active, collective form and leading to genuine democracy.

The thrust of Nietzsche's work in its own time, with its injunctions against compassion for the suffering, was to counteract the moral force of anarchism and socialism as well as encouraging the masters to stamp out the serious threat posed by revolutionary politics in the late nineteenth century. *Beyond Good and Evil* (1886) combines loathing of the bourgeoisie with derision of socialism and democracy, a typically modernist combination of revolutionary and reactionary sentiments. (Scheler also explicitly abhors socialism as the worst of all falsifications of moral values.) The diagnosis of *ressentiment* is a key part of Nietzsche's campaign against socialism: The irrational plebeian envy presumably characteristic of the Judeo-Christian tradition, in his view, persists in the disguised religion of socialism. (Karl Marx certainly has more in common with Christian pity than any capitalist does; when he called religion the opium of the people, his point was to transfer its moral values into the secular realm via democracy. Brantlinger, in *Bread and Circuses,* discusses the long-standing popularity of the accusation that radical politics depend on a quasi-religious faith, pointing out that this is essentially true of all ideologies, and that some respectable theorists believe there is nothing wrong in the first place with a combination of utopian politics and theology.)

When the moral appeals issued out of *ressentiment,* whether Christian, liberal, or socialist, cause the master not to act forcefully, he demeans himself by refraining from stomping on inferior persons to the full extent that Nietzsche thinks the bosses should. It is "absurd to ask strength *not* to . . . crush, become master." (This problem with Judeo-Christian mercy has largely been eliminated by right-wing fundamentalism in our own time, however, led by televangelists working in close concert with big business to destroy empathy and tolerance.) *Ressentiment* works on the bad conscience that developed with the repression or internalization of instincts, or aggressive energy, that allowed human society to come into being. That necessary inhibition of cruelty, a premoral sense of accountability and guilt, subsequently made the slave revolt in the form of morality possible. (This inexact sort of "genealogy" would later allow Foucault to treat historical change as contingent, or as a product of chance rather than self-conscious human agents.) Through religion, then liberal and socialist politics, the slave's "secretly smouldering emotions of revenge and hatred" have enfeebled "the birds of prey" by persuading them that they are "responsible for being birds of prey." The "vindictive cunning of powerlessness" says "let us be good! And a good person is anyone who does not rape, does not harm anyone, who does not attack." Self-realization by the "overman" and the restoration of a properly aristocratic order, therefore, would consist of the masters (or birds of prey) exercising "the lust to rob and dominate" while "taking mischievous delight . . . in the misfortune of others"—pretty much the behavior of corporate capitalism in the United States at present. Nietzsche sounds much like contemporary apologists for the behavior of big business, such as most economists, judges, and politicians: "There is nothing strange about the fact that lambs bear a grudge towards large birds of prey: but that is no reason to blame the large birds of prey for carrying off the little lambs." [33] (I recommend this line to probusiness jurists: it would make a nice learned citation in the current effort to limit corporate legal responsibility—indicating how shockingly unconscionable it is that Nietzsche remains the icon of so many leftist academics, an influence that accounts in large part for their perverse complicity with contemporary social Darwinism.)

When one knows what Nietzsche stands for regarding anger and resentment, finally, his successors in both music journalism and academic postmodernism look pretty objectionable—and postmodernism not very "post." Gilles Deleuze's well-known treatise *Anti-Oedipus* (1972; trans. 1977), written along with Felix Guattari, continues to execrate *ressentiment,* which is singled out as serving the unchanging, circular system of power and dissent perceived by all the French postmodernists. They reproduce Nietzsche's picture of the historical futility of revolutionary hope, locked in an endless drama, the closed circuit with power: The "founders of empires [both] invented vengeance and incited *ressentiment,* that counter-vengeance" that is never acted upon. Indicating just how retrograde French postmodernism actually is, recent neoconservatives such as Michael André Bernstein have used the theory of *ressentiment* to describe the same seamless, circular system: "Every word the Nietzschean slave utters, every value he posits, is . . . formulated entirely in response to and as an anticipation of the responses he will elicit." [34] The "neocon" point is that within such a closed loop, excessive abuse of authority can only lead to madness, and given that delusional state, any assignment of blame for one's suffering is purely arbitrary. That supposed leftists essentially agree indicates the sad state of postmodern theory, in posing as critique but actually amounting to complicity.

In *Nietzsche and Philosophy* (published in 1962 but not translated until 1983, when academic postmodernism heated up), Deleuze's earlier, more extensive description of *ressentiment* sounds exactly like journalists writing on angry music: reaction to one's situation "ceases to be acted in order to become something felt." In other words, a person angry at authority will be satisfied simply to be indignant and never act on that indignation. This is precisely the argument of rock critic Jon Pareles, for example, in the establishmentarian *New York Times*: "All [listeners] want is to feel that someone else is as angry as they are. . . . For a little while it feels like actual power—until the music stops." Pareles directly reproduces Nietzsche's description of pain seeking momentary release from consciousness through the wildest possible emotion. Sarah Ferguson observes in grunge rock fans the same limitation to brief-lived, unenacted anger: "Simply identifying and acknowledging your damage is empowering." [35] Anger, presumably, does not result in any further action or greater consciousness.

In academia, Cornel West, highly esteemed on the Left, has approvingly cited not only Deleuze's *Nietzsche and Philosophy* as the originary text of poststructuralism and assaults on grand narratives but also Nietzsche himself on the theory of *ressentiment*. West's comments on the unenacted militancy of hip-hop music have clearly registered that theory, as well, and its articulation in the postmodern thesis on commercial incorporation prostituting anger: "Rap music is the exemplary postmodern cultural phenomenon, [s]moothly packaged for mass consumption in the name of militant opposition to the status quo, . . . without illuminating what occasions the provocation." Such an observation is nothing new in the history of academic criticism on popular music; Theodor Adorno made the same point a half-century ago. He may now be seen as an important intermediary between Nietzsche and postmodernism in his view that the "so-called releasing element of music is simply the opportunity to feel something"—namely, frustration on which one never acts. Adorno even mistakenly calls it "bad conscience," [36] after Nietzsche, actually meaning *ressentiment*, which in Nietzsche's scheme is the more recent historical outgrowth of bad conscience. (Adorno's essay on the "culture industry," in *Dialectic of Enlightenment,* is likewise full of Nietzschean terminology: "herd instinct" and "slave morality" as well as the same mistaken use of "bad conscience.")

Among U.S. theorists of postmodernism, Jameson is odd with respect to the theory of *ressentiment*. He discusses it extensively in his books *Fables of Aggression* (1979) and *The Political Unconscious* (1981), noting in both that intellectuals like Nietzsche who invoke *ressentiment* against others are invariably full of it themselves. But Jameson only finds *ressentiment* ironic when it comes to the complexities of literary figures such as Wyndham Lewis and George Gissing; in writing on postmodern mass culture, however, Jameson directly reproduces Nietzsche's thesis that expressions of defiance and rebellion only feed abject complacency and inaction. Jameson's postmodern step is simply to erase any intellectual depth in *ressentiment,* where Nietzsche considered slave morality quite rationally and effectively calculated. Like other Marxist followers of French postmodern theory, Jameson succumbs to the syndrome of observing *ressentiment* among the masses because of his own resentment, in his case of their failure to launch the class revolution. This is precisely where so many Marxist intellectuals have come to grief, as evidenced by Jameson's mentor Adorno. He complains about fools who "turn their hatred rather on those [like Adorno] who point to their dependence than on those who tie their bonds." [37]

Besides his greater estimation of the achievements of *ressentiment*, Nietzsche differs considerably from postmodernism on crucial issues involving language. As opposed to the antifoundationalist and poststructuralist view that the arbitrary relation of language to the world makes the expression and enactment of any "truth" impossible, first of all, truth can still be determined in Nietzsche's system, if in a very negative sense. Truth consists of the actions of those able to exercise the will to power—truth, that is, is what they do, what they make the truth. On this voluntarist basis, emphasizing the will over reason, Nietzsche considers language (or the expressive forms of the intellect) inferior to the will to power. *On the Genealogy of Morality* says that the "doing is everything" and the "doer" of any action "is invented as an after-thought" through language. In keeping with the theory of *ressentiment*, Nietzsche holds that the weak stick to talking about their subjectivity rather than acting; for the strong, action comes before expression and rationalization. This very evidently contrasts with his postmodern followers who treat language (or discourse) as fundamental to the exercise of power.

In substituting discourse for Nietzsche's masters exercising the will to power, the postmodernists are right in one respect—power does need language, contrary to Nietzsche. But power's need for language exists precisely because human agents are trying to exercise power, contrary to postmodern theories about abstracted, sublime power. Nietzsche's comments on language quite rightly place language in the context of social relations—if between slaves who need language and masters who don't, hence the inferiority of language in his view. The will to power, says Nietzsche, is exercised through nothing but "driving, willing and acting, and only the seduction of language (and the fundamental errors of reason petrified within it), which . . . misconstrues all actions as conditional upon an agency, a 'subject,' can make it appear otherwise." The last part of this statement, on the fictitiousness of the subject, is reproduced in highly selective, misrepresentative fashion by all the notable postmodern theorists, among them Butler, Derrida, and Foucault. The selectivity lies in the fact that the first part—on "driving, willing, and acting"—makes it clear that Nietzsche is a voluntarist and hardly believes there are no effective human agents, as in postmodern accounts of power. There are still powerful people (such as the robber barons, then and now) doing what they like.

The weak person, presumably, due to an inability to act, is the one who "needs to believe in an unbiased 'subject' with freedom of choice" and in an existence interpreted through language, specifically in moral terms.[38] Thus, supposedly, inferior persons filled with *ressentiment* are all talk and no action. Real freedom is for the few, or the minority on top who do what they want without worrying about any justification, who don't stop for discourse, or to talk about themselves the way the weak do as their only precarious means of self-preservation.

Postmodernism discards Nietzsche's masters for no real reason beyond postmodern fatalism about the unfathomable operations of power. *On the Genealogy of Morality* hardly justifies Foucault's description of Nietzsche revealing language to be "an enigmatic multiplicity that must be mastered" in the attempt to understand not what was said, but *"who was speaking"*—or the "enigma" of power's exercise.[39] There's nothing enigmatic or multiple about the fact that Nietzsche thinks only the weak need language in the first place.

We see the difference between Nietzsche and postmodernism in Judith Butler's derivations from Nietzsche in *Gender Trouble* (1990), the core text of queer theory, which Alan Schrift praises for avoiding "a voluntaristic notion of a subject who wilfully decides" to adopt a subversive gender position.[40] This equation of voluntarism not with the will but with the concept of the subject would seem to be necessary to make Nietzsche fit the postmodern template. Schrift, like Derrida and others, can concentrate on Nietzsche's objection to the fictitious subject based on the inauthenticity of language, without acknowledging its perfectly voluntarist basis in his preference for a will to power unfettered by discourse. Schrift actually discards Nietzsche's reference to "driving, willing, and acting" in order to cite the sentence on the "seduction of language" and subjectivity as proof that Nietzsche is not a voluntarist.

But there is, finally, a fundamental continuity between Nietzsche and postmodern theory. In eschewing the subject, Butler describes an agentless subversion of identity through the sheer proliferation of gender possibilities (multiplied especially by homosexuality) and actually cites *On the Genealogy of Morality* about the "doer" being a fiction and the deed everything. Neither Schrift nor Butler seems to find it disturbing that the purported fiction of subjectivity (or identity or selfhood), enacted through language, is described by Nietzsche as a tool of vengeful weak people that causes the strong to hesitate over their agency, or to consider their moral responsibility for their actions. Given Butler's basis in Nietzsche and in Foucault's late development of ideas about Nietzschean self-creation, at least some of queer theory would seem to be open to the charge of elitist individualism that Kay Soper levels at Foucauldian feminism.

Some postmodern theorists claim there is a "good" Nietzsche that can be separated from his repugnant elitism; others, like the Foucauldians above, don't seem to find any problems in the first place. The fact that the "bad" Nietzsche so little disturbs contemporary theorists indicates the objective shared by

Nietzsche and postmodernism: Both would like to bury the social element of language, or the contest between agents that occurs through language, because it includes resistance as well as power. Nietzsche feared and loathed insubordination among the masses, and now, as Laura Kipnis argues, postmoderns have given up on them. In *The Will to Power* (trans. 1967), Nietzsche declares the fundamental objective of his philosophy to be an ordering of social rank, and postmodernism involves an "ordering of rank," too, as the example of Paul De Man (in Chapter 1) indicates: a division between people educated (and cynical) enough to be suspicious of identity and those who don't know better than to be all too certain of theirs. Theorists of the frailty or even the fiction of identity clearly exempt themselves from the anonymous mass, or they wouldn't write with such a clear sense of mastery and publish like everyone else who wishes to assert an identity (or to promote oneself professionally, etc.).

The fatalistic Nietzschean strain in French postmodernism has had an unfortunate influence on cultural studies in the United States, as evidenced by the work of an academic more extensively concerned with popular music, Lawrence Grossberg. Grossberg has in essence been broadcasting Deleuze's work on the theory of *ressentiment* without acknowledging its reactionary Nietzschean component: In *We Gotta Get Out of This Place* (1992), Grossberg actually argues that cultural studies needs to be synthesized with Deleuze, his frequent coauthor Felix Guattari, and Foucault. Although Grossberg's work doesn't bear much looking into, as a result of his alliance with French theory, I must do so anyway because he may have played a considerable role in Jameson's thesis on the futility of anger migrating into music journalism (although I suspect Simon Reynolds was more influential in this regard). Having worked assiduously to become the CEO of cultural studies while occasionally appearing in journal forums with well-known music critics and scholars such as Simon Frith and Greil Marcus, Grossberg is unquestionably known to journalists; recently, I saw a passing reference to him, in *The Village Voice*, as a "cult studies stud."

In crossing cultural studies with French postmodernism, Grossberg obeyed the professional impulse to stake out ever more extreme ground. Jameson, in essence, had already gone beyond Nietzsche in finding the depth of responses to defiance diminished by mental incapacity and even schizophrenia—Jameson denies much rationality to resentment, that is, where Nietzsche found the morality created out of *ressentiment*, designating good and evil, all too rational. Grossberg simply took the final logical step when he bluntly announced in 1988 that "meaning [or political ideology, reason, etc.] and affect have *broken apart*" (emphasis added), a thesis that subsequently became a mantra in his publications.

The disconnection of emotions like anger from any intellectual insight or political significance has supposedly resulted from the triumph of neoconservatism, which he holds in unhealthy awe. As a result of being broken apart, in his view, neither emotion nor ideology on its own offers any political hope:

> The relationship between affect and ideology . . . has become increasingly problematic. . . . It has become increasingly difficult, if not impossible, in other words, to make sense of our affective experiences and to put any faith in our ideological constructions. . . . Postmodernity, then, points to a crisis in our ability to locate any meaning as a possible and appropriate source for an impassioned commitment.

Grossberg's grand thesis, on the disconnection of passion from meaning, is reproduced ad nauseum in music journalism. As a result of that disconnection, presumably, we crave emotion alone, without consequences, exactly as Nietzsche had it.

The basis for this cynicism lies in Grossberg's conception of "authentic inauthenticity" (or "ironic nihilism"), typified for him by the meaningless, transparently calculated emotional intensity of a Bruce Springsteen. (My students have convinced me that this criticism of Springsteen has dated to the point of irrelevance; his career can hardly be reduced to the fiasco of 1984, when the congenial sounds on the lyrically acerbic *Born in the U.S.A.* allowed Ronald Reagan to construe Springsteen as a patriot.) The mass media create universal indifference by peddling nothing but the simulation of emotional commitment, divorced from reality; thus the "difference between reality and image has disappeared." As in the political arena since Ronald Reagan, we presumably prefer performers who clearly only pretend to care about anyone: "If every identity is equally fake, a pose that one takes on, then authentic inauthenticity celebrates the possibilities of poses." [41] When Grossberg says we are all "anesthetized," however, echoing Nietzsche, it becomes apparent how much of this is merely recycled modernist pessimism.

In *We Gotta Get Out of This Place*, Grossberg's thesis on the split between emotion and ideology is further developed through a poststructuralist schema. To understand his tactics, it helps first to know that Peter Middleton, in *The Inward Gaze* (1992), concludes that the terms *affect, emotion, feeling,* and *passion* have become interchangeable. He found no consistent differentiation of them in his exhaustive survey of the treatment of emotion throughout the history of modern aesthetics, philosophy, and psychology. Grossberg, in contrast, sharply distinguishes *affect* from *emotion.* Affect is depicted as one of those overarching structures or totalities, typical of poststructuralism, that determines the possibilities for our actions and expression—including our emotions. Affect, he tells us, "is a socially constructed domain," an abstract "prepersonal intensity." Organized in particular by the "consumer industries," affect preexists and conditions the individual's (or subject's) responses to music. Like language in poststructuralism, affect shapes the "various fragments" of our identity and locates us "within various circuits of power"—all without our realizing it, of course. Ignoring the contrary views of feminists and many other scholars about the origin of emotion in social relations, Grossberg breaks off emotion as an internal or personal matter determined by the larger structure, affect: "Our emotional states are always elicited from within the affective states." Emotion is quite inauthentic and weak, as a result, just another product of structures emanating from power.

Grossberg does relent somewhat regarding his earlier thesis on the disconnection of affect and ideology, holding instead that affect disarms us by rendering ideology "invisible behind a screen of passion." (Even material reality disappears, he claims, the classic postmodern picture of dematerialization and fragmentation.) Affect is still accompanied by "ideological narratives," that is, even if they're invisible, because affect "can never provide its own justification, . . . can never define, by itself, why things should matter." [42] To be motivated, we need ideology or articulation and reason. But even on this account Grossberg is entirely unreliable, due to his apparently complete ignorance of the scholarship on emotion. He inadvertently reverses the view of the eighteenth-century philosopher David Hume, much admired by recent scholars, that emotion *alone* provides motives; reason, or intellectual activity like ideological narratives, would have no motivation without emotion. (This is still insufficient, though, because Hume doesn't break with the treatment of emotion and reason as two distinct kinds of experience.) Grossberg, in contrast, treats even affect, superior to mere emotion, as quite dumb—both stupid and mute—in relation to ideology. His work differs not at all, therefore, from the derision of emotion for two hundred years in masculine aesthetics and philosophy, to which Hume is widely considered an honorable exception. The only thing "post" about Grossberg is that he cancels out reason (or ideology), too: Affect or passion is not only inarticulate but has completely supplanted political ideas, which are thus invisible. Detached if not quite utterly disconnected from one another, neither the emotions nor the meanings available to us offer any political hope. He has a useful theory of "affective alliances," describing the often widely dispersed audiences for hip-hop and rock music, but because affect and meaning are disconnected, in those affective alliances "we live and act in ways over which we have no control and about which we may be unaware." [43]

The preference of some people for transparently inauthentic emotional gestures, however, does not mark some new postmodern epoch so insipid that any ideology whatsoever, progressive or reactionary, has become irrelevant. Emotions and ideology (or the beliefs, meanings, and values to which we subscribe) could never cease to mutually constitute each other. Our common sense is a matter of how we *feel* as well as what we think and of our notions of the right ways both to feel and to think. In Grossberg's argument, in contrast, Reaganism triumphed through sheer feeling alone, making ideology irrelevant and thus leaving the Left helpless to respond in traditional political terms. This is another classic instance of complicity masquerading as critique, of postmodern theory produced by the Left actually collaborating with the people in power by reinforcing a fatalism they would like us to feel. If ideology really no longer mattered, conservatism would be just as helpless as the Left to make its case, and the political arena would be highly volatile, open to every conceivable view if indifferent to them all. And even if politics were indeed a matter of affect or passion rather than ideas, that too ought to volatilize the political arena because emotions are difficult to control. In actuality, of course, politics aren't very volatile but quite one-dimensional because conservative corporations dominate mass communication and political institutions. Corporate America, as a result, sets *both* an emotional and a political agenda favorable to the status quo (as all the feminist commentators on emotion surveyed in Chapter 5 have observed). Rage, for example, receives massive corporate sponsorship if it is Rush Limbaugh's, and his affect of meanness and ridicule is unquestionably accompanied by an elaborated ideology. (Other capitalists, fortunately, are willing to settle for making money off Courtney Love.)

But observations like these, says Grossberg, are too easily "reassured by the difference between postmodern nihilism and conservatism." [44] The two in his view have become virtually identical, instead, because conservatism learned to exploit postmodern irony and inauthenticity. Notice, however, that although he has affect and ideology broken apart for most of us, as a result of the new conservatism emphasizing affect over ideology, his point is that the success of conservatives themselves lies in *fusing* postmodern nihilism (or ironic, inauthentic affect) with conservatism (or ideology). Even if the effect is to make ideology irrelevant, in other words, the triumph of conservatism is cast as a concomitant domination of emotion and ideology alike. We are "uncontrollably . . . pulled toward the right," as a result. [45] But when he discusses the possibility of resisting conservatism, in contrast, he trots out the thesis that emotion and ideology have broken apart universally, making political resistance impossible since neither is sufficient on its own. If one asks why rock and rollers can't also marry emotion and politics—or why their emotions, like anger, aren't rational and meaningful in themselves—the problem with postmodern theory in general becomes apparent: It has complete faith in the people in power, and none at all in the people opposing them.

Thus Grossberg claims that even the most harrowingly rebellious popular music merely supplies more fodder for jaded consumers, just another meaningless choice in tastes: "The production, through consumption, of affective identities further dissociates any possible relationship between taste and politics." This unhelpful anticapitalism dates to the eighteenth century, of course, but as postmodernism it has cropped up repeatedly in music journalism, in the notion that because we purchase our music, our responses to it are inauthentic, without meaning or political significance. Judging from Grossberg's categorization, angry music is an example of "grotesque inauthenticity," in particular, which allows only "negative" affective investment in "the destructive." [46] I cite these terms because the key rallying cries of anarchism and the avant-garde for more than a century have been *negation* (of conformist common sense) and *destructive passion*. The well-known line of anarchist Michael Bakunin holds that the destructive passion is the creative passion, and he wrote with regard to attacks on common sense (what I call cultural anarchism), not throwing bombs. By detaching "negative" or "destructive" emotions from any meaning, therefore, Grossberg isn't just announcing a bleak new epoch, he's discarding the whole avant-garde tradition of artists trying to change the world.

In the name of his own version of radical politics, self-confessedly a pessimistic brand obsessed with terrorism and random death, Grossberg seeks to cut off the possibility of an avant-garde more deliberately than any force outside academia on which we could blame the postmodern condition (whatever it really is). For Grossberg, rock music is "part of the dominant mainstream culture, . . . losing its power to encapsulate and articulate resistance and opposition." It can only offer a typical postmodern rejection of grand narratives, or ideologies, that express hope for the future: "Rock's articulation within the 'end of ideology' makes it extremely difficult for it to enter into . . . political resistance." From the very beginning of the postmodern period, in fact—which he dates with the 1950s and nuclear terror as well as television and Elvis Presley—"Youth was subordinated to its already defined place within a social narrative that was told before it arrived." Thus rock music simply cannot construct "a space outside of everyday life," or outside of vapid consumerism, that is, his very reductive notion of the extent of everyday life.

Such a conclusion has been typical of aesthetics over the past two centuries and its impossible insistence on complete freedom from capitalist culture. Grossberg is presumably a postmodern who knows no "outside" exists, as most of his discussion of the inescapable monolith of power suggests, yet when it comes to defining resistance, he falls back on the modernist ideal of artistic autonomy or detachment. All he adds is classic poststructuralist fatalism over the structure absorbing the subject: In general, the "affective individual" only finds "temporary space for itself within the contexts that have been prepared for it." As with many postmodern theorists, what little freedom of action is acknowledged looks very slight in the wake of all the theoretical arguments about the power of the social system as a whole. Grossberg, as a result, very confidently tells us that for a large portion of the population "there is a feeling of helplessness: what can anyone do?" (He also claims that everyone thinks everyone else is going crazy in some way, a thought that had never occurred to me.) Ultimately, we are told, "rock cannot escape everyday life, it can only serve as a reminder of its imprisonment." [47] But academic postmodernism itself, it seems clear, more perfectly embodies the futility it assigns to everyone else.

It is not surprising that music journalists' hatchet work on disaffected persons also echoes Nietzsche; it just points out how commonplace his views really are. But in reproducing the arguments of postmodern academics, music journalists have indeed directly absorbed Nietzsche as well. When Grossberg says "it has become increasingly difficult, if not impossible, . . . to make sense of our affective experiences" and act on them, [48] he's of course been reading postmodern theorists like Deleuze, Foucault, and Jameson who know Nietzsche perfectly well. So does Michael André Bernstein, who asserts that with repetition—that often ridiculed feature of popular songs—resentment becomes something "vile," only "a parodic falling-off of the energy once released by a forceful word." [49] The neoconservative Bernstein reaches the same conclusion as the quasi-Marxist Grossberg, in other words: the expression of anger and resentment is weakly derivative in the postmodern epoch and thus no longer holds any meaning.

When Grossberg does resort occasionally to actual concrete evidence for this theoretical claim, he turns to a shallow nonexpert, the novelist Bret Easton Ellis, cited a number of times in *We Gotta Get Out of This Place* on the futility of contemporary youth. Grossberg even tells us that conservative scholar Allan Bloom is largely correct about youth and its debilitation by popular music and consumerism! [50] For the most part, though, Grossberg's very slight, highly selective evidence consists of idiotic moments from television, hardly much of a cultural survey in a book supposedly revolving around rock music. This tactic is much like Baudrillard's: telling us the world is exactly the way it appears on television, or taking the dominant culture's own self-presentation at face value and merely reproducing it. As the rest of Part 1 makes abundantly apparent, such tactics are typical of academic and journalistic postmodernism in general. What we saw in an elite literary scholar like Fredric Jameson, moreover, turns out to be true of music journalists as well: Much of postmodernism is not really "post" at all in its warmed-over rehash of romantic and modernist prejudices.

# CHAPTER 3

# Collaborating With the Oppressors

*Postmodern Academics on Music*

An example of Jameson's influence in academia is the seemingly compulsive, certainly misleading citation of him in Barry Shank's 1994 book *Dissonant Identities: The Rock 'n' Roll Scene in Austin, Texas.* Jameson, says Shank, "recognizes that commercial culture is an important site for political struggle," although judging from the evidence I provided earlier, Jameson clearly believes just the opposite. At the time Shank wrote his book, so many commentators held that Jameson provided productive insight into postmodern culture that I'm sure Shank must simply have been disgorging scholarly common wisdom rather than misreading Jameson. Genuinely odd, however, is the fact that Shank mentions the historian George Lipsitz along with Jameson. It is Lipsitz, of course, who criticizes the one-dimensional pessimism of some postmoderns as "collaboration with the oppressors," a description perfectly applicable to Jameson.

Shank relies more heavily, though, on another founding father of postmodern theory, the psychoanalyst Jacques Lacan (also a prominent influence in Jameson's essay "Postmodernism"). Lacan has us driven forever by a "lack" of fulfillment of desire in our relations with other people, a futility beginning with our initiation into language. He recasts Freud's Oedipal drama as the acquisition of language: An infant learns that it does not have a parent's total devotion but must share love with the other parent as a part of becoming conscious through language of its difference from Others (with a capital O). Differentiating persons and things, in other words, requires differentiating words themselves in order to name people and objects. A passage occurs from the "Imaginary Order"— feeling that the world is whole (or an extension of oneself, in the transitional "mirror phase") and that all desires are met—to the "Symbolic Order," the empty world of language in which "real" experience outside language becomes inaccessible. Because words (or signs) have no direct, natural correspondence with objects, language only operates in the absence of things, and thus communication, desire, and wholeness can never be realized. We wind up caught in a double bind: Our sense of selfhood (or our difference from others) amounts to a fiction because it couldn't exist without language, but once we've acquired that fictitious sense of individuality we obviously can't go back to the fullness or "plenitude" of the "Imaginary" realm.

Shank uses Lacan as others have for some time now, to argue that postmodern young people do not make a very full transition from the "Imaginary Order" to the "Symbolic Order." From the counterculture to the stereotypical Generation X, postmodern youth has supposedly remained infantile in its demands for instant, constant gratification. Where neoconservatives such as Midge Decter lament young people's refusal to accept "deferred gratification" and decry our culture's hedonism, Shank finds adolescents to be perfect postmoderns: Advanced capitalism, obviously, depends on consumer hedonism. Thus he's no happier than the "neocons."

Shank's conclusions are perfectly in keeping with Jameson, as a result, and just as unhelpful to the interest in "political struggle" they supposedly share as theorists of postmodernism. Postmodernity, says Shank, is like adolescence, in "a heightened awareness of the pure possibilities of representation combined with an *absence* of social power and the *inability* to enforce discursively the qualities of these representations" (emphasis added). Plenty of affect is available in those possibilities, but they remain "pure" in the sense of being unrealized, receiving no articulation, and thus prompting no action: "Timbral and rhythmic articulations of noise into sound, affectively charged with the erotic undertones,

. . . support an extreme nonconscious sensitivity to the transformative effects of signifying practice." To put it less densely, we respond quite strongly but remain "nonconscious," having little or no idea what is happening to us. This holds true for our experience of both specific performances and the general processes (or "signifying practices") in which meaning is made.[1] Our affect lacks intellectual depth, in other words, as Jameson claims, so Shank assigns affect to desire.

According to another analysis based in Lacan, by Fred Pfeil, postmodern young people are the products of "de-Oedipalization," or a more indulgent nurturing that has led to self-indulgence. As in Shank's book, that is, the transition from the "Imaginary Order" to the "Symbolic Order" is incomplete. Pfeil's intention is to put a positive spin on the matter by taking the feminist view that emotional relations have become more vital, as a result—where Marxism would only see advanced capitalism creating more hedonistic consumers. The resulting diagnosis, however, sounds uncomfortably like that of neoconservatives who blame society's ills on Dr. Spock and permissive parenting. I'm not sure this reversal works any better than Baudrillard professing to find the masses revolutionary while repeating all the reasons for which modernism denounced them (such as female-like passivity).

In Pfeil's case, de-Oedipalized young people are found to swing from "a deliriously dispersed self-exaltation" to "rage" at the inevitable denial of some of their desires.[2] At one extreme, that of delirium, the fulfillment of desire seems possible, for young people are not fully absorbed into the "Symbolic Order." But, caught up in the quest for pleasure, they can only sense the "power" always threatening to intervene as an abstract, invisible force—the classic postmodern sensibility of intellectuals here attributed to Generation X—hence the swing to the other extreme, impotent rage. If postmodern self-indulgence is highly volatile, therefore, it is not terribly well controlled or focused; as Jameson and Grossberg have it, that anger is disconnected from political articulation. The psychoanalytic view would add that the self-absorption of de-Oedipalized young people is what keeps the anger internalized and unenacted, except through more pursuit of consumer goods and entertainment calculatedly directed at the enraged. There is a schizoid split between actual affective experience and the prepackaged (or rationalized) outlets it finds (like angry music).

Douglas Coupland's 1991 novel *Generation X* is essentially a précis of all of the above ideas, as well as a gloss on the Jamesonian view of the world. The "world has gotten too big—way beyond our capacities to tell stories about it"—as in Jameson's "impossible totality." So the characters tell stories incessantly, in an effort to grasp their situation. In keeping with the postmodern stress on fragmentation, however, those stories are never more than "a fragment of your own horror," said to be the most vital, appropriate form of storytelling possible. Coupland predictably treats the consumer society as the cause of that fragmentation, although he spews out brand names as eagerly as a Bret Easton Ellis.

The futile effort to grasp the postmodern age leads to something like the end-of-history thesis, in the paradox of "historical underdosing" and "overdosing"—living in a period "when nothing seems to happen" and "too much seems to happen," respectively. The resulting paralysis is typified by "addiction to newspapers, magazines, and TV news broadcasts," as wallowing in seemingly chaotic change becomes a substitute for making history. Although Coupland scarcely celebrates the postmodern world, calling it "hell" more than once, and gets in some admirable abuse of boomers and yuppies, his closeness to the likes of Jameson is evident in Coupland's favorable, nostalgic citation of a modernist, Rainer Maria Rilke.[3] Rilke's typically elitist extolment of the "solitary man"— implicitly the poet or intellectual aristocrat—seems jarring in a novel presumably about young people trying to create a sense of community and indicates how thoroughly Coupland's outlook resembles that of his academic sources.

In contrast with Coupland's cynicism about history, Pfeil insists that youthful outrage at authority might still release "historically new and progressive social forces."[4] But postmodern culture continually works to diminish that possibility, he adds, by diverting new energies into consumption—the conventional postmodern thesis on incorporation. Pfeil does repudiate the argument of Jameson, Grossberg, and others that rebelliousness results from a psychology, essentially that of arrested development, that precludes any political significance. Expressions of resistance bound up with pleasure should not be discounted, although Pfeil doesn't seem convinced that they take very strong forms, given his citation of musicians like Laurie Anderson, Philip Glass, and the Talking Heads as exemplars in handling the postmodern condition. (And it is debatable, as will be seen, whether there is actually a postmodern rock music.)

Other postmoderns simply believe that nothing has changed since the 1960s, as capitalism has continued not simply to court but actually to construct the alienated young hedonist. The relentless Tom Frank insists that youth culture "à la Pepsi," perpetually channeling alienation into consumerism, has been unvarying since the counterculture:

> The discovery of the rule-breaking boomers merely cemented the victory of the advertising revolution, and the discovery of their successors [Generation X] in the '90s has breathed new life (and new imagery) into the basic wisdom established during those years: hipness is the lifeblood of mass culture.

The "rebel profile" of youth culture never varies from "the consumerist hedonism . . . of the '60s original." [5]

In actuality, youth culture has evolved considerably in its sophistication since the 1960s originals in the counterculture. As numerous critics have pointed out, the failure of much of the counterculture lay in its easy equation of consumer freedom—the right to wear clothes and hair any way one wished, to consume drugs and music, and to have sex unimpeded—with political freedom, even revolution. By the mid-1970s, punk emerged in large part out of disgust with hippies, especially the institutionalization of rock music in corporate hands: "The man can't bust our music!" declared CBS record sleeves. Johnny Rotten made a point of ridiculing not only mindless dope smokers but also the notion that flared (or bell-bottom) jeans connoted nonconformity. His working-class hostility toward hippies had direct roots in subcultures contemporaneous with the counterculture like the hard mods, or early skinheads, and the glam or glitter subculture epitomized by David Bowie fans. It is typical of the abstraction and historical imprecision of postmodern theorists that they can flatten out this history of youth subcultures into one long, dismally identical parade of "youth culture."

Pfeil's description of the combustible relation between self-gratification and anger is fairer, but I would add that many young people make a conscious *choice* between them, and that when they do so they choose the latter. Anger is *always* based in a judgment on a situation and is never "blind" rage. In contemporary music, anger is quite intentionally focused on a culture offering what Pfeil rightly calls the "intrusive and monotonous" pleasures of instant gratification, "a menace to be resisted." [6] As one of my students put it, in defending seemingly cacophonous, repetitive musics like hardcore punk and industrial, "This is the way the *whole culture* sounds to us." What sounds like irredeemable noise to the uninitiated is in fact a deliberate commentary on the cacophony of the *rest* of our culture—what passes for normal, like the media screeching about O. J. Simpson. The noise of angry music is the same avant-garde force described by Richard Huelsenbeck in *En Avant Dada* (1920): "Every movement naturally produces noise." He believed, furthermore, that "noise is a direct call to action," not a sign of anger without political significance.

Psychoanalytic schema, finally, aren't really necessary to explain what has been an evident ideological development—and one that does not strictly involve the young, either. Fed by a hyperactive, voracious mass media, our culture's conscious values stress the instant gratification of quick, big-bang victories, whether in Hollywood, in the Persian Gulf War, or on Wall Street. So the solution to poverty is to build more prisons and orphanages in which to lock up the unruly poor; trying to attack crime at its roots, through social programs, promises results only over an extended period of time in a hazy future. Ralph Nader once observed that it was the Reagan administration that seemed to suffer from arrested adolescence in its self-interested lack of concern for anyone else and preference for resolving conflict with force. It doesn't make much sense, therefore, to use youth—with its connotations of newness—to prove that post-modernity is an unprecedented condition. And it doesn't help combat self-centeredness to argue that a terrible new epoch has brought some deep, virtually unalterable psychological dysfunction.

In contrast with poststructuralists like Lacan, I've always felt that language sometimes sparks some very satisfying encounters with other people, including authors and singers, as well as very intense conflicts, especially with authoritarian types. (In a colloquial nutshell, that's the dialogical linguistics of the literary theorist Mikhail Bakhtin and of Walter Benjamin's materialist description of language, both of which I elaborate in Chapter 6.) Lacan would call my experience "misrecognition" for thinking I could connect with other people. His finding, however, like so much of poststructuralism, relies on ignoring any actual social experience (as Bakhtin pointed out several decades ago about structuralist linguistics) by dismissing it as a figment of one's imagination. Pfeil and Shank actually feel somewhat the same way I do—although Shank waxes romantic about the intuitive inspiration of musicians—and thus they undermine themselves by latching on to a postmodern icon like Lacan, who doesn't.

When younger (which is to say thirtysomething) academics approach contemporary popular music from a postmodern perspective, the results are inevitably disastrous, even more so when journalists get sucked into the game. An extraordinary case in point is *Present Tense,* a 1992 book on hip-hop and rock music combining scholarly and journalistic efforts. The book was originally a special issue of *South Atlantic Quarterly,* a journal not coincidentally edited by Fredric Jameson. The editor of the special issue, Anthony DeCurtis of *Rolling Stone,* is a former literary scholar, and his cynicism about the music business seems perfectly in keeping with postmodern academics. After focusing solely on superstars, he concludes that "you'd better be willing to . . . smile and make nice with the powers that be—or you might as well go back to the bars." To this I have one word to say: Nirvana. *Present Tense* is a good example of a slew of academic work (like Lawrence Grossberg's) and journalism, written around 1990 and 1991, that was immediately rendered obsolete by Nirvana's break-through. But DeCurtis's later obituary for Kurt Cobain in *Rolling Stone,* predict-ably, continues to insist on the supposedly desperate battle to uphold one's "integrity" while making music for "a mass audience." [7] If Cobain killed himself over dealing with large record labels, which I doubt, a contributing factor must have been so many writers similarly harping on the issue of selling out.

But I felt compelled to write my book well before I traced out the hounding of Cobain (recounted in Chapter 4), when I found rock and roll declared identical with poststructuralism in *Present Tense*. A scathing review by Daniel Harris of postmodern accounts of Madonna could easily be turned on *Present Tense*: In the very act of "spurning the pieties lavished on the canon, academics demonstrate how incomplete the postmodern break with traditional forms of artistic analysis [like modernism] has been, how abysmally they have failed to take popular culture on its own terms." Postmodern theorists offer apocalyptic conclusions, instead, based on their "most cherished tenet—that . . . there is no stable and empirically verifiable 'reality' behind the vagaries and impermanence of language" (as poststructuralism has it). Journalist Mark Dery's misguided effort to fit in with his academic compatriots in *Present Tense* typifies the influence of such foolishness. (And the endorsement of R.E.M.'s Michael Stipe on the dust cover indicates that musicians have been sucked in, too.) Before Dery's interview with postmodern icon Laurie Anderson, whose recent work is in fact quite political, he insists in all seriousness that "reality is undergoing a gradual process of *dematerialization*" (emphasis added), confirming what critics have suspected was the postmodern agenda.[8]

The academic postmodernist component of *Present Tense* begins with Paul Smith's essay on the ironies that resulted when the group New Order, hardly establishmentarian, was commissioned by the English Football Association to write a song promoting the 1990 World Cup. Smith concludes, on the basis of the lyrics alone, that the resulting song "World in Motion," in its "annulment of the resistant energies of its own cultural context (football culture's violent antagonism, and neo-psychedelic subculture's alienation), can be understood as a symptom . . . of the ease with which subcultural forms and energies can be made to contribute to and participate in . . . the military-industrial-sports complex." [9] This is another fine example of critique so one-dimensional that it collaborates with the oppressors. Smith's repeated references to the "cancellation" of "resistance" in youth subcultures, besides being condescending, only reinforce a defeatism the multinationals would like us all to feel.

The essay following Smith's, "Rock & Roll as Cultural Practice" by David Shumway, is trickier to disentangle, but the implications of his poststructuralist approach bear the same gloom. Shumway begins from a perfectly sound position, describing rock and roll in terms of both the "sign system" (or "semiotics") available to music and videos and the actual social activities of musicians and audiences. Performers and listeners, he says at the outset, have conscious control over both production and consumption. But the essay proceeds to concentrate entirely on *visual* performance, from early television to music videos, including a silly, though tell-tale swipe at the lack of "resistance" to the Monkees. Shumway has no interest, it turns out, in either the music or its audience. In this regard, his focus on visual media, or the most abstract forms associated with rock, is strategic: The enormous variety of *musical* "signs" available is obliterated by concentrating on the clear limitations of the "sign system" found in videos. (That limitation is the fault of the simple advertising function served by music television, I should stress, not some defect in the medium of film itself.) To put matters in the theoretical terms implicitly at work, the visual emphasis allows the semiotics (or structuralism) to mutate into poststructuralism. The *conditions* of making meaning, that is, through abstraction from the real social exchanges that go on among performers and audiences, are made the *causes* of expression. The "social" part of rock and roll disappears.

Thus Shumway concludes that one should not attempt "to stabilize rock meanings by reference to the intentions of singers, songwriters, or musicians," who are only—incredibly—artificial "constructs," "performing units," and hence merely "texts," not active agents. This jargon is typical of postmodern theorists for whom there is no empirical reality beyond language, which constructs us without us acting on it. The various codes and media of rock and roll, says Shumway, produce the performer; the structures, not the person, generate the performance. When the long-forgotten audience, the place where the most genuine social exchanges go on, finally reappears briefly, it is described as passively "positioned" by that performance.[10] Because the performer's own volition had nothing to do with that performance in the first place, either, we are a far cry from Shumway's opening invocation of active agency.

None of this is very surprising, given the fact that Shumway is a specialist in the work of the postmodern icon Michel Foucault. The foremost problem with the postmodernism in *Present Tense,* however, is not its recourse to French theory on the relation between structures (like power in the abstract, in Foucault) and subjects (us). The worst form of indebtedness in the collection, instead, lies in a distinctive residue of modernism; once again, postmodernism does not look very "post" at all. The more long-standing fatalism of modernist aesthetics actually underlies Shumway's concerns and subsequent essays by Robert Ray and Michael Jarrett. Jarrett, citing Ray—indicating the academic insularity at work—even invokes Baudelaire, the original modernist, specifically his conception of the "dandy" or intellectual aristocrat that has helped underpin so much subsequent elitism. To understand how ridiculous this is in a book about rock and roll, it helps to know that Baudelaire's disparagement of photography, for giving the "mob" access to both the viewing and the making of art, marks the origin of contempt for mechanically and electronically reproduced culture.

Baudelaire's intellectual aristocrat certainly seems analogous to the practitioners of "contemporary theory," as Jarrett claims in his "self-indulgent" amalgamation of poststructuralism and rock.[11] But the relevance of Baudelaire's elitism to "contemporary music," as well, is mystifying. Jarrett's subsequent comparisons of Jacques Derrida and one of his epigones, Gregory Ulmer, with Parliament and the Beastie Boys not only rely on dubious affinities in method but invoke long-standing techniques like montage, a tactic that has led some critics to ask exactly what the difference is between modernism and post-modernism. The revolutionary avant-garde of the early twentieth century is also collapsed with postmodernism, in the equation of Derrida's and Walter Benjamin's very different theories of montage by both Jarrett and Ray (licensed by Ray's colleague Ulmer in yet another instance of insularity). In "The Author as Producer" (1934), Benjamin considers montage a matter of different cultural forms learning from one another, especially literature from mass culture, in the interest of progressive political results. Derrida, on the other hand, in writing more recently on montage, natters on about the "castration" of texts being the only option in Baudrillard's world of simulacra or endless reproductions. (Derrida clearly displays, like Jameson, a nostalgia for romantic and modernist ideas about artistic originality—and Benjamin's whole point decades earlier was to get over it!) At no point, furthermore, do Jarrett and Ray acknowledge in citing Benjamin that he considered their icon Baudelaire the originating point for modernist condescension toward "mechanically reproduced" forms like popular music.

At the heart of Shumway's essay, as well, is "the problem of authenticity" (or originality).[12] Like the other supposedly "post" modernists, he perpetuates the divide drawn by modernism between commerce and art, the contempt for mass-reproduced art dating to the eighteenth century. No performer interested in political resistance can surmount the problem of working in a commercial medium, according to Shumway, even when commerciality is put on ironic display. Shumway's example of a conspicuous self-marketer, David Bowie, rigs the discussion, however. If he sometimes flew in the face of propriety in his musical and sexual alterations, Bowie took himself quite seriously and was never antagonistic toward the music business. The tactic of making a mockery of promoting "stars" was most notably developed in punk, instead, specifically by Malcolm McLaren in his work with the Sex Pistols.

In more recent rock music, given the extensive history of the form by the 1990s, authenticity can in fact be attained "only by . . . reflecting upon one's limits and potentials," Johan Fornäs has argued. In his view, "reflexivity is almost identical with authenticity. [O]ne now has the best chance to attain social and subjective authenticity if the symbolic contexts [of music] are made conscious." The contexts he has in mind are those of explicit discourses about the relations between music and audiences, "a form of identifying discourse in which authenticity appears as an option and a construction rather than as a given fact." In light of such activity, it makes no sense to cling any longer to the romantic definition of authenticity as spontaneity, "as naturalness or as related to any absolute and autonomous origin" outside of commerce. At no point in history was creativity ever entirely independent of commerciality (the ideal of "indie" punk rock); in fact, Fornäs notes, the romantic notion of authenticity was hardly spontaneous in the first place, for it required some degree of self-consciousness and self-reflection. One can discover, admittedly, a disconcerting note to Fornäs's argument: The view that "a 'creative artist' is not expressing him or herself in a natural way, but is involved in a self-conscious and calculated activity" appears in Keith Negus's *Producing Pop* (1992) as "the perspective of marketing" directors at record companies.[13] I don't wish to endorse their actual practices—but better to be a realist than a romantic. By abandoning realism (or calculation and reflexivity concerning one's identity) to the capitalists, obviously, the romantic tradition has led many would-be artistic rebels on an essentially thoughtless quest for independence, ill-defined (or unreflective) in its impossible, absolutist insistence on complete freedom (or autonomy) from commerce.

From a more realistic point of view on authenticity, for example, the appropriation of "much of the language and 'style' of independent labels" by corporate recording companies and their subsidiaries "takes place in a much more complex arena than just indies and majors." Rather than verifying postmodern obsession with the defanging power of the multinationals, the relation between art and commerce in making popular music remains a fraught, "powerful site of cultural negotiation," argues Stephen Lee in a history of Wax Trax! records. The employees at that record company "gradually found themselves warming to the idea of some sort of major label affiliation [after] a sober summary of all that was wrong with the independent system" and its abstract, "Romantic myth of the artist." This reconsideration was hardly complete capitulation to commerce, especially since fans continued to find a "sense of community" in identifying with Wax Trax! and its ideology of fairness to artists and with its industrial dance music, a genre particularly notable for its socializing force. Considered from a sociological perspective, therefore, rather than romantic ideology, "being an independent label represented a contested space where meanings of culture [or creativity] and commerce interacted." Holly Kruse likewise finds that however disputable the concept of indie music may be, it is not insignificant that musicians and audiences understand their involvement "as something that both identifies them with and differentiates them from individuals and groups in other communities." [14] If we look to the uses of music rather than the music as an isolated text, in other words, we find some semblance of authenticity—an authenticity consisting precisely of reflexivity, or reference to individual and group identity.

Keith Negus also wishes to get past the "confusion and debate about the meaning of independence—did it refer to the record label, or a type of music and attitude?"—and romantic "dogma which overemphasizes the degree of conflict" between indies and majors. He finds "a web of major and minor companies," instead, in which some of the minors "experience a large degree of autonomy." Negus has been criticized for seeming to justify corporate practices by glossing over the actual degree of exploitation that takes place in such arrangements. Executives at the minor or subsidiary companies, in particular, are presented through their own self-accounts as largely well-intentioned "cultural intermediaries," beleaguered by the romantic suspicions of artists and fans alike. But one such executive's description of the "loose-tight" relation between majors and indies—"loose in terms of creative freedom, but tight in terms of financial control"—is honest enough and indicates how alternative music can indeed exist if economic independence is a whole other matter. [15]

Shumway's own romantic absolutism, in pitting authenticity against commercial calculation, is actually borrowed from music journalists who have absorbed the incorporation thesis, such as Simon Reynolds (whom I discuss in my next chapter). Along with *Melody Maker* colleagues Paul Oldfield and David Stubbs, Reynolds dismisses the Situationist premise of McLaren and other punks and postpunks (especially "New Pop Entryists" of the 1980s, like the Pet Shop Boys) that the spectacle (or mass culture) could be demystified and undermined by putting contrivance and hype on display. [16] I agree that the spectacle continues to function despite such exposés, even thrives on them—but better its machinations be highlighted than not. Everyone worries about the problem of incorporation because punk put it on the agenda in the first place, furthermore, and it seems both petulant and hyperbolic to insist that because the problem didn't get resolved immediately, we've reached the end—not only the end of rock but the end of history, as Reynolds believes. Noncommercial authenticity has never existed, except in the nostalgic minds of aesthetes, because every work of art requires production and distribution, however modest in scale, in order to exist, and once it does exist there is no way to guarantee it can't be exploited for commercial ends. The most difficult experimental works of modernism, for instance, fed right into advertising.

But Shumway casts the impossibility of authenticity, unsurprisingly, as some recent, postmodern loss. The result he discerns in popular music—the "constructedness" of performers and audiences as an array of "texts" (rather than free human actors)—is based on his presumption that there is no "primary" text in rock. If rock music "cannot be identified with any one of its many codes or products," in other words, there is no identifiable primary moment at which one could even raise the issue of authenticity. Robert Ray similarly holds that "everything that was directly *performed* has moved away into a *construction*." [17]

This sentence mimics the Situationist Guy Debord, who wrote in *Society of the Spectacle* (1967) that "everything that was directly lived has moved away into a representation." As we saw with Jameson and Baudrillard, such selective citation belies the fact that Debord also thought that one could do something to inject authentic negation into an inauthentic world. *Society of the Spectacle* is often invoked in this incomplete, misleading fashion to endorse bleak versions of a postmodern culture of images or representations (as in Jameson's essay on postmodernism), more properly attributed to Baudrillard. He and the Situationists both collaborated in the late 1950s with the great theorist of everyday life, Henri Lefebvre, whose expectation of spontaneous "moments" of eruption is suppressed in Baudrillard's portrayal of passive masses. In *Comments on the Society of the Spectacle* (1988), as a result, Debord broke a long silence to condemn the "empty debate on the spectacle" conducted by postmodernists reproducing the spectacle's own self-presentation, in which "everything is said about the extensive means at [the spectacle's] disposal, to ensure nothing is said about their extensive deployment." [18] When someone like Baudrillard describes the pervasiveness of the mass media only in the abstract, that is, without examining the tensions in their actual use, he leaves an impression of unchallenged power.

But the writers in *Present Tense* aren't really postmodern anyway, of course; in fact, they directly echo the modernists of the Frankfurt School. Shumway's lament for the "primary" (or authentic) text is the clearest example of this anachronism: The specific notion that no primary text exists in popular music dates to Theodor Adorno. Adorno's concept of a primary musical text derives from his idealization of the contemplative audience for classical music, an audience that ostensibly works from a distinctive first-time (or primary) hearing of a piece through subsequent revisions of that initial impression. The popular audience, however, is presumably utterly distracted and inattentive. Thus there is no original or primary moment in its experience because a song always remains the same (as a Led Zeppelin album title does actually put it), or identical over time.

Adorno's contrast between popular and classical music was first revived by none other than the best known of U.S. theorists of postmodernity, Fredric Jameson. In an essay well known to academics, "Reification and Utopia in Mass Culture" (1979), he avows that only the Frankfurt School's analysis of mass culture has any validity. With regard specifically to popular music, Jameson's language is virtually identical to Shumway's:

> We never hear any of the [music] produced in [popular] genres "for the first time"; instead, we live a constant exposure to them. [Thus] it makes no sense to try to recover a feeling for the "original" [or primary] musical text, . . . a very different situation from the first bewildered audition of a complicated classical piece.

Without that original or primary text, says Jameson, there can be no "living and authentic culture," [19] a dismissal of any possibility of authenticity replicated by Shumway. Shumway even gets the classical component into his essay, in fact, in an otherwise inexplicable contrast of classical and popular music, so derivative of Jameson that he commits careless fallacies, such as the observation that classical music doesn't breed superstars.

Shumway's resemblance to Jameson makes clear the problem with *Present Tense* and with postmodern analysis of mass culture in general: their direct derivation from the Frankfurt School. We have seen the idea of the simulacrum, the reproduction without an original, in Baudrillard; now we find it in Shumway reproducing Jameson on the absence of a primary text in popular music. But it was Adorno, in fact, who first made the point decades earlier, in his prewar "Culture Industry" essay, that "only the copy appears." The inescapable conclusion, therefore, is that postmodern theory has been a smokescreen allowing intellectual cynics to perpetuate the Frankfurt legacy, as Elayne Rapping points out in an essay on studies of television: "Postmodern disdain for the old Frankfurt School approach to media—the view that mass art is hopelessly degenerate and the tool of the ruling classes—[often reveals], at heart, trendy revisions of Frankfurtian elitism and pessimism about the ability of average people to be anything but passive cultural dopes." [20]

Shumway's paralysis over authenticity and primary texts (works of art autonomous from commerce, that is) is simply unnecessary, for it only reflects the scholarly specialist's own disengagement from the living social processes of popular culture. If the best hip-hop and rock songs function more as "events" or news, argues Simon Frith, or as immediate commentary that seizes and even changes the moment, their social consequence and use matters more than their formal essence as *either* a work of art or a commodity.[21] The authenticity of popular music, in other words, lies precisely in its repetition or circulation, as it enters into actual lived experience. The gross error of the Frankfurt School theorists, as many have noted, is their unexamined elitist presumptions about that supposedly merely secondary popular life.

Rock music is difficult to treat as a primary text not because it presents no authenticity at all but because it contains a number of moments of authenticity—the imprint of corporate bosses, A & R men, producers, and lawyers, to be sure, but also that of musicians, performers, and audiences. Only a lamely disengaged, overintellectualized, armchair approach to the music could reduce the resulting volatility to an absence of any concrete object of study and of any contention. I don't go to many shows myself, nowadays, but I feel justified in suggesting that many academics need to get out more. Perhaps then we could overcome the problem identified by Antonio Gramsci, the one other Western Marxist theorist besides Benjamin and Brecht who is not an utter pessimist:

> The popular element "feels" but does not always know or understand; the intellectual element "knows" but does not always understand, and in particular does not always feel. . . . The intellectual's error consists in believing that one can know without understanding and even more without feeling.[22]

Yet Lawrence Grossberg, the dean of postmodern academics writing on popular music, explicitly insists that feeling and understanding can no longer be connected.

The result of meaningless feeling, authentic inauthenticity, characterizes for him "all of contemporary rock" after the last fling at authenticity represented by punk. But punk and its avant-garde notions of politicizing rock music, as the Sex Pistols illustrate, already measured authenticity in part by self-reflexive honesty about commerce. Like other romantic modernists in postmodern clothing, Grossberg wishes to lament noncommercial authenticity, and thus he posits a sharp, immediate decline, in the 1980s, into "self-conscious parodies" of the ideology of authenticity (apparently those of New Pop)—as if that development were not a logical evolution out of punk. Nowadays, "authenticity is seen as just another style," and that widespread, self-reflexive realism, far from healthy, supposedly leads in every instance only to cynical "image-marketing," however ironically and satirically executed: "In the end, rock, like everything else in the 1990s, is a business." [23] When was it not a business, though? And, to reiterate, does the lasting significance of punk not lie precisely in putting the machinations of the music business in the foreground—making it clear that any claim for authenticity had to involve self-reflexivity—so postmoderns could worry inordinately about them?

I detail in the next chapter how Grossberg's key thesis, that affect and meaning have broken apart, helped influence the largely condescending critical reception of the group Nirvana, whose success resurrected punk. At this point, I simply want to note how closely Grossberg's pessimism was linked to a dismissal of the punk legacy in the first place. That's not to say his argument is very compelling, for he relies in large part on the ludicrous hack Bret Easton Ellis. Ellis's well-known first novel, *Less Than Zero* (1985), and subsequent work helped establish the myth of Generation X through a nihilistic, "numbing invocation of designer names, eateries, [and] personal care products." As one reviewer aptly sums up the positive critical response to Ellis's first book, "The less one was willing to think of kids, it would seem, the more one thought of Ellis." [24]

That observation applies very well to Grossberg, whose low opinion of contemporary youth culture leads him to a high estimation of Ellis—out of convenience, at least, to treat Ellis's contrived cynicism as authoritative. Grossberg uses Ellis specifically to describe the supposed bankruptcy of the "punk method" in the 1980s, as a result of punk's original antagonistic expression of nihilism being incorporated into the banal nihilism of the consumer society. [25] In an essay cited by Grossberg, "Twentysomethings: Adrift in a Pop Landscape" (1990), Ellis claims that "if some visceral rebellion remains" in forms like punk rock, "contemporary subversiveness is all on the surface. [P]assion and affect are simply not worth the trouble." [26] This appears to be a direct paraphrase of Jameson's view that expressions of defiance are fabrications feeding complacency—yet another instance of that supposedly general postmodern phenomenon, the closed circuit of expressive possibilities, that is really only characteristic of postmodern analyses and their endless repetition of one another. Ellis's essay was published in the *New York Times,* indicating once again the close fit between establishment media and the ideas of Marxist theorists of postmodernism such as Jameson and Grossberg.

But Ellis's formulation is illustrative in a more specific way, given his role in helping define Generation X. Thanks to others like Douglas Coupland and

Richard Linklater, Generation X, slackers, and the like have become identified with precisely the combination of attitudes described by Ellis: a punk rock taste for deviance trivialized by postmodern cynicism over the commercialization of rebellion and cheapening of emotion. Jason Cohen and Michael Krugman's *Generation Ecch!* (1994)—which came to attention after endorsement by Courtney Love—exemplifies this particular postpunk mode, simultaneously satirizing and endorsing cynicism among

> a bunch of rebellious losers. It's no accident that the phrase "rebel without a clue" has become a bigger cliché than "rebel without a cause."
> It's sad to say, but looking at *GenEcch* through the pop culture that formed them [sic], as well as the books, movies and music the generation has produced itself, seems to validate conservative old fart Allan Bloom's bellyaching about the accelerating vapidity of post-TV youth [which Grossberg also endorses] and their complete lack of depth, smarts, feeling or history.[27]

Cohen does successfully collapse the whole concept of Gen X but not simply because he demonstrates the role of the mass media in defining it. That exposé is far less revealing than his own scarcely differentiated invocation of *ressentiment,* which indicates that cynical (if hip) postmodernism derives directly from the fetid imagination of modernist elitists such as Friedrich Nietzsche and Theodor Adorno.

In citing Ellis on the irrelevance of affect, Grossberg winds up in a contradictory position because he knows full well there is still a desire for passionate music. His own argument everywhere else is not that no one troubles with emotion but that strong affect and any meaningfulness (or ideology) are disconnected. The failure of popular politically conscious groups like U2, R.E.M., and Midnight Oil results from "a radical disassociation of the music's political content and the band's political position from the emotionally and affectively powerful appeals" denied by Ellis.[28]

But that political failure is exactly what a punk (or avant-garde) position could have predicted. The problem is not that audiences get absorbed by emotion and fail to register political statements in music but, instead, that the music of groups like those above *lacks* a sufficiently outraged affective power. Their rock and roll, in other words, is pretty conventional stuff (not that I don't like R.E.M. quite a bit anyway). That's not to say that they possess no affective power at all, nor that affect and meaning are dissociated in their music—just that there is stronger stuff available in both emotional and political terms. But that's precisely where Bret Easton Ellis comes in, used to trash stronger musical options while Grossberg keeps his distance from such fatuously unexamined cynicism. Like so many others, his whole system—attempting to equate *postpunk* with the *postmodern*—went by the wayside in 1991, thanks to Nirvana, even before the publication of his magnum opus (*We Gotta Get Out of This Place*) on the 1980s.

Another academic postmodernist, Steve Redhead, writing on rock music in Britain in *The End-of-the-Century Party* (1990), adopts an approach similar to Grossberg's. Redhead uses the incorporation thesis to ridicule any residue of punk aesthetics, in another good example of postmodern gloom over the consumer society. He finds that *counterculture* now refers largely to the shop "counter" over which one receives the music. Even punk in 1977 "was easily incorporated after a few short months"—most critics are more generous—"and packaged for the pop and youth culture museum." Any "notion of rock culture as resistant or rebellious," therefore, is "not capable of capturing the changes in youth culture and rock culture from at least the late 1970s onwards." Those changes have been a result of "the policing, regulation and reorganisation of the cultural industries themselves"; the multinationals' control over music is near absolute. Discussion of cultural politics on the part of young people is no longer feasible, therefore, because "the contribution of the marketing strategies of the major corporations in the cultural industries" is preeminent.

Citing Baudrillard on hyperreality, Redhead finds that deviance in popular music and related youth subcultures "dissolved in the 1980s" into a world in which images and signs, in visual and musical styles, have become detached from any meaning. There is now merely a "transitory, fleeting adherence to lifestyles"—without commitment, in other words, just as Grossberg has it. (Redhead doesn't refer to affect, but the similarity to Grossberg on this point indicates how much Grossberg, too, owes to Baudrillard.) Youth culture is "notable not for opposition," therefore, "but for its role in selling everything from Levi 501 jeans to spot cream."

Redhead is not a confirmed follower of Baudrillard, however; he still believes the "social" exists. His postmodern pessimism derives less from abstract theory than from the "political economy" position, which concerns the politics of economic machinations. This fixation on the business end of mass culture (to reiterate Chapter 2) leads to the excess known as productivism, or the view that the corporate control of production determines how a musical text turns out, as well as how an audience behaves. But the standard postmodern picture of hyperconsumerism (linked, typically, to the triumph of Thatcherism in the 1980s) leads Redhead to conclude nonetheless that the music scene does indeed display the characteristics of Baudrillard's hyperreality.

Redhead, as a result, celebrates—where Grossberg laments—a postmodern music equated with being postpunk, in the specific sense of being "Post-Political." This portion of Redhead's argument, indebted to Simon Reynolds, is a fine example of the frequent, perverse circularity in which academics follow the lead of younger journalists whose work on rock music derived in the first place from academic postmodernists. Because "radicalism, rebellion and resistance were confined to the dustbin of history" in the 1980s, Redhead adopts Reynolds's apocalyptic postmodern line about end of history, derived from Baudrillard: "At the end of the millennium, . . . 'music to end the world to' is increasingly the only music which makes much political sense"—in being beyond politics, that is. The best music consists of pastiche, or the recycling of existing musical texts made possible by sampling. We will shortly see how much the concept of pastiche (or an indiscriminate combination of texts) owes to romanticism and modernism; postmodern theorists, however, treat it as the artistic manifestation of contemporary fragmentation. Yet many uses of sampling clearly practice montage as Walter Benjamin describes it—a politically conscious recovery of the past. Sampling in hip-hop music, for example, often explores black culture and popular music in self-evidently purposeful ways. But Redhead, astonishingly, claims that hip-hop typically denies history.

In keeping with the supposed antipolitics of postmodern music, the deviance of the audience lies in the "Baudrillardian excess" of imitating hyperconsumption. Pursuing "extremely volatile affinities and identities" through fashion somehow leads to "new practices of the self" or play with "new subjectivities," befitting the "increasingly speedy change and transformation" of the cultural marketplace. As with Baudrillard, in other words, all the evils that modernism detected in capitalist culture are transformed, with a wave of the wand, into virtues. The result, however, is very little different from the older subcultural sociology (like Dick Hebdige's *Subculture*) that Redhead dismisses for its perception of resistance enacted through style. He may strip away the older political reading of a coherent "self-generating process" in youth subcultures. But Redhead ultimately idealizes youth culture just as much as earlier sociologists, in lauding his new hyperhedonists for casting themselves into the "rapidly changing velocity of Pop Time" that obsesses him. This last bit of exaggeration about dramatic cultural changes in the 1980s is common in postmodern theory. It leads Redhead to clearly insupportable claims that bands have a harder time getting noticed now, and a harder time staying on top, thanks to the velocity of their turnover,[29] when in fact new acts break through all the time and often have sustained careers. In the final analysis, he merely provides yet another example of how the emergence of a new generation of rock groups in 1991, especially grunge and the new punk, undercut postmodern treatises on music before their ink had dried.

One academic, however, Andrew Goodwin, was notably resisting postmodern theory at the same time. His well-known collaborator in some work, Simon Frith, has always been skeptical as well about academic excess, particularly the divide drawn between authentic art and commerce by latter-day romantics. As for postmodernism, he finds that it "really describes the condition of the critics not that of the world they watch." But Frith's work in the 1980s arrives at postmodern cynicism nonetheless, if on an empirical rather than a theoretical basis. What is possible for us as consumers, says Frith, "is a result of decisions made by musicians, entrepreneurs and corporate bureaucrats, made according to governments' and lawyers' rulings, in response to technological opportunities." His view clearly tends toward productivism, in arguing like Jameson, Shumway, and Redhead that corporate interests determine the nature of popular music. Frith may acknowledge musicians and entrepreneurs, but he does not mean petit entrepreneurs, apparently, for he treats the significance of the independent record company as a punk myth. The indies are worried over too much, to be sure, but their importance is far from mythical.

Frith also illustrates another result the postmodern incorporation thesis has had in popular-music scholarship, the gloomy "economism" of concentrating exclusively on institutions involved with the economic or production end of music. He and Lawrence Grossberg, along with a number of his other coeditors and coauthors, have been churning out books on governmental as well as industrial policy regarding popular music. Convinced that only crunching numbers and reviewing case law and statutes provide any valid, useful insights, political-economy types seem to consider the music itself and its audiences a weak link, at best, if not an overromanticized irrelevance. Thus the largely mythical cultural populism has become a particular object of economist scorn. In the pre-Nirvana gulch of 1988, Frith proclaimed in *Music for Pleasure* that cultural studies had become an anachronism, now that "the rock era is over." [30]

Combating the more genuine problem of the anti-intellectual populism in British journalism devoted to popular culture, Frith (and Jon Savage) have called more recently for "a grasp of pop both as an industrial and as an aesthetic form," [31] and the emphasis is unquestionably on the former: His most positive finding of late is that technological breakthroughs like the sampler fuel the most important new music. Technology matters more than the artistic initiative involved in exploiting it, in other words, and thus musical change is driven not by musicians but by new opportunities that technology opens up for consumers (like portable machines). Where the romantics among postmodernists fetishize authenticity, Frith is nearly as absolutist in prioritizing commerce: Any concern with creativity in music and subcultural style should "giv[e] way to the material struggle for a piece of the new musical action," based on devices "that increase consumer control." The music that people get to use, however innovatively they use it, appears to be little more than a reflex reaction to that new marketplace. A would-be avant-garde musician or group desiring to achieve some social significance, in other words—let's say Rancid—is ground between corporations and their consumer society, a view making Frith difficult to distinguish from more theory-based postmoderns. Any authenticity heard in music, in his ultimate judgment, is "determined by the technological and economic conditions of its production," [32] a textbook instance of productivism. Frith is more interesting and humane, as a result, on the occasions when he returns to writing as a "fan" on artists and audiences and finds more of a dialectic between creativity and commerce.

In contrast with Frith's economic determinism, consistent with the post-modern obsession with overarching structures, Andrew Goodwin outright rejects nearly all postmodern theorizing about popular music. In the essay "Popular Music and Postmodern Theory" (1991), he targets exemplars of postmodern music such as Fred Pfeil's triumvirate—Laurie Anderson, Philip Glass, and the Talking Heads—as musicians whose impact is conveniently overestimated by scholars. Those musicians' techniques, furthermore, such as ambiguity and self-reflexivity (in a strictly textual sense), are actually based in modernism, Goodwin points out. In the more specific matter of supposedly postmodern musical tactics, there is nothing new or postmodern about departures from song structure and tonal rationality, either. In a nutshell, as I have been arguing, if such practices constitute postmodernism, it is evidently nothing more than the persistence of modernism.

As opposed to the writers in *Present Tense,* who declare rock and roll and postmodernism identical, Goodwin argues that postmodernism might be better understood as "a parasite *description* of post-war pop, rather than an explanatory paradigm." Tim Brennan also finds an essentially parasitic relation in the frequent scholarly association of hip-hop with postmodernism. While we have seen scholars such as Cornel West repudiate hip-hop on that basis, Brennan has in mind the questionable relocation of hip-hop that occurs even in the most informed, positive postmodern accounts, which act "too much the agent[s] of alien black youth in the fuddy-duddy surroundings of the academy." Is it really elevating to make hip-hop conform with academic paradigms? He concludes, therefore, that "we need a different theoretical apparatus than the familiar one of postmodernism." [33]

Goodwin's case against postmodern parasitism goes much further, assailing the fundamental logic of many academics who write on popular music: "Postmodernism employs eclecticism and intertextuality [or pastiche]; rock music is eclectic and intertextual; *ergo,* rock music is postmodern." The primary spurious result of treating virtually all contemporary popular music as postmodern, along these lines, is to lump together "an extraordinarily divergent, and incoherent, profusion" of music. A good example of this tendency is Redhead's and Reynolds's amalgamation of sampling (in both hip-hop and dance music), shambling bands (such as the Mekons, Shop Assistants, and Smiths), and postpunk groups as postmodernism. All rock music is made identical by postmodern critics not just in terms of pastiche, Goodwin notes, but also with regard to the thesis on "excessive affect," or emotion split from meaning. As a result of viewing emotions as unreasonable, the postmoderns insist on abandoning reason in analyzing music; thus even favorable music criticism is condescending, in assuming its subjects possess very little rationality, or intelligence. Goodwin also finds quite odd, finally, the use of popular music to prove the all-encompassing grasp of the corporate world, concluding that postmodern cultural theorists are essentially guilty of collusion with it.

Goodwin's most damning point, however, is that the universalizing pronouncements of postmoderns actually depend on a very narrow focus, "bracketing out vast areas of contemporary pop that contradict [postmodern] theory." Thus we get the Madonna industry in scholarship, uninterested in the rest of popular music. More significantly, as Goodwin emphasizes, the general denial of "authenticity" depends on "leav[ing] out too much—indeed, the absences are precisely what allows each account to seem coherent." [34] The absence of much reference in postmodern work to specific groups and musicians, outside of a few undeveloped, clichéd references, is apparent in the work of the two academics most obsessed with authenticity, Grossberg and Shumway. Claims about the absence or impossibility of authenticity clearly require that postmoderns ignore new, more challenging music, another respect in which their work is hardly as up to the minute as it pretends to be.

Goodwin's response to postmodernists is to point out that popular music fans continue to distinguish art from pop, or serious, committed music from trash; contemporary music is most definitely not all the same for anyone attuned to it. Goodwin's point also works against postmodernism in other respects. For one thing, the distinction of good and bad popular music indicates that the belief in cultural hierarchies (or levels of quality) has not disappeared due to eclecticism, pastiche, and so forth, as postmodern theorists claim. It is important to note, though, that postmoderns have in mind one specific distinction of cultural levels, the romantic and modernist system pitting the fine arts against mass culture. Obviously, contemporary music fans are not traditional elitists and thus are hardly concerned with perpetuating the distinction of "high" and "low" culture. Their distinction of good and bad music is often based on a more or less explicit political standard, instead—just the opposite of modernism and its loathing of mixing art and political engagement. The political standard does sometimes revert to the romantic and modernist distinction of good art as noncapitalist, however, as in the preference for music on independent record labels.

The political distinction of good and bad popular music is nonetheless essentially like Walter Benjamin's and Bertolt Brecht's original distinction, in the 1930s, between avant-garde popular art and commercial fodder. In stressing that mass culture held both good and bad possibilities, they meant to move beyond modernist absolutism about good art having to be entirely free (or autonomous) of capitalism. The original avant-garde of the 1930s, in other words, *already was* "post" modern. Postmodern universalizing about hip-hop and rock music—the view that no expression of outrage or social concern is authentic—has the deliberate effect, therefore, of closing the door on the avant-garde, on the real postmodernism. That is why, logically, we continue to find modernism posing as postmodernism, especially in the absolutism about capitalism and its universal incorporation of creative expression. Fredric Jameson, for example, claims that the Benjamin-Brecht position no longer addresses the conditions of our own time, one good reason why Goodwin would find Jameson's "efforts to grapple with rock music from within an account of the postmodern condition . . . empirically quite unconvincing."

Goodwin himself does not use the term *avant-garde* but, instead, describes every aesthetic idea from the modern period as modernism. This is unfortunate, for he clearly retains the avant-garde idea of angry, discomforting voices disrupting the processes of commercial culture—Brecht's alienation effect, Benjamin's shock effect—dismissed by Jameson. "Today's rap music, like punk rock before it," Goodwin emphasizes, "encounters extraordinary difficulty in gaining airplay and media exposure precisely because its *sounds,* as much as its sentiments, are not conducive to a commercial environment." But in concluding that such music "is, in the classic *modernist* tradition, disruptive" (emphasis added), he fails to correct the strategic collapse of the avant-garde into modernism by scholars.[35] This time-honored strategy involves stripping away the emphasis of the revolutionary avant-garde on political outcomes and treating it as purely artistic innovation like the rest of modernism. (Peter Bürger's *Theory of the Avant-Garde,* published in English in 1984, was a watershed in challenging this academic common wisdom and has been much maligned as a result.) In Colin MacCabe's *James Joyce and the Revolution of the Word* (1978), for example, as in the film theory MacCabe promoted in the journal *Screen,* Brecht is reduced to a formalist essentially identical with Joyce—practicing nothing more than a self-reflexivity (in the narrow textual sense, although MacCabe deems it revolutionary) that indicates the difficulty if not impossibility of expressing any authentic identity.

But in distinguishing the "realism" (rather than avant-gardism) of punk and its offspring from the "modernism" of performers like the Talking Heads, Goodwin's heart is clearly in the right place. His use of the term *realism* echoes Brecht's broad political sense of realism being a matter of "laying bare society's causal network/showing up the dominant viewpoint as the viewpoint of the dominators," which implies the transmission of some sort of content, as opposed to MacCabe's version of Brecht. Formal innovation certainly matters as well; artists accomplish this realist objective by addressing new social problems with "new techniques. Reality alters; to represent it the means of representation must alter too."[36] *Realism,* in other words, means keeping up with changes in the perception of *reality* brought about by new cultural technologies (or "bad new" art forms, as Brecht puts it). At most, modernism exploited new forms for traditional elitist ends, much as postmodern theorists take dire, apocalyptic readings of the world off of television.

Music videos, in particular, have been an object of fascination for postmodernists, as examples of eclecticism and pastiche. Goodwin, therefore, particularly decimates postmodern theory in *Dancing in the Distraction Factory: Music Television and Popular Culture* (1992). MTV has been an obsession of academics intent on verifying their worst suspicions about the postmodern condition, or, in a few cases, their excessive optimism about it. I have not addressed MTV up to this point, however, largely due to my concern with the subject of emotion, more fundamental to music's tactile, sonic impact than the visual images added by videos. But I have also not taken on academic postmodern work on MTV because Goodwin has already effectively demolished it.

First of all, he points out, video did not suddenly inject eclecticism and pastiche into rock music. Ever since Elvis Presley married country, gospel, and rhythm 'n' blues, rock and roll has been an odd combination of styles. When the first wave of rock and roll stars figuratively and literally died off, it was English art-schoolers, playing the music of black American bluesmen, who revived the music. In making rock and roll still more eclectic by reading it through European aesthetics, especially romantic idealization of the artist, by the end of the 1960s the English had helped transform rock and roll into the more stately "rock music." And with punk's attack on art rock in the mid-1970s, finally, the European avant-garde (particularly the Situationist International) emerged into mass and popular culture for the first time. Rock music, in other words, has always been wildly eclectic pastiche, and to discover in the mid to late 1980s that it is postmodern seems suspiciously opportunistic.

To make music videos, or visual pastiche, the basis for asserting that rock music became fully postmodern in the 1980s (and less radical or avant-garde than punk, in essence) is even more suspect. From the moment Elvis appeared, rock and roll has relied heavily on film and television. Shumway thus has to backtrack and make even the innocuous Monkees—actually a great pop band, whoever was making the music—part of the postmodern horror show, although he does at least acknowledge the long history of music video. Goodwin points out immediately, in *Dancing in the Distraction Factory,* that "pop has always stressed the visual. [T]he fundamental importance of performance imagery . . . is not new." Even music videos, more recently, are usually far more considered than postmodern theorists allow. Simply in the promotional or advertising function of videos, there is a "fundamental continuity of music television with [traditional] practices inside the music industry." In treating music videos as pastiche, or a senseless (or depthless) combination of fragments, postmodernists willfully ignore the fact that "music television makes sense (not nonsense)," as promotional material, "both for consumers of pop and for the institutions that control its production." [37]

When it comes to pastiche, finally, Goodwin cites Franco Moretti on romantic and modernist irony, which long ago instituted the kind of "blankness" now attributed to music videos. For postmoderns to discover romantic and modernist practices in MTV indicates once again, of course, how little is new about the postmodern. Moretti describes the esteemed work of art, since romanticism, as one made as indefinite—or blank—as possible, through difficulty, impenetrability, and so on. The "irony" lies in occupying two places at once: the external public world (including mass culture) from which one's images and subjects must necessarily be drawn and the internalized private world of art. The romantic and modernist frame of mind "sees in any event no more than an 'occasion' for free intellectual and emotional play, for a mental and subjective deconstruction of the world as it is." It is romanticism, modernism, and now their postmodern epigones, therefore, who are "incapable of a decision." There is no difference in the past two centuries, moreover, in the fondness of the academic, aesthete, or intellectual for attributing that "spell of indecision" to everyone else. [38]

One reason why academic postmodernists writing on popular music have been complicit in that arrogance, and inadvertently with the journalists examined in the next chapter, has been identified by Houston Baker in a fairly hilarious criticism of black scholars who have appeared in courtrooms and the mass media as "instant experts" on hip-hop. Baker finds that academic hucksterism, motivated by "the allure of name-recognition," leads to saying

> whatever you will about emergent popular cultural forms simply because you are an adult scholar and feel that nobody will challenge you since your colleagues are too busy deciding which Chardonnay to serve at the next dinner party, [which] is as bogus, sloppy, and irresponsible as you wanna be.[39]

Baker has in mind Henry Louis Gates Jr.'s defense of 2 Live Crew's *As Nasty as They Wanna Be,* but the fate that Baker assigns to academic celebrities passing overly casual, misguided judgment on mass culture—a "foolish closed-loop credibility"—seems even more pronounced in the case of cynical Marxist theorists of postmodernism such as Fredric Jameson. When he started showing up in music journalism, the closed loop of postmodernism became a self-fulfilling prophecy.

# CHAPTER 4

# Kurt Cobain Died for Your Sins
## *Postmodernism in Music Journalism*

As in well-intentioned academic work like Barry Shank's, there are obviously inherent contradictions in a recent celebration of alternative rock that favorably cites Fredric Jameson's "landmark essay" on postmodernism. In *Manic Pop Thrill* (1993), journalist Rachel Felder professes that she "assumes Jameson's conditions and goes from there," although where one could go from such a hopeless position is difficult to imagine. Felder has in mind a specific postmodern condition, actually, the erosion of distinctions between high and mass culture noted by many critics. Jameson, we have seen, hardly celebrates that erosion, as Felder seems to think, but instead complains about the loss of high culture's distance or autonomy from mass culture. That Felder is out of her element on this particular subject is apparent: She turns the modern/postmodern divide into a conflict between somehow "high modernist" commercial musicians, though modernism defined itself against commerce, and "postmodern" alternative rockers on indie labels.[1] She appears to have in mind an analogy with punk's opposition to mainstream rock in the 1970s. But punk's do-it-yourself ethos rejected pretensions about artistic virtuosity—the actual quasi-modernist element in rock—more than corporate financing, which punk groups were in no way averse to seeking, even though they parodied the process of "selling out."

Far worse, however, has been the absorption of Jameson's and Lawrence Grossberg's arguments by mainstream music journalists. That absorption may not have been direct in every case, but there are clearly music journalists, especially Simon Reynolds writing in *Melody Maker*, who have been influential conduits for academic postmodernism. (It's not surprising, therefore, that Reynolds is now published by Harvard University Press.) However it came about, the importation of postmodern theory into music journalism became apparent in 1991, when the postmodern thesis on the meaninglessness of emotion was directly reproduced in a spate of articles precipitated by the first Lollapalooza tour, Nirvana's breakthrough with the *Nevermind* album, the rise of the Riot Grrrls, and the proliferation of gangsta and radical rap music. Echoing (I won't say plagiarizing) each other quite closely, the articles posited a dysfunctional disconnection between "rage" and meaning in the new music. The visceral emotional impact of the music, from this view, is undercut by either inarticulate or indecipherable lyrical content. The journalists making this argument, however, betray the classic self-contradiction in ridicule of supposedly weak-minded emotions: a clear motivation by fear of the actual danger that anger poses for authority.

Prior to 1991, establishment media hectored new music like hip-hop for its lyrical content, a traditional pastime. Even an infamous article titled "The Rap Attitude," published in 1990 by *Newsweek* and distributed to Congress by groups urging music censorship, had little to say about the music's actual "attitude," or anger. The article borrows a number of subjects and its title from a 1989 article with a very different tenor, "Wanted for Attitude," Dave Marsh and Phyllis Pollack's account in *The Village Voice* of efforts to censor hip-hop, which states approvingly that "anger and resentment are at the center" of gangsta rap groups like N.W.A. The *Newsweek* article, however, makes only one passing reference to "free-floating rancor" (inarticulate anger, that is), although in a sign of things to come, it is supplied by an academic well read in postmodern criticism, Todd Gitlin. The article chides hip-hop and heavy-metal lyrics for their obscenity and concludes, contrary to its own evidence, such as Public Enemy, that the songs are "mostly empty of political content"—apparently very narrowly defining the political as elaborate party platforms and so forth. The article's own politics are apparent: Just a year before Nirvana sold ten million or so records, unquestionably bridging working- and middle-class youths, *Newsweek* sneers at alienation in heavy metal and hip-hop as a purely "working-class and underclass phenomenon." It is difficult to tell, as a result, whether the writers are being ironic or simply condescending when they refer to "millions of American youths who forgot to go to business school in the 1980s." [2]

This smugness didn't last long, for it became increasingly apparent that more affluent young people purchasing a resurgent punk music felt just as alienated by shrinking opportunity. Heavier artillery was needed, and at this point the importation of postmodern academic theory began in earnest. The watershed event was the appearance of articles in August and September 1991 in the *New York Times* and *Newsweek,* respectively. The first, "Now Is the Summer of Our Discontent" by Jon Pareles (popular-music editor for the *Times*), concerns the first Lollapalooza tour, a surprising success organized by Jane's Addiction. The tour featured a diverse group of performers including the industrial group Nine Inch Nails and the rapper Ice-T, a deliberate statement about their common outrage. Pareles's article does not actually concern Lollapalooza, however; the tour serves as the occasion for an editorial on the condition of youth music in 1991.

Pareles's awareness of postmodern ideas is evident at the outset in his gloom over consumer society's ability to make even the strongest emotion just another commodity. As in academic postmodernism, commercial incorporation is said to split emotion from meaning, making the performers' anger inauthentic and thus no genuine basis for commitment:

> This is the summer of rage—or, more precisely, the summer when rage sells. . . . [A]dvertising has helped convince people that they can forge an identity through consumption, and they can fill in that sense that something's missing with the right brand of running shoes or jeans or beer. Or an album. So people consume rage as entertainment.

The idea that choices in musical taste are no more important than the choice of shoes stretches matters quite a bit, like most of postmodern theory. It makes no sense whatsoever to claim that people make the same emotional commitment to their Nikes that they do in listening to music.

Pareles more sensibly observes that rage is simply "big box office" in mass culture in general. But he goes too far in concluding that Nine Inch Nails, Nirvana, and hip-hop are thus identical with sitcoms like *Roseanne* and *Married With Children* and radio talk-show hosts like Rush Limbaugh and Howard Stern. The "nastier and nastier put-downs" dispensed by these radio and television figures, "cackling with self-satisfaction all the while," couldn't present a more complete contrast with angry music. Never hateful toward anyone besides authority, even at its worst that music is no more than self-loathing (with the exception of a few less compelling performers like Axl Rose who dabble in homophobia and racism).

The more significant point, however, is that Pareles makes all anger identical by enlisting the postmodern thesis that emotion and meaning have become entirely detached. His declaration that rage is "as inarticulate as it is widespread," it seems to me, clearly reflects an awareness of Grossberg's thesis that affect and meaning (or ideology) have broken apart. The adherents of angry music, Pareles claims, "don't much care who or what that rage is aimed at. All they want is to feel that someone else is as angry as they are." That concern to share common feelings, in an affective alliance, is exactly what popular music has always been about—the discovery that there are still people one would like to talk to. But now, implicitly thanks to the postmodern condition, those feelings are meaningless and outright irrational, bereft of any content or intelligence. So there is actually nothing being communicated.

At this point, I must emphasize again that emotions are in fact *never* without meaning and that Pareles, like the postmodern academics he's absorbed, is rehashing an elitist aesthetic perspective dating to the eighteenth century. The odd thing is that Pareles stops to document the good reasons why young people are enraged: In "an economy in which real income hasn't risen since 1973, they can look forward to moving back in with their parents after graduating and competing for low-paying service jobs. . . . The future seems circumscribed." So why does he tell us their anger is unreasonable? In Pareles's case, his exploitation of academic postmodernism seems to be quite congenial with his personal tastes, especially a nostalgia for folk music of the 1950s and 1960s, the sort of attitude that has fed a new generation's loathing of baby boomers. It is simply amazing to find a rock critic in the 1990s invoking folk music as a standard: "Forget protest songs," Pareles laments, "with their topicality, their hopeful suggestions and their attempts to convince the uncommitted." More important than noticing the nostalgia, however, is to detect the priority he places on intellectual effects, or lyrical content. Along with the dismissal of emotion and the loathing of commerce and consumerism, this is all Kant. In 1996, finally, Pareles turned the same apparatus on the new wave of women in rock: "The music business has decided to get behind the Angry Young Woman, [turning] audacious aspirations into a systematic shtick"—end of subject.[3]

A month after Pareles's original article on merchandising anger, John Leland published a similar jeremiad in *Newsweek,* indicating the influence of the *Times* in setting the agenda for establishment news media. Leland starts with the same contempt for meaningless angry music, presumably a matter purely of consumerism, thanks to its incorporation into commerce: "Adolescent rage, and the appetite for it, finally get their own shopping holiday." The expression of that rage is presumably only a commercial calculation aimed at meeting tastes conditioned by "the violent dysfunction of a generation." Like Pareles, Leland paradoxically indicates at the same time some perfectly good reasons for youthful outrage, although in his case he is so interested in issuing dismissals that his short list is quite muddled. It's not clear how youths in the 1990s have been ravaged by Vietnam, as he claims, although in lumping that war in with alcoholism, drug abuse, and divorce he may have in mind the effects of dysfunctional parents who came of age during the Vietnam War. The danger of police brutality for black males that he cites, however, is certainly good reason for outrage in hip-hop music.

But rappers and rockers lose their moral force, he finds, because they "no longer present themselves as hopes for a better future"—a complaint like Pareles's nostalgia for protest songs. I would've thought the refusal of musicians to hold themselves out as icons is quite healthily honest, or "authentic." But Leland prefers, ironically, the transparent pretense of idealism represented by the "We Are the World" single, concerned with starvation in Ethiopia in the mid-1980s. "We Are the World" is in fact the one genuine instance cited of the phenomenon for which angry music is being indicted: a self-promoting pose of emotional commitment manufactured for mass consumption. (The song is also an appalling declaration of who the world revolves around—wealthy First Worlders.)

As a result of hip-hop and rock music cultivating rage above all else, according to Leland, both are "reduced to often violent survivalism, . . . locked in a static battle" with authority. This locked embrace bears an uncanny resemblance to the French postmodern picture, in which battling authority is merely a delusional drama serving to reinforce the closed circuit of power. But Leland in no way means to pursue that logic; he likes authority too much. Thus he castigates young people for their somehow unreasonable belief that "authority is actively destructive." It seems to me this is something that one can quickly confirm by looking at, for example, efforts to end protection of the environment, the calculated erosion of the economic status of most Americans—let alone that of homeless families and inner cities left to rot—and plans to take children from poor families and place them in orphanages.

But Leland's article in *Newsweek,* apparently for the sake of originality, also adds a highly revealing twist. To the rage of heavy metal and hip-hop, he counterposes its complete opposite, a saccharine element in popular music epitomized by Mariah Carey. Leland quite rightly disses one song of hers in particular, a banality actually titled "Emotion," a smug testimonial to feeling good (because you're married to the president of Sony, apparently). By introducing Carey along with romantic balladeer Michael Bolton (whose greatest success has been with the secondhand emotion of warmed-over cover versions), Leland is able to appeal to a hazy middle ground described, significantly, in terms of reason: The "two camps—one brutal, the other unrealistically gentle— [both offer] unreasonable responses to the world, pulling ever deeper into their own unreason." [4] Here again is aesthetics dating to the eighteenth century: Reason or intellectual contemplation is the proper response to art; emotion is bad because it is entirely unreasonable (which is not the case at all). To pit the angry and the saccharine camps against each other, therefore, does nothing to enhance Leland's credibility. He may not like moronic music utterly devoid of any emotional challenge, but in dismissing emotion altogether he might as well be—take your choice—Kant, Adorno, or Jameson.

Leland's article is a fine example, as well, of the continual effort of corporate media to stereotype anger and deviance among young people in negative terms intended to reaffirm the status quo. This tactic was identified two decades ago by British sociologists like Stanley Cohen, in *Folk Devils and Moral Panics* (1972), and the group in Birmingham's Centre for Contemporary Cultural Studies, in *Resistance through Rituals* (1976) and *Policing the Crisis* (1978). The inescapable conclusion that one draws from the *Newsweek* article, however, contrary to its author's intention, is that the enraged camp in hip-hop and rock, far from unreasonable, is quite *rationally* directed at the feel-good culture represented by the likes of Carey, which wants to accommodate us to the world of the multinationals.

Shortly after Leland's and Pareles' 1991 articles, as if to confirm the fears that led them to adopt postmodern contempt for emotion, Nirvana emerged to make 1991 "the year punk broke." Nirvana's success with undiluted punk anger thus fueled a rapid proliferation of the thesis on the split between emotion and reason/meaning/ideology. Leland's response to Nirvana in *Newsweek,* in 1992, was to rehash the incorporation thesis by ridiculing the "feeding frenzy" of major labels searching for another Nirvana (also described in the alternative-music magazine *Spin,* right down to the same choice of phrase). "What's new," he mocks, "is that this one is for punk-rock acts, distinguished largely by their stance against the record industry. Suddenly, this stance is worth something." As in his earlier article, and much like Pareles, Leland lumps together all expressions of anger to suggest that they're all part of the same marketing triumph: "The '90s are shaping up as the decade of anger: angry women, angry African-Americans, angry gays, angry taxpayers." He concludes, however, that punk is uniquely attractive to corporate music executives because punks are white males and thus more mainstream. The music industry can exploit their "anger without [feeling] guilt," as a result, as opposed to marketing the stronger stuff implied by the list of angry groups like blacks and women.[5] That list, in essence, allows Leland to give the usual postmodern clichés a veneer of multicultural concern. It seems odd, though, to drive a wedge between punk and women in an article featuring a picture of Courtney Love and a sidebar with Love's group Hole and Babes in Toyland.

The *Times* weighed in on Nirvana with an article in September 1991 titled "A Band That Deals in Apathy," which concedes at the last possible instant that "there are a number of issues the band strongly supports." This concluding point is coupled with the notion that Nirvana nonetheless represents "pledged nihilism," and no effort is made to resolve the discrepancy. The *Times* became actively hysterical and vengeful, though, when Nirvana reached number one. Three articles in January 1992 alone chalked up the group's success to "careful orchestration" by their corporate record label, as an article titled "Is Hit Album a Fluke or a Marketing Coup?" put it.[6]

But Simon Reynolds's "Boredom + Claustrophobia + Sex = Punk Nirvana," which appeared in November 1991, had already done a complete hatchet job. Reynolds's findings are entirely in keeping with the earlier Pareles article, but I should note that Reynolds had long since introduced postmodern ideas into music journalism. If anything, Pareles's postmodern article owes a considerable debt to Reynolds; in giving him the Nirvana assignment (among others), obviously, Pareles knew Reynolds's work. One reason why I think Pareles relies as much or more on Grossberg, nonetheless, is Reynolds's difference from both of them in his treatment of the relation of emotion and meaning. As a strict poststructuralist, citing Baudrillard, Foucault, Jameson, Lyotard, and Nietzsche in *Blissed Out* (1990), a collection of articles from 1985-1989, Reynolds is actually explicitly opposed to meaning, in contrast with older critics like Pareles. Reynolds instead prefers indeterminacy and irrationalism—not only in lyrical content, however, but also in the emotion produced by music. The purported split between affect (or emotion) and ideology (or reason) is fine with him, in other words, as opposed to Grossberg's and Pareles's pessimism over the matter.

According to Reynolds, in fact, the postmodern displacement of "depth and meaning" is actually quite subversive. Jameson is cited on the waning of depth—a problem of affect, of course—and though his misgivings are acknowledged, Reynolds's otherwise favorable construction of the matter is probably responsible for a younger journalist like Rachel Felder thinking that Jameson can be reconciled with alternative rock. The Pixies, perhaps the leading indie group of their day, are said by Reynolds to "provoke emotional responses you *can't pin down*" (emphasis added), or an affect without depth or meaning, that is: "All that remains is the urge to holler, shriek and whoop it up for the arbitrary, unnegotiable hell of it." [7] Even in the midst of a culture stressing restraint, apparently, such emotional outbursts have no meaning (or social significance) beyond relieving emotional pressure. In forming the Breeders and giving similar music a distinctly feminine cast, however, former Pixies bassist Kim Deal clearly feels that sonic roar can open up expressive possibilities for women—and as a result has been far more appealing and successful than the Pixies were.

In keeping with his preference for indefinite emotion, moreover, Reynolds habitually disparages anger, which he ridicules as the legacy of punk's faith in the direct expression of outrage. His dismissal of any association between rock and rebellion offers perhaps the clearest evidence available that the fundamental basis of postmodern theory is an abandonment of political agency: in Reynolds's explicitly Foucauldian universe the idea of directly opposing power is a delusion only serving the dominant order. So if he differs somewhat from other postmoderns on the repercussions of the split between affect and meaning, ultimately he reaches a quite similar conclusion on the futility of open dissent. And Reynolds was quickly widely influential: By 1988, the alternative press was chastising devotees of punk for perpetuating concepts like "subversion" and "rebellion," which "no longer plausibly apply to rock or pop culture in general [because] they all depend on a certain [discredited] dynamic of opposition"—a précis of Reynolds's work.[8] This attack on the sham of rebel rock conveniently and dishonestly ignores the fact that punk highlighted the problem of commercial incorporation from the start (see "Complete Control" by the Clash). Punk has continued to seem both vital and volatile for two decades because its ideals of rebellion have always included self-awareness regarding incorporation. Like Bertolt Brecht's theater, it wishes for a different world but in actual practice dwells on the way things are now, trying to raise the question of whether they have to be that way.

Reynolds and Joy Press, in contrast, argue in the 1995 book *The Sex Revolts* that the best artists actually rebel against the very notion of rebellion. Nonpolitical psychedelic music, in particular, presumably realizes that rock music can never be a revolutionary art but merely that of the weak postmodern rebel "secretly complicit with the Order" in the closed loop of power. (The terms in this case actually come from a modernist, Jean-Paul Sartre, whom scholars of emotion such as Peter Middleton consider quite reactionary for underwriting

Nietzsche's concept of *ressentiment*.) Some of the groups that Reynolds endorses as properly postmodern psychedelia, however, such as Sonic Youth, don't agree at all with his premises. Kim Gordon, the group's bassist, says that she writes from the standpoint of anger, in the interest of transgressing what's appropriate for women (and men, too)—a distinctly punk attitude.[9]

Reynolds's favorite groups, such as A. R. Kane, My Bloody Valentine, and Sonic Youth, appeal to him because their electronically enhanced wash of sound approximates an acid trip, like the original psychedelia of the 1960s. Their equally spacey lyrics are disjointed to the point of schizophrenia, which *Blissed Out* celebrates on the model of postmodern theorists such as Gilles Deleuze and Felix Guattari, prominent figures in *The Sex Revolts* as well. The effect of psychedelic music, claims Reynolds, is somehow to "dissolve systems" by being "suspicious of words, reluctant to spell it out, [and] eager to be spellbound, to succumb to oceanic feelings, to go with the flow." *The Sex Revolts* argues that music of this sort approximates a desirable, radical return to the mother's womb, adding postmodern feminism to the standard postmodern dissolution of identity championed in *Blissed Out*: Psychedelic experience in your head leads to "trips out of yourself." [10] But even shamblers and shoegazers such as My Bloody Valentine continue to represent something oppositional. As Reynolds acknowledges, for instance, British indie rock (or Steve Redhead's "Post-Political Pop") made a point of retaining punk's antipathy for apolitical hippies even when harking back to the 1960s, as in the second coming of the Summer of Love in Manchester. Reynolds, predictably, considers that "anti-hippie consensus" part of a "stifling orthodoxy" deriving from punk and its notions about opposition.[11] Instead, he quite highly esteems the 1960s and drug-enhanced bacchanals, an even lamer nostalgia than Pareles's.

The notoriety of this vapid 1960s nostalgia on the part of Reynolds and his colleagues at *Melody Maker*, Paul Oldfield and David Stubbs, is attested to by their inclusion in *Zoot-Suits and Second-Hand Dresses* (1989), a collection edited by Angela McRobbie. McRobbie wished to bring to academic attention a new form of cultural journalism, but in the case of Oldfield, Reynolds, and Stubbs, rehashing Foucault et al., there is very little that academics would consider new, except for the process of running popular music through the postmodern meatgrinder. The most interesting thing about these postmodern journalists, instead, is how clearly they reproduce the roots of postmodernism in the late eighteenth century and romanticism. Blaming punk (like Reynolds) for making rock music somehow "small and common" by giving people expectations that music could pose a social "threat," Stubbs wishes to rekindle "mystery and fascination" in the form of "function-less, far-out noise—a new 'purity.' " [12] Although he and Reynolds associate this rekindling with a return to the 1960s, pure art without a social function has been the ideal of aesthetes for more than two hundred years now. The perpetuation of that ideal, in fact, is what crippled the counterculture intellectually: Rock writing from the late 1960s happily extolled modernists like Baudelaire and his concept of the dandy withdrawn from social concerns, an enemy of democracy.

So when Reynolds describes himself as a poststructuralist in *Blissed Out,* his additional profession that he seeks "certain ancient truths" is a revealing admission that postmodernism isn't doing anything new. By the time one encounters frequent references to musicians who have "the Gift" accorded by "the unequal distribution of brilliance," it becomes apparent that Reynolds is only recycling the romantic notion of the artist's unique inspiration. Reynolds's usefulness, in fact, lies in making clear how much postmodernism shares with the original romantics, in pitting that abstract value of originality against the material values of commercial culture. There is a heavy residue of modernist elitism in Reynolds, too, in his calls for "perpetual aesthetic innovation" (constantly making it new, that is, as Ezra Pound put it) and a "remystification" of art (à la Stubbs) that would restore its "worship." Worshipping art, of course, is what conservatives like William Bennett, Allan Bloom, Lynne Cheney, and Hilton Kramer insist we should do—so much for Reynolds's cutting-edge pose.

Thus the postmodern concepts in *Blissed Out,* as in so many other cases we have seen, mask a deeply reactionary regression. The wholesale repetition of academia in Reynolds's postmodern laundry list ought to be suspicious in itself, though. We hear that "power operates by inculcating us in the art of self-policing" (or creates and absorbs us as subjects, as in Foucault); that carnival (or laughing and cursing at authority, as described in Mikhail Bakhtin's *Rabelais and His World* and performed by Bikini Kill) is thus only "a brief intermission" actually reinforcing "the other side of normality and control," in the closed circuit of power; that the do-it-yourself ethos of punk and subsequently sampling in hip-hop, as well as independent producers, are all inescapably "vertically linked to the major record companies" (the incorporation thesis); that life "shatters into fragments" thanks to the media overload of hyperreality diagnosed by Baudrillard, which causes the schizophrenia lamented by Jameson but advocated by Deleuze and Guattari; and that with the resulting " 'end of history,' " revolution means an "endless, discontinuous [phenomenon] constantly accessible, in your head, as psychedelic experience [that] *can't* be turned into a new order" (emphasis added), or be the basis for social change, in other words.[13]

Given Reynolds's long-standing loathing of punk for expressing instead a concerted antiauthoritarianism, it comes as no surprise that he reacted hostilely to its revival with Nirvana's success in 1991. That revival plainly and simply gave the lie to the postmodern ideas he was pushing as musical state of the art in the late 1980s. He has willingly joined hands, as a result, with conventional critics who find the group's anger inarticulate and irrational:

> Nirvana's rage is mostly unspecific and apolitical, and at times verges on the incoherent. It provides a catch-all catharsis that fits in perfectly with the directionless disaffection of the 20something generation. . . . If "Nevermind" is about anything, it's about the agony of blocked idealism, the way anger festers when it can find no constructive outlet.[14]

The presumption that Nirvana's music is in no way a "constructive outlet" is odd, and far too easy. Whatever one thinks of a particular group, musical expression is unquestionably an act of construction, or creativity, and to wave away that act is astonishing.

Once Nirvana became a test case for the new rage in rock and hip-hop music, the observation that Kurt Cobain's anger was utterly incoherent spread like wildfire through the news media and music press. (The ridiculous form this argument often took—that it's hard to understand Nirvana's lyrics—is one that should have been settled years ago concerning popular music; in Part 2, I discuss the meaningfulness of emotion as a matter distinct from lyrical content.) Even periodicals devoted exclusively to alternative music underwrote the conclusion that Nirvana represented senseless emotion. *Option,* for example, found that Nirvana's songs represented "a frenzied search for meaning among kids who have been given no tools for contemplation." [15] This lament over the lack of contemplation by the audience for popular art is also found in Kant's *Critique of Judgment,* and it's distressing to find that writers strongly supportive of grunge and punk music could be so retrograde.

The basis on which Reynolds finds Nirvana's anger incoherent, unsurprisingly, is the notion that the consumer society incorporates and renders all expression trivial: "As Nirvana knows only too well, teen spirit is routinely bottled, shrink-wrapped and sold, . . . in an industry that's glad to turn rebellion into money." The music writers in the *Times* never tire of this line; in an article on Green Day more than three years later, we read once again that "by embracing and accepting their anger and alienation, popular culture neutralizes it." [16] That Nirvana understood this and placed the problem fully in view, as many groups have since punk first laid bare its own merchandising, is of no moment. Somehow, the criticism of capitalism, in the closed circuit of postmodernism, merely reinforces its operations—unless, as always, intellectuals are performing the criticism.

I think just the opposite is true, for as we have seen ad nauseum, it's intellectuals who are so fatuous as to help perpetuate the beast they complain about by endlessly lamenting its inevitability. Nirvana, in contrast, went so far as to record its subsequent album *In Utero* with hardcore-punk producer Steve Albini, to ensure music that would survive close scrutiny for signs of commercial compromise. If largely a self-serving myth created by Albini, the resulting rumors of conflict with their record company (David Geffen's DGC) were far more public than any academic treatise on the evils of incorporation. It may not have amounted to a hill of beans, in the final analysis, other than selling several million more units. "Smells like corporate spirit," sneered *Newsweek,* which seized on the incident to question Cobain's integrity, citing an unnamed source's claim that far from defiant and angry he "enjoys making millions and millions of dollars." [17] But *at least Nirvana tried,* unlike postmodern cynics.

Cobain's reward for his efforts, from the moment the group reached number one in the record charts until his suicide two years later, was to be hounded by the obsession of both mainstream and alternative music journalists, as well as fans, with the prospect of Nirvana being ruined by the embrace of a corporate record label. The single unrelenting theme of coverage of Nirvana concerned the supposedly tormenting dilemma of retaining one's integrity while selling a large number of records. An excuse for ridicule in the establishment press, in the music press this theme was a source of usually well-intentioned concern, although also a target of hip cynicism. In the final indignity, many commentators on both sides attributed his suicide to the agony of celebrity and commercial success. The postmodern vultures feasted on his corpse in a far more damaging, influential fashion than Andy Rooney's moronic demagoguery on *60 Minutes* about Cobain's torn jeans (in the course of which Rooney admitted he had never heard of Cobain before).

I thought at the time, in April 1994, and right up until I wrote this section of the book almost a year later, that attributing Cobain's suicide to commercial success was ridiculous—he had suffered from a debilitating, clinical case of depression long before he had a hit record. But after reviewing two years of journalism on Nirvana, I am sorely tempted to conclude that everyone harping on the possibility of Cobain being tamed by commercial absorption (or incorporation) did have something to do with his suicide. I even considered subtitling this whole book "Kurt Cobain Died for Your Sins." If it were indeed true, as an obituary in *Time* observed, that Nirvana's success tortured him,[18] it's no wonder why: Friend and foe alike hectored Cobain about his success from the moment Nirvana hit number one.

Given the plethora of commercial periodicals and fanzines devoted to alternative music, it would be sheer speculation on my part to claim that the postmodern view of Nirvana was generally endorsed. I did, however, find an essentially similar postmodern posture in two very different publications, *Spin* and *Maximum Rock 'n' Roll*, the former the literally and figuratively slick magazine that dominates coverage of commercial alternative music, the latter the leading voice of a subcultural network committed to hardcore punk. Little if any reference to Nirvana is found in *Maximum Rock 'n' Roll*; out of strident, romantic anticapitalism (or a near absolute division of art and the marketplace), it only covers music on labels truly independent of the corporate embrace. Shortly after Cobain committed suicide, in fact, *Maximum Rock 'n' Roll* put a picture of a young man holding a gun in his mouth on the cover of a special issue devoted to the exploitation of punk by major labels—but only one writer even grudgingly uses, as he puts it, the " 'N' word." [19] (The same issue, not coincidentally I suspect, also contains a favorable review of *The Baffler,* that popularizer of academic postmodernism.) *Spin,* as a result, is more useful in demonstrating the chain reaction fueled by postmodern ideas that greeted Nirvana's extraordinary breakthrough. With the outer limit a refusal even to mention Nirvana, when we see *Spin* worrying over the incorporation of Nirvana it's safe to assume that many more radical fanzines reviled the group—oddly mirroring the *New York Times,* much as the Left and the Right have traditionally wound up on the same side in their loathing of commercial culture. The puritanical anticapitalism of *Maximum Rock 'n' Roll* is genuine enough, whereas the aesthetics of the *Times* only amount to the traditional sham of romantic idealism, but when the two wind up on the same ground, something is obviously amiss.

Two articles on Nirvana that appeared in *Spin* in early 1992, immediately after Nirvana hit number one, obviously have postmodernism on their minds. Their authors, Lauren Spencer (in January) and Nathaniel Wice (in April), both offer the standard description of directionless, dysfunctional anger undergoing commercial incorporation, but their judgments differ considerably. Spencer is more charitable, which may have everything to do with her being a woman. Although she worries that the band "has a tenuous handle on the realities of its rise to prominence," she concludes that "Nirvana is hardly the product of record company-inspired, corporate rock-controlled rebellion." But Spencer's article is certainly typical of the general obsession with this issue, and the response she elicits from Cobain indicates that he was immediately plagued by doubts about his authenticity: "Maybe this could be the disclaimer article," he hopes. "What we're gonna do now is let the kids know that we haven't sold out." On the specific subject of anger, Spencer rejects the notion that the apparent apathy of Cobain's lyrics cancels out the anger in their actual vocal performance: "His lyrics have a sheen of naïveté that just barely contains his anger." [20] In acknowledging Cobain's own views on the essential irrelevance of lyrics, Spencer gives the lie to critics like Jon Pareles. When he eventually got around to doing a number on Nirvana, Pareles conveniently cited Cobain directly only once, on his view that "none of my poems are coherent at all [because they] have no themes," [21] to confirm Pareles's earlier view that lyrical limitations cancel out anger. Cobain's point, however, as in Spencer's article, was to downplay the significance of lyrics and to highlight the importance of emotion.

Nathaniel Wice's article in *Spin,* with the insinuating title "How Nirvana Made It," is a bit of nastiness that could've been written by Pareles. Wice starts from the hardline postmodern stance that "the major labels have taken over and expanded alt[ernative]-rock into a market force." Nirvana's label certainly played some role in breaking the group, but the key words here are the bleak "taken over," which lead to descriptions of Nirvana listeners "wander[ing] zombie-like into record stores." How Nirvana could be so easily taken over is made clear by Wice's all-too-familiar judgment on Cobain's "vaguely incoherent, antisocial lyrics." Their incoherence apparently cancels out even the slightest interest on Wice's part in their emotional performance; he makes no mention of the anger described by virtually every other critic. His conclusion typifies the reception of Nirvana across mainstream and alternative media, in pessimistically prodding Cobain to prove his genuineness: "It remains to be seen what of Nirvana's world will survive as the band gets absorbed into the mainstream." [22]

An article on the Sex Pistols in the same issue, however, indicates how divided the opinions of alternative-rock journalism were on Nirvana. As part of a retrospective based on a poll determining the most important rock bands in history, the article favorably compares the Sex Pistols' "dramatization of real emotions" with Nirvana's "lifting the lid off a raging mass of social and political discontent"—a celebratory view entirely at odds with Wice's. The same divided perspective later appeared within the course of a single obituary for Cobain, by Gina Arnold, which begins by arguing that the vigil for him in Seattle dispelled forever the idea "that Nirvana's core audience did not understand his message." Shortly thereafter, though, she pillories Nirvana for "the band's *inexplicably dutiful* agreement to change the album cover of *In Utero* for acceptance at the Wal-Mart chain" (emphasis added). [23] Cobain had argued quite reasonably that the change was necessary to reach young people in small towns, but even in death he couldn't escape the charge of complicity with the corporate beast.

For the most part, in *Spin* at any rate, a similar obsession with commercial incorporation won out. One article published six months before Cobain's suicide concerns the "fierce toll" and "endless complications" of celebrity and success, actually beginning with a prophetic death wish for Cobain: "Fame has a vaporizing effect." In the same issue, Howard Hampton plays the postmodern side of the street just three years after pillorying Fredric Jameson (see Chapter 2). In a review of *In Utero,* Hampton finds that after "Nirvana suddenly gave punk the face of profit, . . . [f]ame has aged Cobain's plaintive rasp, as if celebrity were some kind of public dungeon that turned his shout into a prisoner's, looking for an echo in solitary confinement." [24] With so many others harping on the same theme, and since every writer knew that Cobain was depressed, sick, unstable, and hence susceptible to suggestion, I could see a case for charging the whole lot with assisted suicide.

*Rolling Stone,* surprisingly, which by all accounts lost touch with alienated young people some time ago, strikes me as much more generous than *Spin* in its coverage of Nirvana. In yet another article in January 1992 on Nirvana's commercial breakthrough—with a predictable headline on "the demons of fame"—Chris Mundy takes a familiar postmodern position: Commercial success "cast[s] overwhelming shadows of doubt over Nirvana's self-image as underground, antimainstream operatives." But he also acknowledges that the members of the group were unhappy with "the media depiction of them as rock brats simply mirroring the nihilism they rail against, rather than concentrating on their sincere effort to focus attention on such problems as sexism and repression." (Simon Reynolds in the *Times* is a perfect example of the reductive treatment Nirvana resented, in his list of terms—*apolitical, incoherent, unspecific*—"for kids who don't know what they want.") Bassist Chris Novoselic is prominently cited on the fundamental antiauthoritarianism of Cobain's emotional performance: "The most anti-authority guy I know is Kurt . . . out there yelling at the top of his lungs. . . . A big factor has been a lot of social and political discontent." Mundy, unfortunately, follows up with a reference to "blind rage," undercutting this "focused frustration." [25] Whatever the article's strong and weak points, however, in the final analysis *Rolling Stone* proved well beyond its readers, who subsequently filled its letters column with anti-Nirvana rant.

In an article in April 1992, Michael Azerrad dwells on Nirvana's "runaway success," noting that friends of the band "worried about how the band was dealing with it all"—a personal pressure on top of that inflicted by journalists.

But Azerrad, the author of *Come as You Are: The Story of Nirvana,* takes a much different approach than the usual abuse of Nirvana for being signed to a major label, letting Cobain define the issues to a considerable extent. (I suspect Azerrad's presence at *Rolling Stone* had a good deal to do with its general moderation.) Azerrad cites Cobain's own insistence that he was not finding fame as difficult "as it seems like it is in interviews and the way that a lot of journalists have portrayed my attitude." Cobain even gently chides fans suspicious of Nirvana's commercial success:

> I don't blame the average seventeen-year-old punk-rock kid for calling me a sellout. . . . I understand that. Maybe when they grow up a little bit, they'll realize there's more things to life than living out your rock & roll identity so righteously.

Being able to reach as many people as possible may be more important and is "pretty much my excuse for not feeling guilty about why I'm on a major label, [rather than] denying everything commercial and sticking in my own little world." (Sticking to one's own little world is the ideal of romantics, modernists, and now postmodernists, I would add.) Cobain's success clearly did not entirely consume him, and so despite the provocations of many journalists, a charge of assisted suicide would give them too much credit. He took his life for personal reasons involving his mental health that I know very little about and would not presume to speculate on.

Azerrad also presents a much more positive assessment of emotion, including the question of whether song lyrics are very important to a music's impact. The difference in his article, once again, is that he allows Cobain to set the agenda, namely that "the message isn't necessarily in the words":

> Most of the music is really personal as far as the emotion, . . . but most of the *themes* in the songs aren't that personal. They're more just stories from TV or books or movies or friends. But definitely the emotion and feeling is from me.

The producer of *Nevermind,* Butch Vig, is also cited on the importance of Cobain's emotional performance:

> He's not necessarily a spokesman for a generation, but all that's in the music— the passion and [the fact that] he doesn't necessarily know what he wants but he's pissed. . . . I don't exactly know what "Teen Spirit" means, but you know it means *something* and it's intense as hell.[26]

Azerrad's generosity on the subjects of anger and incorporation contrasts not only with other journalists but especially with the work of academic postmodernists who never permit performers to speak for fear of being contradicted.

That same generosity marks a lengthy special issue of *Rolling Stone* on Cobain after his suicide. Of particular note is scholar Donna Gaines's testimonial to the "Fucked Generation" produced by the "unsurpassed social violence and humiliation" of the 1980s. Thanks to the "gruesome landscape" of "AIDS, global warming, unemployment, and homelessness," young people have come to "acknowledge alienation, deep loss, and rage as normative conditions of living." These emotional conditions, in other words, are far from apathetic, inarticulate, or incoherent. The young may experience "an existential terror too horrific to put into words," but that is precisely what Cobain captured so profoundly in the way his "anger and moral outrage" transcended the words in his songs. Through music like punk and a variety of other activities, the Fucked Generation manages to take on "the brutality agenda—exposing the lies, fighting the bullshit"—a fight that Gaines sums up as the best kind of anarchism. Her conclusion on Cobain's suicide is harsh for an accurate, humane reason—his abandonment of his audience: He betrayed "an unspoken contract among members of a generation who depended on one another to reverse the parental generation's legacy of neglect, confusion, and frustration." [27]

The sort of aging baby-boomer horror at Nirvana that one might expect from *Rolling Stone* but doesn't find did appear in very revealing fashion in the New Age sampler *Utne Reader.* As Andrew Ross indicates in *Strange Weather* (1991), New Agers are exemplary postmoderns in opposing orthodox rationalism. They don't like the Enlightenment legacy either, that is, specifically institutional science, countered with mysticism and psychotechnologies including everything from tarot cards to holistic medicine. Thus we find in *Utne Reader* a reversal of other postmoderns' pessimism in which the supposed irrationality (or incoherence, at least) of Nirvana's anger is condoned. The writer, Dick Dahl, asks how one explains "the phenomenon of Nirvana, a Seattle trio several light years removed from mainstream radio that shot past the heavily marketed and neatly merchandised likes of Michael Jackson and Mariah Carey, [achieving] the seemingly impossible?" I should think the question answers itself, as is the case when John Leland also poses the same opposition as some sort of mystery: The preference for Nirvana's outrage has everything to do with rejection of the corporate machinations that produce fodder like Carey and Jackson.

Dahl does not accord the anger of postmodern youths this much intelligence, however. Even if he approves of the irrationality he finds, in time-honored

rock-critic celebration—"maybe it's just great rock 'n' roll and we don't need
to make anything more of it than that"—his findings are hard to differentiate
from the condescension of academic postmodernists. Nirvana's music, he tells
us, emerges from the "dark intellectual valley [of] mindless adolescence" and
thus is "loud and wild and it doesn't 'mean' much of anything." [28] Placing the
word *mean* in quote marks is clearly intended to highlight the split of affect and
meaning, as a postmodern theorist such as Lawrence Grossberg would put it,
that results from the supposed mindlessness of youthful anger.

The main reason why I've cited *Utne Reader,* however, is that it followed
up its first report on Nirvana with the most extreme of the postmodern obituaries
on Cobain, a despairing piece by Sarah Ferguson that has been circulating among
students at my school as some sort of authoritative statement. (As if to comple-
ment her cynicism, the next issue of *Utne Reader* promoted the camp escapism
of Lounge music and the Cocktail Nation subculture.) Obituaries in establishment media, in contrast, actually moderated their usual ridicule; the *New
York Times* allowed a younger writer to assert that Cobain's "railing screams . . .
were as big a part of the emotion he conveyed as his words were"—even though
ultimately the emotion is described, as usual, as "rootless anger and dysfunction." *Time* offered the same postmodern final word on Cobain's inarticulate
rage, an anger and passion that supposedly always remained inchoate.[29]

Ferguson goes much further, though, in pouring the tragedy of Cobain's
personal problems into the classic postmodern mold. The results illustrate very
well the close relation between the incorporation thesis and the closed circuit of
power popularized by French postmodernism:

> What Cobain's suicide in April and the whole trajectory of his band's success
> prove is the inability of youth to own their own rebellion. The loop taken by a
> new musical style from the underground to the mainstream is now so compressed
> that there's no moment of freedom and chaos when a counterculture can take root.

A number of obituaries similarly argued that Cobain blew his head off because
he was signed to a major rather than an independent record label. In anticipation of this lame rationale, I have objected throughout this book to the residual
romanticism of drawing such an arbitrary divide between different scales of
capitalism.

Ferguson's inclusion of virtually every tenet of postmodern theory is
unusual though. Of particular note is a classic exaggeration of the evils of
consumer society: "The fact that this generation bought *The Brady Bunch* myth
in the first place is testament to the totalitarian nature of commodity culture."

Under the supposedly totalitarian rule of consumerism, "dreams and desires [are] manufactured and controlled [from] an early age." Dire claims like these are such a reflex in postmodern writing, however, that Ferguson has no business indicting grunge fans for thoughtlessness. To find that they "lack a clear sense of authentic experience," moreover, thanks to the impossibility of a "counter-culture" that would provide real "freedom" [30] once again introduces the hoary wish for some impossible authenticity (or autonomy) entirely removed from capitalism, as seen earlier in Fredric Jameson and David Shumway. Ferguson's rhetoric about totalitarianism and mass culture, in fact, is similarly indebted to Theodor Adorno in particular.

One reason for Ferguson's gloom, I should note, is her work on homeless street punks in Seattle and their alienation and despair. But the majority of the ten million people who bought Nirvana's *Nevermind* are hardly destitute and living on the streets. An undergraduate student of mine who lived in the "gutterpunk" subculture in Austin, Texas, furthermore, recently wrote a thesis in which she reported that the homeless young people involved had for the most part made deliberate choices in their circumstances, and had an articulate sense of politics, music, and stylistic symbolism. Ferguson's subjects, in other words, hardly prove some universal postmodern condition.

To employ every postmodern critic's favorite evidence, however—absurdities drawn from television like the resurgence of *The Brady Bunch* (as well as shows Kurt Cobain watched, *Leave It to Beaver* and *Mayberry R.F.D.*)—is less forgivable. The objections are clear enough in this case; for one thing, many people watch the reruns, stage productions, and film of *The Brady Bunch* to laugh at the inanity of television then and now. Unfortunately, to some it also signifies how inane the 1970s (and leisure suits, etc.) supposedly were, which is one reason why I keep harping on the fact that the Sex Pistols happened in the 1970s (as Greil Marcus also objected in a recent interview[31]).

I dwell on Ferguson's contrived mention of television, though, because it reproduces the postmodern thesis on the split between emotion and meaning. Young people, she claims, watch shows like the ones above out of a feeling of "mournful nostalgia," refusing to reach for "larger truths." A disjunction between emotion and meaning also characterizes Nirvana's music, which in her view is only "powerless rage, . . . rooted in the feeling of damage." She cites Cobain's song "Dumb," in particular, in which he assumes a persona who ponders whether he is dumb or just happy and concludes he's just happy. Ferguson conveniently takes the song literally, ignoring its actual parody of views precisely like her own with regard to young people. (Cobain in fact told an interviewer that "when I say 'I' in a song, it's not me 90 percent of the time.")

According to her, "Dumb" is about "the terribleness of not knowing the difference" between mindlessness and happiness. Grunge music in general, presumably, is "muddled" by the same intellectual dysfunction: "Kids don't know who to blame," whereas the original punk of the Sex Pistols "knew who the enemy was." Ferguson does admit that grunge "sees the lie of consumer culture," but insists nonetheless, quite self-contradictorily, that it "still yearns for . . . manufactured suburban bliss" like that in *The Brady Bunch.*[32] I would've said, once again, that a song like "Dumb" and a music like grunge are instead a clear, complete repudiation of corporate America's feel-good, "Don't Worry, Be Happy" culture and its efforts to make everyone stupid. I don't think, therefore, that in the final analysis it was very difficult at all for Kurt Cobain to resist incorporation by that culture.

In an article coupled with Ferguson's in *Utne Reader,* Michael Ventura is quite certain about the origins of the darkness that swallowed up Cobain. An excerpt from his book on the "endarkment" of life, an egregious New Age treatise, reinforces Ferguson's (and Dahl's) portrait of mindless youth by rejecting any historical and social context as an explanation for adolescent rage. Young people, says Ventura, are "obviously not in control of their refusal; they *have* to refuse us, no one knows why" (sic). The reasoning behind his absurd claim that "no one knows why" young people rebel against their elders reflects the essential conservatism of New Agers. I want to dwell on their clearly reactionary tendencies to suggest a similar dark streak in postmodernism.

Ventura's denial of any social explanation for youthful anger is entailed by a denial of history itself. (In postmodern theory, these denials usually take the form of the "end of history" line.) He claims that the "psychic structure" of the young "has remained constant for 100,000 years." Never mind actual historical work like Patricia Meyer Spacks's *The Adolescent Idea,* which demonstrates that the very concept of adolescence has only been around for about a century, and can be attributed to quite material forces like the consumer society and the field of psychology, which registered the effect, for example, of compulsory education postponing adult responsibility. According to Ventura, in contrast, the "same raw, ancient content" has surged through youths' psyches throughout human history; the young have always been equally "extreme" in their rage, never understanding it because of its purely instinctual nature.

The basis for this antihistorical notion is the work of appalling men's movement types like Robert Bly (author of *Iron John*). They lead Ventura and others to conclude that the young need the "excruciating rituals" with which "for tens of thousands of years tribal people everywhere have greeted the onset of puberty, especially in males" by teaching some vague, mystical "dark knowledge." [33] On the face of it, considering the source, this is male backlash, desirous of men becoming "real" men again. Treating anger as an involuntary condition ("rage") requiring a radical remedy is very much in keeping with traditional fear of emotion as feminine and irrational. But in essence this masculinist scheme is fascist, appealing to the pure, mythical past of a tight social order based on ritual ceremonies. The fact that some postmoderns also excise social and historical awareness, as in abstractions about power derived from Foucault, indicates their own "endarkment," or dark side. (The specific form of that darkness, we have seen, derives from Nietzsche.) And, finally, since Ventura's terms seem very close to a branch of modern psychology that obliterated historical differences—C. G. Jung's work on the universal archetypes in the collective unconscious—once again the postmodern looks suspiciously like warmed-over modernism.

To return gratefully to a male feminist, Kurt Cobain, I want to note one honorable exception to the condescending obituaries for him in the mainstream press, a piece by Robert Hilburn of the *Los Angeles Times*. Hilburn directly addresses the seeming paradox that "even the parents who grew up on rock 'n' roll find it difficult to relate to today's angry young bands." He sensibly attributes this development to the advancing history of rock and roll, and the inevitable fact that new generations are going to make music their parents will hate, just as the parents once did. More significant, though, is that Hilburn provides a number of good reasons for anger without dismissing them, unlike most academic and journalistic postmodernists: "broken homes, unsympathetic schools, generally hostile environments, and bleak job prospects." He even goes so far as to include ample evidence of the thoughtfulness of musicians, like Chris Cornell of Soundgarden and Eddie Vedder of Pearl Jam, on the lost "pillar" of stable families, as Cornell puts it. Their articulate comments, like Kurt Cobain's, indicate why academic postmodernism never allows them to speak and often doesn't even mention their existence—all the cherished postmodern theses would collapse.

Hilburn's conclusion on the continuing vitality of rock music also strikingly flouts postmodern common wisdom: "The over-30 crowd that closes its ears to this new generation's best music" misses a chance to gain perfectly meaningful "insights into the disillusionment" of contemporary youths. As opposed to postmoderns dating the death of rock with the end of the first punk era, he draws a continuous line between the Sex Pistols, groups in the 1980s like Black Flag, Hüsker Dü, and the Minutemen, and ultimately the mainstream breakthrough of punk with Nirvana. According even to better critics like Simon Frith, such breakthroughs—Elvis, the Beatles, punk—were no longer possible by the

1980s. Hilburn, in contrast, chides those who are missing "what is proving to be one of rock's golden ages: a repeat of the energy and relevance of the late 1950s, mid-1960s, and late 1970s/early 1980s." [34]

The bulk of post-Nirvana journalism, however, has been in keeping with the importation of academic postmodernism. The thesis on the split of emotion and meaning quickly became a bludgeon to use not only on latter-day male punks and grunge-rockers, but especially on the female punk of the Riot Grrrl groups. In 1993, *Rolling Stone*'s Chuck Eddy declared Bikini Kill's first record (including the song "Carnival") an unmusical collection of "yowling and moronic nag-unto-vomit tantrums." Although I have a feeling *tantrums* is a word angry women call to Eddy's mind, he professes not to have anything against anger, complaining that the group "cages its rage in silly editorial doggerel . . . instead of letting the rage work on its own." [35] But this dichotomy drawn between emotion and ideology is perfectly in keeping with the postmodern view that the two have split. The application of that thesis to the Riot Grrrls, moreover, offers a striking example of its continuity with modern aesthetics and the feminine terms traditionally used to dismiss art appealing to feeling rather than the intellect or reason. Theodor Adorno, for example, couldn't mention jazz without invoking castration and eunuchs—to be pacified by mass culture, that is, is to be emasculated, or feminized. The field of aesthetics was pretty vulgar well before postmodernism, in fact, in endorsing the commonplace notion that women are emotional and irrational.

Simon Reynolds, writing on the Riot Grrrls in the *New York Times* in 1992, once again exemplifies the postmodern contempt for emotion, if he does so in enforcing his personal bias against directly angry, political music deriving from punk. In apparent gestures of fairness, he cites Courtney Love of Hole (his main subject, who was about to marry Kurt Cobain) and feminist Susan Faludi on the way gender construction makes anger inappropriate for women, as in condemnation of angry women for being "shrill or hysterical," as Love puts it. (John Leland, for example, wrote in *Newsweek* that Love doesn't sing but "screeches, really.") Reynolds then proceeds to reproduce that sexist condescension. The slippage sets in when he observes that "female anger tends to be implosive" because women are taught to contain their anger. He still seems to be acknowledging realities faced by women but, in fact, has shifted the ground to the internalized, unhealthy condition that Nietzsche called *ressentiment*. It's bad enough that angry music by men and women alike is then described in terms of "perpetual adolescence, . . . avoiding responsibility" (qualities Reynolds esteems in music other than punk, of course). But his conclusion is simply straightforward sexism: "Groups like Babes in Toyland, Hole and the Nymphs take male adolescent tantrums back even further in time—to *kindergarten*" (emphasis added).

This contempt, first of all, makes it hard to argue with the feminist observation that our culture seeks to infantilize women. But the explicit reason for Reynolds's startling condescension is apparent in his description of Love's musical approach as "emotional nudism"—the same postmodern thesis, on anger denuded of reason, he had already used on Love's husband Cobain. One snide comment on the Riot Grrrls is strikingly similar to Reynolds's Nirvana article and to the whole spurious argument that incomprehensible lyrics are a sign of deficiency: Fans "can't always understand the words, but are comforted by the angry quality of [the singer's] voice." They are not discomforted, in other words, as they would be by genuinely avant-garde art. In a subsequent article in *Spin,* he "empathizes" instead with "ethereal girls," or groups like the Cranberries, Cranes, and Lush whose "dreamy swirl pop"—much like the vague emotion he prefers in *Blissed Out*—represents the direct opposite of the "traumatized lyrics and violently cathartic vocals" of Riot Grrrl groups. How ethereality escapes being just as contemptibly "comforting" as the Riot Grrrls, if not more so, is left unexplained.[36] Reynolds's repeated ridicule of angry women out of control is the real problem, though: In reproducing such a traditional form of sexism, his career-long pose of cutting-edge postmodernism collapses.

Thus his and Joy Press's postmodern paean to the liquifying bliss of the mother's womb, *The Sex Revolts,* arrived stillborn. Reiterating Reynolds's earlier praise of ethereality, both in women and in male performers of psychedelia, the book compares such music to the *écriture féminine* of French postmodern feminists, which a number of critics have linked to modernism and its loathing of both mass culture and political engagement (as Chapter 5 explains). To link *écriture féminine* with a mass-culture form like rock music makes little sense, therefore, except to license Press and Reynolds's dismissal of the whole idea of musical "revolt." Their postmodern postpolitics, especially in light of Reynolds's earlier distaste for direct feminine anger, makes the title *Sex Revolts* a deliberate misnomer. The very idea of rock music expressing rebellion has been irreparably contaminated by the past misogyny of male rockers, according to the authors, and can never be rehabilitated by women; a single short article dismisses the Riot Grrrls for playing punk music. The intellectual sources cited most frequently in the book, moreover—Robert Bly, Joseph Campbell, and Camille Paglia, who underwrite a preoccupation with ahistorical, Jungian myth symbols—indicate that Reynolds might best be compared, finally, with another pretentious journalist, New Ager Michael Ventura.

Hip-hop music, in contrast with the Riot Grrrls, has not been indicted with anything like the same condescension. For one thing, Reynolds's infantilizing terms regarding female punk rockers are only acceptable when applied to women, and would be considered racist if applied to hip-hop as well—although recent theorists of welfare dependency come close to invoking old descriptions of black people as children. More generally, everyone acknowledges that much of hip-hop is angry over undeniable racial injustice; as opposed to the easy contempt for white youths and women, virtually no critic has the gall to say there is no reason whatsoever for black anger. As Tricia Rose says, the response instead is fear—"a fear of the consolidation of black rage [in] music, lyrics, and attitude [that] illuminate and affirm black fears and grievances." In music criticism, observes Tim Brennan, that fear takes the more specific form of "an allegorically coded public debate over art and artlessness," in which "unguarded racism enters only through an aesthetic portal." With hip-hop generally synonymous with " 'black youth' in a declining economy," that is, the frequent attacks on hip-hop's supposed lack of musicality betray a deeper racial fear and hostility.[37]

One widespread approach along these lines is to soft-pedal the demonization of black anger by lumping hip-hop together with grunge and industrial, as Stephen Holden does in "How Pop Lost the Melody" (1994), an article prominently featured on the front page of the Arts & Leisure section of the Sunday *New York Times*. In this collective treatment of presumably degraded, cacophonous music, grunge and industrial—or Nirvana and Nine Inch Nails, respectively—replace heavy metal as the balance used to deflect accusations of racism for attacking hip-hop. (Recall the metal/hip-hop combination in *Newsweek*'s "The Rap Attitude.") When Holden indicts music that "surrender[s] melody to beats," it's clear his primary target is hip-hop, which is often criticized on this basis.

On the whole, though, Holden's nostalgic complaint that popular music isn't as good as it used to be simply seems to indicate the conservatism of aging rock critics, which one would expect the *Times* to promote. All the postmodern theses are in place, however, particularly the execration of supposedly mindless anger. Considering the postmodern components of the essay, it seems odd that Holden praises Bruce Springsteen for speaking genuinely of "transcending personal hardship through faith, courage, and hard work"—in essence Ronald Reagan's version of Springsteen in 1984, which led academics and journalists such as Lawrence Grossberg, Simon Frith, and Richard Meltzer to consider Springsteen a classic example of inauthenticity. Holden is otherwise a perfect postmodern, especially in replaying modernist elitism: Nihilism, he says, is "threatening to become the new pop kitsch," or just another commodity—an echo of Clement Greenberg.

We also find, once again, a close relation between the incorporation thesis and berating emotion. Holden attributes the rage of Snoop Doggy Dogg, Nine Inch Nails, and grunge rockers in part to "the unresolvable moral dilemma" that their alienation, defiance, and rebellion will presumably only be "absorbed by television [and] used to sell burgers and blue jeans." The resulting malaise affects "the very form and fabric" of music like hip-hop and industrial—or their emotional tone, in other words. His primary concern is their anger, which he acknowledges is partly a response to other music emphasizing softness and sweetness, like Michael Bolton's and Mariah Carey's. (In citing Bolton and Carey, Holden seems to have read John Leland's 1991 piece in *Newsweek,* and lumping together all expressions of anger certainly resembles Leland as well as Jon Pareles.) But rather than endorse angry music, Holden laments it as "sour misanthropy." Thus he hardly approves of the contemporary sense that "pleasure, if not accompanied by anger and rage, is suspect." As we might expect, Holden instead finds a diminishment in reason and intellect: Contemporary music "trusts the body more than the mind." [38] This makes no sense—when was rock music about the mind, except in the bad days of classical rock in the early 1970s, before punk?—unless one realizes that Holden is reproducing postmodern theory on the split between affect and meaning thanks to the commercial incorporation of anger and outrage.

The ungodly repetition of this postmodern thesis over the past few years suggests that journalists condemn and ridicule anger at authority in popular music because they and their corporate masters are afraid of it. Publications and politicians (like Bob Dole) owned by mass-media conglomerates criticize music often produced by those very same corporations: *Newsweek,* for example, finds it lamentable in "The Rap Attitude" that "major companies are behind" groups like Public Enemy. That doesn't mean the criticism is a charade, however, or just part of the closed circuit of postmodernism. Given the inherent chaos of competition, capitalists are continually forced to bring each other into line when one of their members threatens to arouse the public, whether the abuses involve corruption of government, threats to public health, destruction of trust in markets, or indiscriminately purveying entertainment. The laughable result is that conservatives continually lament irresponsibility in producing mass culture, although the lack of restraint results precisely from the practice of their beloved profit-motive by their friends. They're right to worry, though: As the Situationist International always argued, marketing anger and other forms of dissent is a combustible business; the best stuff gets taken seriously by some portion of the audience, at the same time that fraudulent performances stoke still more ridicule and resentment.

After the preceding two chapters, finally, I don't think there can be much doubt that Marxist theorists, of all people, have provided journalists the means to condemn and ridicule angry music. Out of disappointment at the absence of progressive politics, and especially at the supposed pacification of the populace by mass culture, the intellectual Left winds up, as it traditionally has, on the elitist ground of the establishment. Contrary to the rhetoric of postmodernism, however, there is nothing new in either journalism, which has always performed reactionary service for its masters, or the highest reaches of radical philosophy and theory: Both have long diagnosed resentment of injustice as a disease. Contemporary culture may actually work in large part the way postmodern theorists believe it does: to encourage a taste for strong emotions unburdened by reflection or commitment. But this is just another variation in the long history of efforts by mainstream culture to convince people that anger and resentment are inappropriate—or in this case, frivolous—and such efforts have been under-written by scholarly ideas ranging from social Darwinism to postmodernism. The condemnation of resentment is continually necessary because the anger of disenfranchised groups, including disaffected youths, always presents a threat to the status quo.

# PART 2

# CHAPTER 5

# Emotional Rescue
## *Feminist Philosophy on Anger*

Looking at feminist thought that contradicts male postmodern theorists, it seems the men's effort to persuade us to jump out the window with them is intended to spare themselves a richly deserved public humiliation. The postmodern thesis that emotion has become disconnected from ideology (or reason) is entirely undermined if feminist philosophy is right in arguing that emotions are rational judgments formed out of social interaction (and thus educable in both good and bad directions), that physical sensations are just as important as verbal articulation in those judgments, and that anger is the "essential political emotion." [1]

In the theories of modernists such as William James and Sigmund Freud, hardly abandoned even now, emotion is a matter of physiological and/or unconscious reflexes within the individual—universal or identical among everyone, but at the same time internal or personal. In the worst cases, emotion was held to be a common trait of humans and animals, an instinctive choice between fight or flight, anger or fear, that was in no way educated by experience. Nietzsche and Scheler at least allowed that the emotion of *ressentiment* involved judgments on social relations, although they assigned it an essentially feminine passivity, the common view of emotion in general. Postmodern theorists continue to reproduce the old body/mind split, obviously, in their detachment of affect from ideology, or emotion from reason. Postmodern work that does take the body seriously has its liabilities, too—often a similar fatalism—and an adequate grasp of emotion, I will argue, provides a more adequate critical position.

Emotion, properly understood, is the whole works involved in evaluating a situation: our cognitive appraisal of it, our physical feelings about it, and our subsequent choices in expressing our approval or disapproval and acting on it. Knowledge is always accompanied by feeling, and vice-versa; we don't know anything about an event without feeling something about it and don't feel anything about an event without knowing something about it. I should add once again that anger may regrettably find its express meaning in authoritarianism, bigotry, and violence or may actually be directed into commercial fodder for consumers. But to misidentify the cause of one's anger, in the intentional process of choosing an object on or through which to express it, is hardly the same as a complete detachment of emotion from cognition and meaning.

With a proper understanding of emotion in judging popular music, the tacile and verbal elements of a performance would no longer seem so distinct. The divide we have seen drawn between visceral anger in music and its presumably feeble lyrical expression simply doesn't hold up if that anger in and of itself is already a significant *cognitive* discovery—even just of the possibility of being angry, a critical matter particularly for young women. If emotion is never without meaning, it is simply impossible for affect to have no depth or for affect and meaning to split apart, as theorists of postmodernism such as Fredric Jameson and Lawrence Grossberg claim about punk rock and other expressions of anger. The confidence of such sweeping pronouncements, untroubled by their complete ignorance of the substantial body of work on emotion, reflects the roots of postmodern theory in romantic and modernist contempt for mass and popular cultural forms. In the name of a new epoch, we get assertions backed up only by their implicit appeal to tradition.

I stressed the larger historical context in Part 1 as a check on postmodern claims that treat both themselves and the contemporary social situation as profoundly distressing, unprecedented, even apocalyptic. My next chapter also returns briefly to the modern period, but to figures like Mikhail Bakhtin and Walter Benjamin, whose distaste for romantic idealism led to theories of language with an unusual, progressive emphasis on emotion. For the most part, the historical coverage in Part 2 is much less broad—but also much more positive. For very encouraging reasons, feminist scholarship defending emotion has had a chronology quite similar to that of music by angry young women. Feminist interest in anger and the politics of emotion has emerged over the past decade or so, from Julia LeSage's "Women's Rage" (1983) to a boom in 1988-1989 led by Morwenna Griffiths, Alison Jaggar, and Elizabeth Spelman in work usefully summed up in 1991 by Miranda Fricker. Some men have contributed, too, from Peter Lyman's essay "The Politics of Anger" (1980) to Peter Middleton's *The Inward Gaze* (1992). The dates in their case, as with the female scholars, essentially coincide with the hiatus in punk rock, from its purported demise in the early 1980s to its resurrection around 1991.

It turns out that underneath the Reagan-Bush years, which seemed like the meanest, lowest decade in my experience (maybe because I was in graduate school for half of it)—a meanness currently persisting under different management—feminism was preparing an antidote while punk persisted despite its obituaries and proved to hold new expressive possibilities, especially in the hands of young women. In light of the obvious constriction of economic opportunity for the young, it should come as no surprise that after being buried under the authoritarianism of the 1980s and its feel-good onslaught on deviance, the expression of anger as a form of refusal and resistance has sprouted up all over the cultural map, accompanied by a spate of denunciations in establishment media. The compatibility of academic feminism and punk rock, in efforts to fuel a resurgence of anger at injustice, is evident in the Riot Grrrl groups. Because a number of the Riot Grrrls are college graduates, I think it's fair to say they represent a literal fusion of feminism and punk, both of which they know quite well.

I emphasize the common ground of academic work on emotion and the Riot Grrrl groups because my main concern in Part 2 is the lessons they provide, in tandem, for a more sensible evaluation of popular music than that found in either academia or journalism. Such an approach would be reasonably authentic to its subject—not overintellectualized, that is, and especially not insensate to the emotional impact of music. Understanding emotion would allow us to mediate between what have seemed the irreconcilable experiences of the body and the mind, in moving from listening to music to writing criticism about it. The legacy of romantic and modern preference for the intellect is nowhere more explicit in the postmodern era, we will see, than in recent literary criticism that focuses entirely on the "poetry" of rock music, or its lyrical content.

That a recognition of the intelligence of emotions is needed in popular music criticism as well as in academic work reflects the fact that everyday common sense and the common wisdom of many intellectuals are quite similar. The layperson's beliefs about the abnormalities of women, in fact, have played a considerable part in shaping the sexism of many academic studies of emotion: "Over the years in biology, psychology, sociology, sociolinguistics, and other fields," anthropologist Catherine Lutz points out, much research "has been implicitly based on everyday cultural models linking women and emotionality." Both academic and everyday common sense consider emotion a purely physical "disturbance of the rational order of being" to which women are particularly susceptible. That disturbance presumably "flood[s] away reason with tears or blind[s] it with rage." Everyday common sense does also "value emotion as a sign of authenticity," notes Peter Middleton, but strong feelings, given their association with the body and with women, are not always assumed to be connected to the cognitive component of emotion. Feminist psychologists report, however, that it "is not usually difficult to persuade people" to recognize the cognitive component: "The notion of appraisal of the situation before or concurrently with the experience of the emotion accords with everyday experience," whatever "the irrational or passionate character of the experience or action that may follow." [2]

That would seem to make laypersons much more flexible than the sciences, which still largely replicate everyday common sense about the location of emotion in the body. I dwell on this point to refute the view that emotion is largely a physical matter, but I believe there is something more at stake as well. The physical sciences, in particular, have failed altogether to explain emotion, which gives the lie to the faith in science so often urged on laypersons by a high-tech society—the belief, that is, that if science has taken up a subject it must have successfully penetrated it. The futility of biological explanations for emotion, therefore, supports a crucial argument in feminist philosophy for the importance of emotion to political freedom: the physical feelings in emotion remain free to some extent from explanatory systems (or discourses or ideologies), whether scientific or political ones. Emotion is simply much less accessible than either conscious or unconscious thought-processes are, especially to discourse about emotion, whether that discourse consists of "objective" analysis or disapproval.

Neurobiology, for example, has searched fruitlessly for the originating point of emotion in the brain: "Nothing—let me repeat, nothing—can be definitively said at this point about the chemistry of emotion," one medical expert has concluded.[3] The backwardness of neuroscience is evident in the reception of Antonio Damasio's *Descartes' Error,* published in 1994, which was hailed as a breakthrough for its discovery that "feeling [is] an integral component of the machinery of reason" exercised in evaluating situations—even though cognitive philosophy and social psychology have been making the point for more than three decades. (An article in *New Scientist* in the same year also breaks, finally, with Descartes's priority on the mind in writing "I think, therefore I am.") Evidence that neurobiology has no good explanation for emotion, as Damasio acknowledges, is the broad, imprecise net that he casts beyond the limbic system, the focus of previous research. Emotion, he tells us, results from "activity in a number of specific brain systems interacting with a number of body organs," an observation any layperson could make. The same sort of imprecision occurs in the views of clinical medicine, physiology, and psychiatry on the specific emotion of anger, traditionally viewed "as a rather uninteresting derivative of aggression and hostility," as Willard Gaylin puts it—or some reptilian part of our brain.[4]

The worst abuses committed by the sciences, however, have occurred in forms of psychotherapy that seek to control and suppress emotions like anger, in keeping with the view of emotion as a physical force overwhelming reason. A supposedly therapeutic ventilation of anger in "heavy doses" of catharsis may first be necessary, says Middleton, but the object is simply to make emotion "visible to the inward gaze of reason" and thereby "free up the mind's reasoning processes." As I wrote this book, for example, a book came out with the title *Anger Kills: Seventeen Strategies for Controlling the Hostility That Can Harm Your Health*—"As Seen on 'Oprah,' " according to an advertisement.

Psychotherapists, however, at least understand that bodily affect "is not just a signal of the presence of [an] emotion," as cognitive philosophy and social psychology tend to assume in concentrating on the rational component of emotion. The physical experience of emotion is not secondary or superfluous, Middleton points out, but a necessary "form of discharge, the means by which the emotion's power to disturb intellectual functions is reduced." [5] We do need this discharge, in other words, or the intellect would be unable to begin the work necessary to discern what caused the emotion. The problem with psychotherapy that stresses catharsis is its notion that feelings require discharge not to seek their social causes but because they're unhealthy symptoms of individual dysfunction that reason must regain control over, to have done with them.

The treatment of anger as a disease (shades of Nietzsche) led one honorable psychotherapist, Carol Tavris, to write *Anger: The Misunderstood Emotion* (1982). In a précis of subsequent feminist philosophy, she argues that anger "is essential to the first phase of a social movement. It unifies disparate members of a group"—let's say fans of hip-hop and rock music—"against a common enemy; the group becomes defined by its anger." Out of "private, unarticulated experience [arises] a feeling of power. [Anger] creates the hope of change," [6] precisely the hope that Nietzsche and his postmodern epigones would like to squelch through ridicule. Understanding why one is angry is the critical matter, in other words, as opposed to the cathartic ventilation and purging of anger.

Like physical science, but with some notable exceptions, the humanities and social sciences have suffered for their failure to transcend the traditional treatment of emotion as a physical disturbance in need of control. Sociology, for example, as a result of its "interactionist" (or "functionalist") interest in how people modify their behavior to suit others, seems much like psychotherapy in emphasizing the "self-regulation" exercised in "learned controls of emotion" necessary for the sake of normalcy.[7] Arlie Hochschild does manage to make a virtue of this approach in *The Managed Heart* (1983), however, in which she studies the emotional burden placed on women in domestic and professional work, especially expectations that they be managers of emotion in the family but display and exploit their own supposed emotionality at work.

Another sociological treatise, Norman Denzin's *On Understanding Emotion* (1984), has a fairly good historical overview of some of the major philosophical and psychological theories of emotion, and he does take the social constructionist position that emotion involves the active appraisal of a situation. But in the final analysis, Denzin casts his lot with Jean-Paul Sartre's *Sketch for a Theory of the Emotions,* which actually denies the significance of emotion in quite conventional ways. Sartre treats emotion as a magical retreat by those blocked from real political action, especially women, with bodily disturbance a primary symptom of this frustration. If this sounds like *ressentiment,* that is indeed the subject with which Denzin wraps up his own book, and he buys into it wholesale. Given his interactionist approach, the subject of emotion inevitably involves the problem of keeping it under control, no matter how much credit he gives it for intelligence.

Historians of emotion have come to grief in similar fashion, as Peter Stearns's otherwise excellent *American Cool* illustrates. Immersed in detailing the increasing instruction in emotional restraint after the 1920s, he can only perceive even "hot" or "intense music" as a sort of safety valve used to discharge emotion rather than confront it, a release serving "to relieve emotional pressures imposed by the new norms" barring strong emotion such as anger. To reduce rock and roll to "intense beat" and "increasing physical volume," though, "with no explicit emotional strings," seems more a matter of personal taste. Even overt "hostility" in music is held to be only a substitute or "surrogate" for anger, feeding a cathartic, "emotion-draining crowd activity" that supposedly leaves "a thrill without emotional involvement." Thus the music offers "no real contradiction" of the dominant culture's "hostility to emotional intensity." But angry music might just as easily be understood to articulate and extend its listeners' emotional lives, which may not be all that restrained either. A brief note in Stearns's conclusion does acknowledge this possibility: With the expression of anger in the United States becoming freer "by the late 1980s, . . . impressions of new outpourings of anger deserve serious assessment." [8]

Postmodern Foucauldian theorists have also weighed in on emotion, and it will come as no surprise at this point to learn that the subject is left fairly hopeless. One such Foucauldian scholar, Catherine Lutz, does provide a valuable overview of a good deal of work on emotion in *Language and the Politics of Emotion* (1990), coedited with Lila Abu-Lughod. Anthropological work like theirs has been helpful in pointing out the variations across classes, cultures, and the sexes in the expression of emotions like anger. Emotion is hardly an instinctive biological function, or a universal, unlearned, internal entity of little interest or use to social analysis.

But, as always with Foucauldian scholars, there seems to be considerably more faith in power and its discourses than in people. Abu-Lughod and Lutz claim at the outset that their primary concern is "how discourses [about] emotion and emotional discourses can serve . . . for the relatively powerless as loci of resistance and idioms of rebellion." Popular discourse about emotions, however, Lutz later tells us, is handicapped by the belief that emotion is "located within individuals" and thus that feelings are a marker of authenticity and uniqueness, providing "access to some kind of inner truth about the self." This is fair enough as a specific historical point, but there is also a more general implication that our orientation to emotion is part of the ruse through which power encourages us to believe ourselves unique individuals, when we are only its subjects. Lutz cites Foucault to this effect: Discourses " 'systematically form the objects of which they speak,' " or us and our emotions.

Biomedical discourses about the need for control of emotion, in particular, by implying that emotion "would otherwise be out of control, something wild and unruly, a threat to order," are held to be responsible for the misguided belief that emotions have some subversive potential. Such a belief simply feeds the postmodern closed circuit of power: "The opposition to self-control will most likely be absorbed into the logic of the existing system and so come to equal not resistance but simple deficiency or lack (of control), [vindicating] authority by legitimating the need for control." Emotional expression with an oppositional intent, like angry music, may also have outcomes collaborative with power because "most audiences" would take lack of self-control of emotion as a confirmation of irrationality, especially in women. But that problem is precisely why artists like the Riot Grrrls are working to educate their audiences' notions about feminine anger, and the effect of the Foucauldian circular worldview is clearly to stymie such efforts. Lutz's conclusion on the need "to recast the association of women with emotion in an alternative feminist voice," therefore, seems highly belated.[9]

Foucault also makes a devastating appearance in a literary study concerning emotion, Anne Cvetkovich's *Mixed Feelings: Feminism, Mass Culture, and Victorian Sensationalism* (1992). Cvetkovich begins with a fair enough point, objecting to a "female politics of affect that too readily celebrat[es] the subversive powers of affective expression." Like Lutz, Cvetkovich finds that even positive "discourse about affect" and political transgression can serve "to contain resistance." When emotion becomes "an end in itself," the celebration of emotion actually installs *control, management,* and *regulation* (frequently repeated terms). The best feminist work on emotion hardly stops short in this way, though, and since Cvetkovich provides no examples, her thesis seems to rely on a straw(wo)man. Licensed by the fashionability of postmodern theory, she brazenly substitutes Foucault—along with Jameson, as the subject is mass culture—for any reference to the scholarly literature on emotion, even feminist work alone. The net result clearly implies that nothing is to be expected of emotion under any circumstances.

For all the postmodern trappings, however, the basis for condemning the celebration of emotion is actually the bugbear of romantics and modernists, the presumably facile emotional appeal of mass culture. Cvetkovich essentially paraphrases Kant, Wordsworth, Mallarmé, and successors like Jameson in finding that mass culture represents "complex social issues in simpler and emotionally engaging terms." It does so universally, apparently, and without simplicity or emotion ever having any virtue. Cvetkovich's postmodern updating is to argue that mass culture does not merely employ emotion, but "actually *creates* affect, . . . actively constructing it." You're only feeling what they want you to feel, in other words. Thus it is quite mistaken to suppose that "mass culture is liberatory because it [might conceivably enable] repressed or forbidden impulses to be unleashed." Such a view depends on what Foucault called a "repressive hypothesis," or the belief that emotion (like his subject, sexuality) has some authentic or natural but currently repressed existence, independent of its cultural construction. Liberating emotion would supposedly be the means to liberation in general. But because there is in reality no realm independent of discourse, the feelings dredged up have already been constructed by one's culture and are thus an inauthentic, carefully controlled (or managed or regulated) dead end. A hypothesis about undoing repression, therefore, becomes "repressive" itself, part of the great circle of power, just as Lutz suggests that opposition becomes collaborative. Once again, however, this seems to be more true of postmodern theorists, given their penchant for assuring us that power thoroughly controls us.

Cvetkovich's use of Foucault also supplies a prime illustration of the liabilities of a historical method based in Nietzsche's concept of genealogy. (His description of *ressentiment* in *On the Genealogy of Morality,* moreover, shows up in Cvetkovich's depiction of women incapacitated by confinement to emotional experience.) Just as Nietzsche's genealogy treats history as contingent, or the discontinuous product of chance, and Foucault generalizes about modernity, Cvetkovich treats the construction and management of emotion through mass culture simply as a given in life since the eighteenth century. This historical generality results in an enormous dilemma, when she assures us that emotion is "not natural." [10] Because she does not say what the nature of emotion was before the eighteenth century, one must choose, apparently, between two completely contradictory conclusions: either that emotion has always been the product of discourse or that emotion used to be natural at some point in the past.

Leaving the appearance of such a choice is the real problem, however, because cultural norms and nature have always mutually influenced emotion. Aristotle, for example, given his great historical distance, no doubt experienced emotion through a very different discourse about it than ours and perhaps also through living closer to nature than us. But when he says in the *Nicomachean Ethics* that anger can have good cause, the emotion he had in mind is hardly foreign to contemporary feminists who cite him while making the same point. A detailed historical study of discourse about anger, Carol and Peter Stearns's *Anger: The Struggle for Emotional Control in America's History* (1986), supports such an assertion: Despite distinct differences in discourse about anger over the last two centuries, in an increasing insistence that anger be brought under control, the authors add that "the biological components of anger suggest considerable constancy." In the more recent *American Cool,* Peter Stearns reiterates that "no resolution . . . is in sight" regarding the balance between the roles of biology (or nature) and of cultural norms (or discourse) in emotional experience.[11]

In the course of his effort to introduce nature into leftist discussions of culture, Sebastian Timpanaro likewise finds in *On Materialism* (1970) that emotional experience has had considerable continuity "even across very diverse social and cultural environments," indicating some biological basis. Only systems based on language alone could deny this continuity, he emphasizes, and poststructuralism is singled out for being "closed" to material existence. (Timpanaro had a considerable influence, in this regard, on the work of Raymond

Williams, discussed in Chapter 6.) In contrast with postmodern certainty that emotion is not natural, virtually all thoughtful work on emotion agrees with him that "nature versus nurture controversies" over the basis of emotion, as the Stearnses put it, have hardly been settled—because physiology and culture are *both* involved. Emotion, in fact, especially in postmodern times, offers us "an important link between the biological and the social" in studying human experience.[12] Cvetkovich's denial of the natural element is simply indicative of the arbitrary judgments Foucault has licensed in postmodern scholars.

The postmodern claim that emotion is entirely the product of discourse, with no natural basis, derives from a similar description of the body that has become widespread in academia, thanks to Foucault. By borrowing from work on the body to analyze emotion, in fact, Cvetkovich in essence reduces emotion to an attribute of the body, no improvement at all on traditional literary criticism and philosophy (though there is a difference noted below). Her primary source, Foucault's *History of Sexuality,* has been criticized, moreover, for the way its male-oriented "austere and clinical ethics," as Kate Soper puts it, "is more or less devoid of any reference to the feelings of women, [such] that emotional responses drop out of the picture altogether." Cvetkovich, in other words, not only construes affect as a matter of the body (or desire) but does so to base her entire account of emotion on a study "without reference to affectivity." [13] Besides this highly questionable transplantation of Foucault, in claiming that emotion is "not natural," Cvetkovich echoes postmodern feminists such as Susan Bordo and Judith Butler, who stipulate that there is "no 'natural' body."[14] In this respect, we find the one difference from traditional dismissal of emotion for originating in the body, but that difference only makes matters worse: The body is now disembodied, or no longer biological, in the ultimate postmodern move to materialize discourse and dematerialize everything else. Because the body is a product of discourse, in other words, the association of emotion with the body actually reduces emotion to a matter of the mind. This pinball action hardly suggests the possibility of an interchange in emotion between body and mind.

In attending to the body, the "new somatics" based on Foucault appears to extend radical politics in a vital way, by expanding our recognition of how power operates. But in actuality it has been "a desperate displacement" of politics, treating the body as a passive object at the expense of its ongoing social relation to other bodies, "the ground of all possible communication" if also that of exploitation. In the new somatics, as Terry Eagleton sums it up, "the body is where something—gazing, imprinting, regimenting—is being done to you." Foucauldian "body talk" can seem a "glamorous kind of materialism," nonetheless, because it constructs "an elaborately coded affair, and so caters to the intellectual's passion for complexity." But in actuality the many scholarly "footnotes to Foucault" simply reflect a despair at the decline of "certain more classical strains of materialism now in dire trouble"—that is, Marxism and its emphasis on social struggle. Thus, body talk is hardly sexy, paradoxically, but is "our latest brand of repression," at least in the sense that the postmodern preoccupation with power has suppressed the human subject.[15]

Adalaide Morris, for example, a literary scholar writing on the body, describes written documents directly "figuring and refiguring the body." This is not to say that paper has taken revenge on us for origami but, as usual, that language is active and we are passive. Because the "material world" has only an "unstable" (or fragmentary) existence apart from language, we should therefore abandon material social life, biology, and nature and ask "not what the body is, but how particular discourses have constructed" or "textualized" and thereby controlled it. As Judith Butler interprets Foucault in *Bodies That Matter* (1993), the seemingly natural material existence of the body is only the product of power relations. But as Kate Soper argues, to reject any natural or "prediscursive reality" and thus "any dialectic or interaction between nature and culture" is to remove "the grounds for challenging [the] construction of gender." If the body is held to be entirely constructed by cultural processes, that is, then its origin would essentially be identical with that of gender, which by definition is a product of social convention. What alternative conception of the body (and through it, identity) could be posed, therefore, that could claim any greater legitimacy than the prevailing "distorting and repressive representations?"[16]

The denial of any natural basis for the body reflects the classic Foucauldian position that power in the modern age "operates on bodies not through direct physical cruelty," as Scott Lash claims, but through discourse. As far as I can tell, though, the police still routinely beat the shit out of people and shoot them, although academics living alone with discourse obviously have less to worry about on this score. (Thus, for Jean-François Lyotard, "terror" lies not in physical violence but in not being able to "speak," or express oneself freely.) The relation between bodies and texts is much more socially mediated, that is—by others such as police officers acting on laws, ideology, racism, sexism, and so forth— than the bookish make it out to be. In dance studies, a field concerned first and foremost with the body rather than starting from written texts, Sally Banes similarly stresses the social give-and-take between the body and power. Expressing impatience with both Foucauldian accounts of bodies victimized by power and postmodern celebrants of a typically diminutive, fragmentary resistance, that of a protean body in flux, Banes argues that "the relationship between bodies and culture [or discourse], like that between bodies and nature, occupies a middle ground between discipline and creative expression." [17]

Banes's formulation, however, does not attempt to express just how the body mediates between nature and culture. In essence this is because the body alone doesn't; the link between these two sources of experience is emotion, in which physical feelings are bound up with judgments on social experience. Given the partial (and I stress *partial*) basis of emotion in the body and assuming that the body has a partially natural basis, emotion is therefore considerably fuller than the product of passively absorbed discourse depicted by footnoters of Foucault. Discourse about emotion certainly influences but does not *determine* the expression and understanding of emotion, which is not so susceptible to mass culture, medical science, and so on, as Foucauldian scholarship suggests. The postmodern take on emotion is deficient, in particular, for a reason highlighted by feminist philosophy: The ability of authority (or power) to constitute emotion through discourse is constrained by the fact that emotion is *not reducible to language*. This is not to say that emotion is entirely independent of language (or discourse) but that the two are interdependent. Postmodern theory is anxious to shut down this and any other dialectic—between nature and society, structure and subject in language and ideology, the body and the mind, and so forth—because of its abject wish to leave everything it touches one-dimensional and without possibilities. The sole entity exempted from this reduction and dematerialization of life, of course, is power, as exercised through discourse.

To find a progressive view of emotion, one must turn to branches of philosophy and psychology, cognitivism and social constructionism, respectively. Cognitive philosophy, concerned with the rationality of emotion, is well represented in Amélie Rorty's *Explaining Emotions* (1980), which features notables such as Robert Solomon and Ronald de Sousa. De Sousa may be the best of the cognitivists, stressing not only the educability or adaptiveness of emotions but also their own educational contribution as "models" or "frameworks in terms of which we perceive, desire, act, and explain," a good argument for the sensibility of angry music. The frequent condemnation of emotions for irrationality, in fact, is due in no small part "to their power to reinterpret the world" or challenge the prevailing version of rationality[18]—the threat dreaded by Nietzsche and his descendents among music journalists.

De Sousa does share one of the liabilities of cognitive philosophy, however: a concentration on the individual self rather than the full social dimensions of emotion. The origin of emotion in interaction with others is acknowledged, but the roles that emotion plays and might play in actual cultural and political strife, for example, are of little or no interest. Social constructionist psychologists—including Magda Arnold, James Averill, Jeff Coulter, Nico Frijda, and Rom Harré—likewise tend to "leave us adrift in a laboratory, not in the real world, and with little appreciation for the cultural determinants of emotion," conclude the Stearnses.[19] (The collective effort *Emotion and Gender* [1992] supplies social psychology with a much needed political interest, as well as a useful survey of the field.) Cognitivism and social constructionism, moreover, are as endlessly repetitive to read as postmodern theory, as a result of their self-imposed limitations.

The views on emotion in my own field, literary studies, are massively surveyed by Peter Middleton in the remarkable last chapter of *The Inward Gaze,* which also manages to include a great deal of work from philosophy and psychology. I can't begin to do justice to Middleton's breadth, so I will simply note what he says about contemporary literary studies. Literary criticism (with honorable exceptions like Paul Ricoeur) has long subscribed to the view linking emotion with the body and the feminine—or the mindless, passive audience for mass culture. Not much has changed in postmodern literary and cultural theory, according to Middleton, in which emotions are still assumed to "belong to the body." But now "the body is widely believed to be an apparatus whose self-awareness is constructed by external discourses," and thus emotion is too, as we saw with Cvetkovich. But if postmodern theory is interested in the body, emotion winds up being set aside because *desire,* manufactured in the subject by discourse, is considered "the only legitimate term for a universal motivational force in human interaction." (Thus, Cvetkovich uses *desire* and *affect* interchangeably, as does Barry Shank in *Dissonant Identities.*) Feeling "lies outside postmodern theories of the subject," as a result, which assume that talk of emotions is "personal, intimate, humanist, sentimental and old-fashioned." [20]

Under the influence of postmodern theory, feminist literary criticism and theory has been no better. The disinterest in emotion of many literary feminists has resulted from an unfortunate abandonment of a central thesis in the original wave of feminist scholarship. Following on the heels of Kate Millett and Mary Ellmann, as well as creative work such as Adrienne Rich's "The Phenomenology of Anger" (1972), critical studies like Sandra Gilbert and Susan Gubar's *Madwoman in the Attic* (1979) famously celebrated all novels by women as direct projections of their authors' anger. Elaine Showalter speaks of anger as a source of "female creative power" in *A Literature of Their Own* (1977); Patricia Meyer Spacks writes in *The Female Imagination* (1975) that "one encounters [anger] everywhere in women writing about their own condition," and that it sometimes provides "a means for growth." [21] But the emphasis on anger dwindled in the 1980s, with exceptions like Audre Lorde's "The Uses of Anger" (in *Sister Outsider,* 1984) and Jane Marcus's *Art & Anger* (1988), both of which continue the simple affirmation of the virtue of anger.

The celebration of anger came to seem unsophisticated to many feminist scholars, as Toril Moi indicates in *Sexual/Textual Politics* (1985), thanks to poststructuralism—the hand of postmodern theory at work again. By "stipulating anger as the fundamental feminist emotion," or even "the *only* positive signal of a feminist consciousness," the notion that "feminists must at all costs be angry all the time" seemed not only to endorse a stereotype of feminism but also to be guilty of "essentialism," or reducing womanhood to a narrow essence. The real problem, though, was not so much the advocacy of anger but "a critical practice that relies on the author [as] the source, origin, and meaning of the text." [22] The baby went out with the bathwater, in other words: Anger became guilty by association with its advocates' heavy-handed treatment of novels as direct embodiments of their authors' intentions and emotions. Such untroubled certainty about the authorial self needed to be rejected, it was felt, as a masculine (or "phallocentric") trait typical of traditional humanist scholarship untroubled by questions about identity, especially concerning its formation through gender (or through assumptions about sexual difference). Anger, unfortunately, was cast out with the rejected critical method. Under the rule of postmodern theory, even feminist literary scholars who deign to examine mass and popular culture typically turn to Madonna—not out-and-out angry but ambiguous (supposedly) and thus a more suitable subject than the Riot Grrrls for postmodern treatises on the instability and fragmentation of all communication.

The preferred model became the antirational, presumably bodily and fluid *écriture féminine,* popularized by French poststructuralists Hélène Cixous and Luce Irigaray. They actually continue to work in a quite cerebral vein, however, preoccupied with discourses, signs, texts, and so forth that "tend to take on a life of their own or become the world," says Jane Flax, as is the case for male postmodern theorists dematerializing everything but language. The quest to discover a uniquely feminine style, or to dissolve gender altogether in one's language, typically remains confined to literary practice, and a practice difficult to distinguish from modernism, at that. Laura Kipnis finds that

> *écriture féminine* and its practice of displacing revolution and politics to the aesthetic refer us back to that very modernist tradition that these continental theorists are presumed to transcend. [I]t is perhaps a measure of the late reception

of Frankfurt School theory in France that [a] return to modernism has taken place in continental feminism.

As was the case with modernism, mass culture "resides outside the vanguard elite" of feminism, which has understandably been unable to capture the "popular imagination." [23] As Rita Felski similarly argues in *Beyond Feminist Aesthetics* (1989), the possibilities for injecting distinctive feminine voices into popular forms is of no interest to literary feminists stuck in an essentially modernist quest for an utterly unique style. At most, we find forays claiming Madonna for poststructuralism and psychoanalytic theory.

Many have found French feminism excessively detached from social experience, in dissociating the body from the mind by abandoning meaning. The body may be reassociated with nature, as a feminine realm contrasting with the male world, but even a postmodern theorist wishing to "decenter" identity, Jane Flax, objects that if "the body is presocial and prelinguistic—what could it say?" [24] The fundamental problem with French poststructuralist feminism, in this regard, can be seen in how much at odds it is with the real fullness of emotion. Given the interdependence of emotion and reason, to resist an excessively rationalized (or calculating) world by abandoning reason is to also abandon emotion. Postmodern theorists, feminists as much as nonfeminists, are left with a body not only irrational but useless: As David Hume points out, there's no motivation without emotion.

With direct emotion out of fashion in literary studies, Jane Tompkins created a sensation in 1987 simply by contributing a conventional autobiographical essay—nonetheless hailed as "revolutionary" [25]—to *New Literary History*. But later work inspired by Tompkins, such as Nancy Miller's collection *Getting Personal: Feminist Occasions and Other Autobiographical Acts* (1991), essentially makes writing personally still another matter to theorize in the abstract. Although Tompkins refers briefly to Alison Jaggar, therefore, the whole episode represents no coming to terms with emotion whatsoever; she goes on to align herself with poststructuralism, declaring that meaning in language has "nothing to do . . . with a particular sound" or tone. She even claims, incredibly, that "sound itself is in a sense constituted by a certain form of *silence*" (emphasis added). [26] We register a word, that is, only because of the difference (or *différance*) of the word's sound from other sounds that we *didn't* hear, that remained silent—and the meaning (or the signified) arbitrarily associated with that sound (or signifier) only kicks in after that, so sound and meaning are quite detached. (As always, language in poststructuralism is treated in the abstract and in terms of isolated individual words, not in the social context of full utterances, the only way language is actually used, in which inflection or tone is a substantial part of meaning.) The only recent, substantive work on emotion I could find in the field of English, besides Middleton's, was a book on composition pedagogy by Alice Garden Brand, *The Psychology of Writing* (1989), which surveys social psychology. If you ask people in English about emotion, they will still refer you back to David Bleich's 1975 treatise *Readers and Feelings,* which simply advocates letting students write about their emotional responses to literature—the subjective approach condemned in W. K. Wimsatt and Monroe Beardsley's infamous essay "The Affective Fallacy."

The work of reviving enthusiasm for anger, as a result, has fallen to feminist philosophy, which, despite its own poststructuralist elements remains a field in which some women can never forget the charge that they aren't properly rational. Rather than cultivating irrationalism in response, the feminists I discuss here have turned the tables by pointing out that the supposedly distinctive characteristic of femininity, always threatening to escape proper control by reason—emotion—is in fact produced by reasonable judgment common to men and women alike. This cognitivist view originated with male philosophers, of course, a debt feminist philosophy always acknowledges. But even cognitivism, given its continuing priority on reason and disinterest in physical sensation and social experience, doesn't suffice to achieve the ultimate objective: to claim anger for women, too, the only emotion deemed more appropriate in men (although they presumably need to control it as well), and to assert the necessity of anger in order for women to empower themselves. As Julia LeSage says, "In the sphere of cultural production there are few dominant ideological forms that allow us even to think 'women's rage' " in any positive way, as opposed to the common indictment of the supposed blind rage of feminists. "It is a task open to all our creativity and skill," therefore, "to tap our anger as a source of energy"[27] —precisely what the Riot Grrrls are all about.

The case for the fundamental political significance of emotion is summed up very well by Alison Jaggar. She begins from the fact that our "emotional constitution" is just as important to hegemony, or the ideological maintenance of the status quo, as our express beliefs. It is particularly critical that our "capacity for outrage" at injustice be kept bottled up (and anger defensive of the status quo unleashed); thus we find anger in music demonized and ridiculed. Delegitimizing outrage at the misery of others serves the ideology of self-interestedness, in particular, or "the belief that greed and domination are inevitable human motivations." In an unjust world, cynicism and passivity thrive in the absence of anger.

Emotion is not easily contained, though. It may include an awareness of the rules and norms of the status quo, but we work continually to resolve the contradiction between authoritarian demands and feelings we find more persuasive. The best evidence in the postmodern world for the existence of agency (or the active construction of identity) lies in "outlaw" emotions, such as anger, that continually arise among various subcultures. Those outlaw emotions are politically subversive in themselves, as an "epistemological" threat—if common sense about feelings were reconsidered, that is, the whole edifice of the prevailing ideology would be in peril. To indict emotional expression for lack of either political analysis (reason, that is) or direct political action (as in passive *ressentiment*) is simply wrong. For many people, social criticism may necessarily begin with outlaw emotions, even just half-formed feelings that provide "the first indications that something is wrong." The discovery that cynical acquiescence is not the only possible orientation to the world might even provide a renewed basis for hope.[28]

In an essay directly concerned with anger, "Anger and Insubordination" (1989), Elizabeth Spelman also starts from the cognitivist view that emotions always bear rational elements of judgment. But she highlights not so much the virtue of anger in subordinate groups, but the way ridicule of their anger confirms the danger it poses to authority. The dismissal of emotion in itself, in other words, whether in postmodern theory or in the *New York Times,* indicates the actual political significance of emotion. Authority fears anger as a sign that "subordinates take themselves seriously [and] believe they have the capacity as well as the right to be judges of those around them"—precisely the capacity that Nietzsche tries to belittle as *ressentiment.* To label subordinates emotional or unstable as he does, and establishment pundits continue to do, is in fact "a refusal to hear that which threatens the legitimacy of one's domination," says Peter Lyman. Nietzsche and his ilk would like to reduce anger at injustice to mere psychology, or a problem of irrational individual personalities, and thereby strip the "collective and active character" of that anger by "blaming the victims for their symptoms." [29] (Lyman, unfortunately, attributes this effort entirely to the descendents of Freud and treats Nietzsche's concept of *ressentiment* as a reliable diagnosis of internalized, "silent rage." [30])

This is not the case just for women either: The familiar association of emotion with women has always been part of its larger association with any subordinate group (as Jaggar also points out). Morwenna Griffiths is explicit about the identification of uncontrolled, unreasonable emotion (and bodies) along class and race as well as gender lines: "Black people, 'primitives' and the working class have been thought to be closer to feelings and nature and to be

more emotional than white, 'civilised' and middle or upper class people." [31]
Spelman's observation that "anger is not appropriate in women, and anything
resembling anger is likely to be redescribed as hysteria or rage instead" can
easily be extended, therefore, to the way in which anger in hip-hop and rock
music is repeatedly cast as insensate "rage" by the *Times, Newsweek,* and every
other periodical reviewed in Chapter 4. The word *rage*—typically accompanied
by *blind*—ought not to be used interchangeably with *anger,* obviously.

To be sure, anger is a particularly salient issue for women, as Spelman
indicates in citing Aristotle, who held long ago that the *man* who "does not get
angry in the right way at the right time and with the right people is a dolt." This
would be an admirable stance, recognizing both the cognitive and social elements of emotion, except that it sets women aside as inferiors. The subordination
of women through "the systematic denial of anger" has been more typical,
leading Spelman to affirm that simply "the existence and expression of anger as
an act of insubordination" matters very much. But she adds another point of
Aristotle's that she considers "important to heed": "To get angry is easy. To do
it to the right person, to the right extent, at the right time, and with the right
motive, and in the right way—that is hard." Spelman's concern is not simply the
frequent difference between the causes of emotion and the objects or outcomes
it finds (a distinction associated with David Hume). Also very troubling, in
deciding how to express anger, is the fact that "expressions of anger by people
in subordinate positions are much more likely to bring on violent reactions" from
people with power. This is a problem I don't want to skate over, either: Given
the propensity for violence in anger defensive of the status quo, "encouraging
persons in subordinate positions to recognize why they . . . ought to be angry
must be done with concern for the consequences of their acting on that anger." [32]
Nietzsche and Scheler considered such circumspection a sign of weakness, but
it needs to be acknowledged as a quite reasonable concern.

Miranda Fricker, whose essay "Reason and Emotion" (1991) is considerably indebted to Spelman, adds a further point salient to an objection frequently
raised against Nirvana, in particular: that one can't hear the lyrics, hence the
evident anger is incoherent and unfocused. Emphasizing anger, Fricker points
out that it is precisely because initial "half-formed feelings" lack articulation—
as rock journalists tell us about Nirvana—that those feelings are "a potentially
subversive force." The asset of such feelings is that they have not yet been fully
subjected to "the accepted form of . . . rational judgment as expressed in
language." Irreducible to language, half-formed feelings thus have a freer field
of operation, "a looser and more flexible relation to the dominant ideology, than
does our reason." Indecipherable lyrics in the midst of angry cacophonous music

might very well be a *virtue,* therefore, and we can certainly understand why the mainstream press continually worries over and condemns such artistic forms.

Fricker may be somewhat overconfident in her view that emotion is freer than reason; Jaggar and many others, of course, point out that the dominant ideology works through emotion as well as reason. In proceeding to focus on anger, though, Fricker does not portray some free play of emotion in general but, like Jaggar, simply insists on the possibility of outlaw emotions. Fricker seems cautious enough on this account, distinguishing two types of anger: "the kind of anger which is politically contextualized and anger whose political significance is not understood." The latter is undeniably characteristic of the experience of many women and young people, and for "unknown" anger to become a political force, emotion and reason need to reciprocate, to mutually constitute one another. She envisions such anger "gradually [being] brought into focus by reason and words," in the process of listening to "each other's stories"—while also respecting the feelings "irreducible to verbal language" that remain. (In *The Rationality of Emotion,* de Sousa offers a similar description of learning to think about emotions by recounting the "stories" of why they occurred.) We should refrain, in other words, from belittling angry musicians and their fans for their lack of immediate, full rationalization, as academics and journalists like to do. With patient cultivation, instead, anger might acquire the "linguistic articulation" necessary to "question the suitability of the publicly available" ideologies and to seek out alternatives or formulate new ones.[33]

Peter Lyman, however, argues that even less articulate angry speech (or music) nonetheless participates immediately in public discourse by inherently questioning "the fairness of the rules of participation in rational discourse." Anger without an articulated ideology, that is, has a peculiar advantage: It highlights the exclusion of deviant voices, certainly, but also, more significantly, the way "reason" itself often represents only "a rhetorical claim by the dominant about their legitimacy," as in condemnations of angry music. Contrary to the critics discussed throughout Part 1, therefore, such music accomplishes a great deal, conveying dissatisfaction with both the limited choices available in public discourse *and* the pretense of that discourse to have a rational view of a rational social order (the status quo, that is). Musicians and their fans unquestionably know full well that the people on top are hardly paragons of reason.

Lyman does stress like Fricker that "new speech [or] a language within which one can recognize one's own experience" requires the transformation of mood into a public language (or discourse or ideology) in which "one can discover that one's anger is shared." That discovery of common anger, of course, often begins with less articulate expression, as in music. But that anger only matters if the result is *"empowerment,* a sense of the possibility of changing fate"—vital in the face of postmodern gloom—"and ultimately, *defiance,* political action." This outcome requires the development of historical awareness, in particular: "In the absence of a critical sense of the past, anger remains vulnerable to manipulation." At a time when corporate culture merchandises anger in many forms, for example, we need to question the relation of any particular expression of anger to the past. Sheerly exploitative crap like talk radio is typically unrooted, or oblivious to the past in denying injustice, while even a more progressive performer like Bruce Springsteen mythologizes and stereotypes working-class experience. In either case, a "manipulative politics treats the symptom, anger, not the disease, injustice." [34] The Riot Grrrls, in contrast, like the best hip-hop music, express a keen sense of the accumulated injustices of history, a significant absence, I admit, in a lot of the white-male music I like, although there are exceptions such as the evocation of working-class life by Uncle Tupelo and its spinoffs, the Bottle Rockets, Son Volt, and Wilco.

Managing to generally "reform the character of rationality" or common sense, as Fricker puts it, is hardly inevitable, finally, when starting from inchoate anger. At the very least, though, we can certainly "explore the possibility of allowing our emotions to be fully and openly social constructions," says Naomi Scheman, as opposed to treating emotion as an internal, personal matter. There is simply no question that "our emotions and our knowledge of them can change"—a view adding a welcome collective emphasis to work on the educability of emotion. Lyman, too, stresses that an "authentic political anger" can only result from self-criticism taking place in "political collectivities," which would overcome the frequent "isolation of anger." [35]

The belief of Fricker and Lyman in the significance of feelings prior to their full articulation in language is vital to a sensible evaluation not just of Nirvana and recent angry music but of popular music in general. Put simply, the immediate understanding of song lyrics has never been critical in rock music. But all too often music criticism betrays its subject due to a problem that many have observed, that writing about music is often as absurd as playing the clarinet about Shakespeare (as I believe John Lennon put it) or dancing about architecture (Elvis Costello's variation). Music works first and foremost in sensory ways (to which emotion is consigned), from this view, whereas language works primarily through cognition (or reason, detached from emotion). Whether in the music press or academia, this dichotomy drawn between the body and reason, between pure form in music and the conceptual content of language, reflects a long-standing problem in the general construction of aesthetic experience: the absence of any serious consideration of emotion. Since the Enlightenment, theories of the aesthetic have veered between a "baroque aestheticism," celebrating libidinal excess (from de Sade to Artaud to postmodernism), and a "brutal asceticism" emphasizing intellectual contemplation, with the latter generally holding sway.[36] As opposed to choosing between either the body or the intellect in our approaches to popular music, therefore, we need instead "a full understanding of the way emotion can act as a mediator between reason and desire," as Peter Middleton puts it.[37]

Griffiths supplies just such an understanding in "Feminism, Feelings, and Philosophy" (1988), using the term *feelings* to highlight the simultaneous, dialectical meeting of body and mind, of physical sensation and understanding, that occurs in emotion. Griffiths's use of the term opposes the wedge that cognitivism drives between emotion "as 'intentional,' that is, of the mind," and feelings, which "are then contrasted with [emotion] and are said to be of the body, [and] irrelevant to understanding an emotion." She also opposes feminists who accept the body/mind division in celebrating women for their emotionality, which merely makes a virtue of the dominant culture's essentialist identification of women with emotion and men with reason.

The significance of Griffiths's argument is that she concentrates on language, a necessary addition to Fricker's concern with emotional activity prior to its full articulation. Griffiths also considers "only partly conscious" or "inarticulate expression" perfectly legitimate and crucial but adds that the interdependence of body and mind, of feeling and understanding, is found in the "intonation" or physical, material qualities of *all* language, however articulate and rationalized. (Peter Middleton likewise finds that all language "has an emotional inflexion.") The body, mind, and language cannot be separated into discrete phases of feeling, belief (or judgment), and articulation, respectively, but are always interacting with one another and always in social contexts: "Understanding depends on shared language which depends on shared feeling; the understanding then contributes to both language and feeling." The authors of *Emotion and Gender* likewise conclude, as do Carol and Peter Stearns, that we find in emotion the foremost link between biological and social experience.[38] That mediation—which was there all along, of course—provides the key necessary to escape the paralysis (or reification) induced by the opposition drawn between the body and discourse by postmodern theory, in which material existence is erased and discourse rules unchallenged.

CHAPTER 6

# The Post-Postmodern Voice
## Emotion and Writing About Music

Acknowledging the socially constituted interdependence of body and mind in emotion—and the manifestation of both, as a result, in the emotional intonation in language—would be a vast improvement on the dismal treatment of the body by Foucault-influenced theorists. We need in particular to get beyond their asocial, antimaterial fixation on the way discourse forms the subject and its body. This isolation of attention has led even less gloomy work on popular culture to concentrate on "individual desires and pleasures, omitting those that derive from and create shared, collective experiences." [1] To get at the sort of social experience that characterizes popular music, in particular, even just in listening at home and imagining other listeners, emotion makes a much more profitable object of study than the mute body. The body viewed in isolation seems a passive instrument overwhelmed or even constructed by discourse, but the body considered in its nexus with the mind and social experience, in emotion, appears quite expressive.

128

Mikhail Bakhtin and Walter Benjamin, working independently, came to a similar conclusion in the 1920s and 1930s. As Morwenna Griffiths would a half-century later, they held that language always involves a material social relation (or dialogue), and thus has an emotive impact indissociable from its cognitive effects. That this self-evident point had and still has to be made at all reflects the abstracted academic uses of structuralism and poststructuralism, from Ferdinand de Saussure in the modern period, the object of Bakhtin's wrath, to Jacques Derrida and postmodern theory. Throughout postmodern work on the body, in particular, the assignment of all power to discourse has led to a suppression of the voice that ought to trouble anyone interested in popular music. Derrida popularized this move, in his argument that the voice, or self-conscious speech, has traditionally and quite wrongly been considered the guarantor of an authentic, living "presence" in the use of language. Saussure, for example, held that the voice united sound and sense (or signifier and signified) and thus ensured a perfect meaning or understanding unavailable in the secondary medium of writing. Derrida argued instead that oral language is hardly superior, but always "already belongs to a 'generalized writing,' " or the "element of undecidability within every system of communication." The slippage (known as *différance*) through the chain of signifiers, in speech as in writing, means that language "can never be grasped by the individual speaker," says Christopher Norris.[2]

One prominent variation on this argument appears in Gilles Deleuze and Felix Guattari's *Anti-Oedipus*: In a murky addition to Foucault's already inexact genealogy of the way legal discourse replaced physical force in controlling the body, they claim that writing "supplants the voice" and "dominates" it, so that "the voice no longer sings." In terms of the reception of song, Deleuze and Guattari elsewhere describe the pathos and precariousness of the "lost" listener who "orients himself with his little song as best he can. . . . A mistake in speed, rhythm, or harmony would be catastrophic because it would bring back the forces of chaos, destroying both creator and creation." [3] This exaggerated sense of catastrophe always awaiting the subject (or the individual) typifies poststructuralism. I knew listening to music could be dangerous if one goes jogging wearing a Walkman and fails to hear traffic, but I had no idea of the apocalyptic disaster my daughter and I nearly brought on when we danced unrhythmically to Weezer's "Undone—The Sweater Song."

Another French theorist, Michel de Certeau in *The Practice of Everyday Life*—commonly misunderstood as a populist manifesto—resembles Deleuze and Guattari in his claim that the old "voices of the body" are now "always determined by a system," leaving only "contextless voice-gaps" that indicate the body's absence from discourse. Thus the "voice of the people" has been utterly fragmented into "aphasic enunciation [of] bits of language." That aphasia, or the loss of the power to use words, results from the voice somehow being universally " 'cleaned up' " by the various techniques of sound reproduction (although music critics universally agree that new technologies are often a source of disturbance, not order). Romantic antitechnologism rears its head again, in other words, and it is hardly surprising, therefore, that de Certeau invokes the simulacrum of Theodor Adorno, Jean Baudrillard, and others in lamenting that the recorded "sound of the body" is only a "copy" or imitation. This is one idea, in fact, for which Adorno is the originating point (and not just a transmitter of modernism): His earliest essay on popular music, "The Curves of the Needle" (1928), claims with regard to female performers "that the gramophone elimi-nates . . . the physical appearance of the body." [4] At least postmodern theorists include men in their indictment.

The perverse impact of postmodern views on the disembodied voice is evident in a recent treatise on the body, Anthony Synnott's *The Body Social* (1993), which is organized around all the sensory faculties (sight, smell, touch) except hearing (and taste). The possibility of auditory communication, astonishingly, appears to have been surgically removed from the body. When one also considers the popularity of postmodern metaphors like the "gaze" and the "panopticon" that stress the evolution of power through visual surveillance as well as discourse (getting closer to Nietzsche's belief that the powerful don't need language at all), it becomes evident that some postmodern theorists wish to shut down the possibility of talking and shouting back.

In treating feminist philosophy regarding emotion as an antidote to cynical postmodern theorists suppressing the voice, it may seem that where I am headed with regard to music is an effort simply to restore discredited notions about the voice and "presence." What I have in mind, instead, is to argue that the voice and authenticity can only be salvaged if they are reconceived more subtly, as imperfect products of a continual struggle. That struggle for authenticity, more-over, involves precisely the dialectic between body and mind that takes place in emotion—an authenticity inadmissible in romantic, then modernist, and now postmodern aesthetics, given their definition of authenticity in terms of resisting commercial culture and its supposedly spurious emotional appeals. But I want first to note that a simple reassertion of the voice would hardly find universal support even among feminists. Cultural feminists concerned with the assertion of feminine identity would not object to a move along the lines of Carol Gilligan's *In a Different Voice* (1986), which concerns the unique qualities of feminine self-expression. One prominent strand of postmodern feminism, however—film studies based in Lacanian psychoanalytic theory—shares Derrida's disdain for the authentic voice, most notably Kaja Silverman in *The Acoustic Mirror: The Female Voice in Psychoanalysis and Cinema* (1988).

In *The Acoustic Mirror,* as in *écriture féminine,* the body (the natural) and language (the social) are deemed utterly divided; physical speech does not authenticate language. Silverman agrees with Derrida that the "metaphysical tradition which defines speech as the very essence of presence" should be abandoned but thinks that Lacan is even sharper in observing that speech not only holds no authentic presence but, in fact, expresses an absence of agency: " 'I identify myself in language, but only by losing myself in it.' " As Silverman sums up Lacan, language "preexists and coerces speech," and thus it "can never be anything but 'Other' " to the subject, who is therefore lost on that alien ground.[5]

The reason why Silverman and other Lacanians divide the body from language, however, is not to end recourse to the voice. Instead, a purely bodily sonority is opposed to speech dependent on language. The body in the voice, or embodied voice, is celebrated for exceeding rational meaning through a tactile "grain" and *jouissance* (in Roland Barthes's terms) or a corporeal *signifiance* (as Julia Kristeva puts it). This approach appears in a number of studies of popular music that are not restricted to the voice: In *Feminine Endings* (1991), for example, musicologist Susan McClary pits the " 'feminine' body" in Madonna's dance music against " 'masculine' intellect" and "the cherished ideal of (white, male, heterosexual, middle-class) rebel rock"—a division much like that in Joy Press and Simon Reynolds's *The Sex Revolts,* although they prefer psychedelic music. A closer examination by Barbara Bradby, however, finds that dance music continues to contain both feminine and masculine elements and actually preserves the Enlightenment equation of women "with sexuality, the body, emotion, and nature" and of men with "the realm of culture, technology, and language." Thus she places considerable weight on Jane Flax's objection to celebrations of the female body that simply reverse the priority on masculine rationality in traditional essentialism.[6]

The dead end here, as Rita Felski argues, is that "no convincing case has yet been made for a gendered aesthetics, for the assertion that . . . certain styles . . . in literature and art can be classified as inherently masculine or feminine." Men and women alike, obviously, produce and consume both dance music and rebel rock. Thus a male theorist of postmodernism such as Lawrence Grossberg can claim that "rock and roll is corporeal, . . . not necessarily involv[ing] the transmission, production, structuration, or even deconstruction of meaning," exactly the virtue McClary attributes to dance music as *opposed* to rock and roll.

Grossberg's division of the body from meaning, moreover, is actually a quite traditional staple of male "rockology," Philip Tagg points out, further indicating how little sense it makes as a feminist claim. And any suggestion by either male or female critics, finally, that the rhythms and sounds produced by the body in popular music do not express "meanings of any cultural or political value," says Tagg, "is an insult to every rock and pop musician" and fan.[7]

More abstract schemas such as Silverman's are only slightly less transparent an "insult"; the abandonment of functional political subjects characteristic of French postmodernism is amply apparent. Silverman extols the body in the voice because it threatens to dispose of subjectivity altogether, by making plain "the most radical of all subjective divisions—the division between meaning and materiality." By highlighting the division in the linguistic sign between the signifier (or tactile sound material) and the signified (or meaning), that is, the voice of the body indicates at a larger level, that of subjectivity, the supposed "partition between the biological body and the body of language [or] the social body." (One can see here the debt owed to Lacan by Foucauldian treatments of language, or discourse, as colonizing and disciplining the body.)

The "acoustic mirror" (a term coined by Guy Rosolato), or the way in which the voice is simultaneously spoken and heard, or departs and reenters the body, "violat[es] the bodily limits upon which classic subjectivity depends," Silverman enthuses, and thus has "potentially destabilizing consequences for subjectivity" (and the whole internal/external, subject/object division of experience). This radical potential involves a return of the repressed, so to speak—namely, the "lost object" of the maternal voice (the "lack" that drives us, according to Rosolato): "Whereas the mother's voice initially functions as the acoustic mirror in which the child discovers its identity and voice"—learning to distinguish inside and outside—"it later functions as the acoustic mirror in which the male subject hears all the repudiated elements of his infantile babble." That "auditory 'afterbirth' which threatens to contaminate the order and system of 'proper' speech," by overflowing the internal/external divide, is the body in the voice. In reducing the embodied voice to "infantile babble" stripped of language and reason, however, Silverman leaves the body with very little to say, much like *écriture féminine*.[8] By simply reversing the traditional elevation of the mind over the body, while still preserving that polarity—the Nietzschean core in postmodern theory—Silverman's results are no improvement on an older elitism.

The mixing of aural and visual metaphors in the "acoustic mirror" indicates the basic problem with postmodern theorists, who *look* at language as an abstract, alien chain of signifiers rather than *listening* to the actual social uses of them, which are always meaningful. This visual bias also indicates that we need to turn to work on music, not film theory, to find much appreciation of the voice. The adherence to psychoanalytic film theory certainly produces disappointing results in a recent collection of essays on music, *Embodied Voices* (1994), edited by literary scholars Leslie Dunn and Nancy Jones. They explicitly follow Silverman, asserting "the voice's autonomy from language, indeed from signification" (or meaning) and speech. With "vocality" reduced to Barthes's and Kristeva's "geno-song, the purely sonorous, bodily element of the vocal utterance," impervious to discursive analysis, the embodied voice is essentially something that cannot be written about—"auditory *jouissance*" strips the listener " 'of all possibility of speech.' " In response to the voice of the opera diva, for example, "the body's libidinal drives emerge in sound unmediated by language, producing a sensation of radical loss" in which subjectivity is supposedly "annulled." With no standpoint from which to write on its professed subject, *Embodied Voices* can only return self-contradictorily to scholarly business as usual, discussing little besides psychoanalytic theory and the verbal content, or themes and meaning, in literary texts and song lyrics.

The subject of emotion is dismissed because of its traditional attribution to women, as if no one had improved upon that perspective, and as a result, Dunn and Jones wind up presenting a more specific contradiction. Silverman argues, we have seen, that the embodied voice highlights the division between the body and language, or society, and *Embodied Voices* tells us that the voice is autonomous from meaning. But then another critic, oddly, is cited to the completely opposite effect that the voice actually articulates "an individual's body to language and society." [9] I agree with this last view and would add that the element of the voice that links the body, language, and society is emotion; with no interest in that subject, *Embodied Voices* understandably winds up muddled.

I have already argued, of course, that emotion supplies a missing link, suppressed by postmodern theory, between tactile vocality and meaning, the body and language, biology and society. With regard more precisely to postmodern treatment of the voice, we might also see that emotion offers a way of establishing a dialectic between the two extreme positions regarding the relation of the body to language: complete confidence in authentic presence, as opposed to despair at inauthenticity "steered by uncontrollable external forces," as Johan Fornäs puts it in an essay on popular music titled "Listen to Your Voice!" He observes that identity in our culture is "increasingly reflexive," with so many external forces conditioning "symbolic self-definition" that it seems impossible to believe in the "authentic subjectivity" of a "genuine voice, . . . understood as something originally given, natural and spontaneous." The voice, certainly, is affected by external conditioning as much as any other attribute of the subject.

Fornäs does not mean by reflexivity, however, the opposite term of authenticity, that one's voice is literally only a "reflex" induced by external forces (such as discourse). He uses the term instead to refer to "reflection" upon individual and social identity, in which we can, in his view, distinguish true (authentic) and false (conditioned) voices within ourselves as well as in others. That reflection on a voice's genuineness would "not [be] possible without a certain amount of authenticity" underlying the judgment—or some sincerely held and felt standard for the authentic, at least. That standard is also partly constructed, not entirely natural, and thus may be perfectly wrong; some people find Rush Limbaugh convincing, of course. Bakhtin's significance, in this regard, lies in describing the material basis on which we might pass judgment on the authenticity of different voices.

In "Discourse in the Novel," Bakhtin holds that with some degree of maturity we begin to work on language as much as it has been working on us, so that it becomes half our own, although still half someone else's. Contrary to Lacan and Silverman, in other words, the whole issue of what comes from inside and what comes from the outside is moot; all we have is the outside, at first, but over time we work on it, such that language winds up somewhere in between— somewhere we can only express as a dialectic. I concede that this process goes on more and less consciously, perhaps even at an unconscious level to some extent, a possibility that Bakhtin rejects out of his loathing of Freudian psychology's ahistoricism. But given the state of postmodern psychoanalytic theory— the pessimism over agency that fuels often impenetrable, sometimes loopy accounts of unconscious sexual motivation, attributed to everyone else without substantiation, and more specifically the simple dualism it sets up between the body and an oppressive language—I'm not too wild about the subject of the unconscious either.

The distinction between the authentic and the reflexive, in Bakhtin's view, is most evident in the tension between authority and subordinates expressed specifically in the emotional accent "present" in every use of language. "Presence" in this material, social, realist sense is not some ideal individual attribute futilely purporting to transcend the limitations of language but, instead, meets halfway with doubts about authenticity. This sort of presence is dialectical, in other words, and in two senses: in the tension between an internally persuasive voice and authoritative discourse, as Bakhtin describes it, and also in the continual self-reflection necessary to discern the difference between the reflexive (or external influence) and the authentic.

Much like Bakhtin, Fornäs observes that "voices and subjects are in a continuous process of development, interfering with other subjects and voices, with the external world and with a range of symbolic systems" such as the structures of language, ideology, and so forth. (Fornäs concedes more to psychoanalytic theory, though, citing Kristeva on the "subject in process.") To this I would add the conclusion in *Emotion and Gender* that "we construct ourselves as agents"—rather than language or discourse constructing us—precisely through the emotions "produced in human beings' attempts to make sense of their world, including their physiological responses." [10]

This material emphasis on the cognitive role of emotion in social experience and the interchange between physical feelings (or the body) and self-conscious reflection (or language) is in a sense "post-poststructuralism," a term Richard Johnson uses to describe cultural studies and its reassertion of the possibility of effective agency.[11] Rather than returning to the autonomous individual voice that supposedly authenticates language (in the structuralist Saussure's view), that is, we should move forward from the fragmentation (if not obliteration) of subjectivity and identity by the poststructuralist obsession with the power of various structures. David Simpson suggests a similar post-postmodern move, in arguing in *The Academic Postmodern* that the subject never died, as some theorists seem to have it, but was simply put on hold while the fallacies of unexamined Enlightenment confidence in the individual were corrected.

Now that subjectivity has been troubled at exorbitant length, it is high time to take the materialist step that Bakhtin suggested long ago (in repudiating Saussure's system) and locate the authenticity of language in the tactile emotive accent it receives in social interaction (through every medium, including writing)—not a complete authenticity but an authenticity continually struggled over. In the contest between authenticity and reflexivity, there is an interdependence or dialectic between structures like language and their users (not "subjects")—between constraint and enablement. Language has no existence apart from its social use, or apart from communication between human beings, and to abstract language into independent, free-floating systems like the chain of signifiers is sophistry.

Emotion, which has its basis in social relations, is the most immediate, material registration of the fight for authenticity. But if the emotion we invest in our voices is the primary way in which we make them partially authentic, or at least half our own, we should be clear that that's not to say that emotion is natural, spontaneous, and unreflexive and thus supplies what language lacks. Instead, as Peter Middleton puts it, emotion is "like language"—and vice-versa—since feelings always contain elements of belief, judgement, and intention developed in social life.[12] In their origin in the cognitive appraisal of social situations and their interaction with reason, that is, emotions involve reflection (or reflexivity) and a struggle for authenticity, just as the voice is hardly spontaneous. But while that reflexive element is susceptible to some extent to external conditioning (e.g., by discourses about emotion), in their physiological component our emotions could hardly be said to preexist us and to develop only through acquisition from external sources, as does language. Although itself the product of a reflective process, therefore, the tactile emotional inflection in the voice (including the written voice) supplies the mediation in language between the body and the mind (or the natural and the cultural) as well as between the individual and society (or the subject and structures).

Bakhtin and Benjamin arrived at their materialist views on language in breaking with aesthetics—a break that marks the real "post" modernism—by repudiating the modernist effort to achieve artistic autonomy through obscure language dissociating sound from meaning, or form from content. (Benjamin's target was Symbolism and precursors such as Baudelaire and *l'art pour l'art,* and Bakhtin's not only romanticism and modernism but the absorption of those movements in Formalist literary criticism lauding poetic "estrangement.") They insisted instead that all forms of communication comprise active, material social relationships between the intention of the author or speaker and the response of the reader or listener. According to Bakhtin's colleague Volosinov, meaning is not only a matter of the conceptual content of an utterance but also "the effect of interaction between speaker and listener produced via the material of a particular sound complex. [That material] is like an electric spark, [with] a meaning quite independent of the semantic composition of speech, . . . imple- mented entirely and exclusively by the power of expressive intonation," or an "evaluative accent"—evaluative particularly with regard to authority. This view adamantly opposes structuralism and its descendents, which remove individual signs from the social context of their actual utterance, in order to claim there is an absolute difference between the signifier (the acoustic image) and the signified (the concept). Language, says Bakhtin, is "social throughout its entire range, . . . from the sound image to the furthest reaches of abstract meaning [in writing]. Form and content are one." Put another way, emotion and reason are in actuality mutually (or dialectically) constitutive in language, just as they are in our lived experience.

Bakhtin and Benjamin (like Bertolt Brecht) are also quite specific about which emotion is most vital: anger resentful of injustice. Bakhtin and Benjamin even invoke music to describe the electricity of language, always loaded with the tension between authority and its active, not passive subjects. From an avant-garde standpoint as much anarchist as Marxist, Bakhtin championed the expression *billingsgate,* or "the right to rage at others with a primeval (almost cultic) rage." The reference here to the "primeval" is unfortunate, seeming ahistorical and asocial, but his interest in anger elsewhere clearly involves "tendentious languages . . . aimed sharply and polemically against the official languages" of the present.[13] Benjamin actually revalued *ressentiment* as a virtue, an act few have caught up with, of course. He finds that "melancholy immersion" is no passive "void," as in Nietzsche's depiction of *ressentiment,* but through "the evaluative word, the judgment" (now stressed by specialists in emotion) "triumphs over every deceptive objectivity of justice."[14] The last phrase is a reference to Georg Lukács's theory of reification, which describes an obscuring of the real injustice of social relations that Benjamin, like Alison Jaggar, addresses as a problem of our emotional constitution.

In more recent work from the 1970s and 1980s strongly influenced by Bakhtin, Benjamin, and Brecht, Raymond Williams describes an "ebb and flow of feeling from and to others," even in writing, which is often "quite physical" in intensifying, quickening, and slowing. His particular interest was the "language of the cry" in avant-garde art forms. That cry "fights to be heard above the news bulletins, the headlines, the false political speeches," giving voice to "sharply polarized states of mind, *angrily* polarized social positions" (emphasis added)—as in the best contemporary music. Given the premium that both Bakhtin and Benjamin place on antiauthoritarian expression, Williams's former pupil Terry Eagleton sums up their materialism in terms of a fundamental concern with "emotive enunciations" like "cursing, fearing, denigrating, celebrating and so on."[15]

Williams, revealingly, has largely been dismissed by postmodern theorists in cultural studies who are anxious to displace materialism like his with Francophile abstractions about discourse and power. Grossberg advocates the marriage of cultural studies with Deleuze and Foucault; a more typical line is simply that no one "really needs or wants to hear [again] the Birmingham-Hoggart-Williams narrative" about the British origins of cultural studies.[16] When we understand the roots of Williams's views in the more materialist members of the original avant-garde, therefore, we see once again that the failings of postmodern theorists on the Left regarding the subject of emotion are only a specific outgrowth of a general loss of faith in a long countertradition in art, hopeful for meaningful social change. Williams had in mind the postmodern suppression of hope when he argued that no social order "ever in reality includes or exhausts all human practice, human energy, and human intention."[17]

A more substantive postmodern criticism of Williams concerns the apparent relation between his recourse to Enlightenment ideals and, suspiciously like white men of the eighteenth century, his lack of attention to gender and race.

Rather than debate the point, I want to note that it brings out what seems to be an irony in the history of progressive work on emotion. Williams stands accused of sexism, but much like Brecht (who really deserves it) is nonetheless virtually unique in his attunement to affective experience, unquestionably a vital precursor of an important development in feminism.

Brecht advocated, in art, a critical approach to emotions as much as ideas; years ahead of anthropology, he found emotion neither identical in "all humanity nor incapable of alteration" or education. Rather than obeying internal or "deeper, more eternal" or universal instincts, emotions are just as easily influenced as ideas are. In describing the "structures of feeling" running through the whole of social experience, including art, Williams lays the same dialectical stress on "thought as felt and feeling as thought," "meanings and values as they are actively lived and felt," and so on. The "true social content" of any expression, such as musical performance, is of "this present and affective kind, which cannot without loss be reduced to belief systems" or fully articulated content. When he speaks of ideology, therefore, he means something "lived and experienced, with or without tension, [that] evidently includes elements of social and material (physical or natural) experience." [18]

This could have been written by any of the feminist philosophers discussed earlier, of course. Brecht's and Williams's incipient feminism isn't paradoxical, though, but reflects the fact that we all continue to have much in common, contrary to postmodern theory. In saying this I do not wish to absorb and subsume feminine experience: We need to recognize the different reasons for emotions like anger—especially the difference between resistance and defense of privilege—and the barriers to expressing emotion posed by gender. These distinctions in lived experience, however, are hardly so absolute as to confirm postmodern theories of fragmentation. Even theoretically speaking, it seems perfectly logical that challenges to *difference* (as constructed in gender) ought in some part to stress *similarities* in female and male experience rather than purporting to shred and atomize subjectivity into some extreme, chaotic difference. As Jane Flax points out, women actually become "prisoners of gender" in overly radical distinctions between the natural and the social, or the "body/nature/female" and language/society/male schism set up by *écriture féminine* and other work derived from Lacan, such as Kaja Silverman's.[19]

The apparent "sex differences in anger" are not irreconcilable but arise because men and women differ in their views of "what constitutes unjust behaviour," with women's views subordinate. If we look past the different judgments on which situations warrant anger, both Carol Tavris and the authors of *Emotion and Gender* conclude, "There are no differences between men and women in how they experience their anger; how they express anger"—thus I can relate to Bikini Kill—"how well they can identify [the reasons for] their own anger; [and] the categories of things that make them angry," like injustice however differently it is defined.[20]

With regard to the voice, as well, there are no "intrinsically masculine or feminine qualities," the editors of *Embodied Voices* note. Recent work "by feminist anthropologists and socio-linguists has demonstrated that there is no single satisfactory explanation—biological, psychological, or social—for the differences between male and female voices." What contrasts we can hear involve "a complex interplay between anatomical differences, . . . culturally prescribed gender roles, and 'the contrasting possibilities for expression for men and women within a given society.' "[21] Distinctions of male and female voices are hardly entirely natural, therefore, or absolute and unchallengeable.

The standard practice of women in rock music, however, is less frequently to dissolve gender differences by simply imitating the male voice, in essence a reversal of the impunity with which men have appropriated the female voice through falsetto. Many female performers wish to retain, revalue, and assert a feminine identity, instead, and not do away with identity altogether à la post-modern ludic feminism. It has thus been more common for female performers to sing in their ordinary voices with the same self-confident, forceful attitude as men, breaking down terms of *soft* (or weak) and *hard* (or harsh, strong, tough, etc.) regarding the timbre of female and male voices, respectively. In referring to the "ordinary" voice, I mean that somewhat shriller pitches often remain distinctive in female singers ("shrill" in the most neutral sense of the word), although punk women do tend to sing in a lower register than, say, Simon Reynolds's "ethereal girls." It's tempting to say that pitch is more a matter of genuine anatomical differences, if only in size, but male rockers are often slight of stature—with the difference that the salaciousness and sexism of performers such as Prince, perhaps the leading falsetto singer of our time, remain undiminished.

Ultimately, piling up examples and counterexamples along these lines—such as P. J. Harvey taking voice lessons to develop a baritone—makes it evident that attempting to associate vocal register with gender is futile and can even lead to embarrassment (as my use of *shrill* illustrates). I think Simon Frith asks for trouble, for example, when he argues that "in rock history low not high voices have sounded odder" in men, that falsetto has predominated except in hip-hop. But settling my disagreement with his view would require a highly subjective rating of the relative importance of different genres and an endless tallying of individual singers. His conclusion is salutary enough, though: If it can be plausibly claimed that the "the least bodily" male voice, the falsetto, is also the "sexiest," then the "time has come . . . to drop Roland Barthes's 'grain of the voice' " and clichés about "the relationship of body and voice and sex." [22] I would add, of course, that what ought to replace unexamined body talk is respect for emotional experience.

In noting the common ground that men and women often occupy in their use of their voices, I am not suggesting some easy rapprochement, on that basis, between men and women. An important caveat regarding sexual relations in general is necessary: As Karen Offen puts it, to "consider as feminists any persons, female or male," they must exhibit "anger over institutionalized injustice (or inequity) toward women as a group." [23] In this regard, male and female singers certainly continue to present striking differences. Offen's definition of feminism also makes clear, in the case of intellectuals, where a line might reasonably be drawn between feminism and the work of Brecht and Williams. But the similarity of their perspectives on emotion to recent feminist philosophy remains, a point I stress, I confess, because my historical coverage has put white males in the foreground again, with more to come in moving at this point to music criticism.

That materialists ranging from the avant-garde to feminist philosophy deem writing as emotive as the voice indicates that it ought to be possible to find an appropriate way to write about music. Differences do exist, to be sure, in the tonal and rhythmic possibilities of writing and verbal performance; writing in no way has the same range. But that hardly justifies the most frequent critical approach to popular music, a "search and destroy mission based on uncovering the particular meanings and messages that mediate between any given popular song . . . and its audience." [24] Even George Lipsitz, who uses Bakhtin to assay a "dialogic" approach in *Time Passages* (1990), sticks largely to an argument for a fuller historical account of the social tensions registered in early rock and roll. His evidence is mostly lyrical content reflecting postwar working-class culture, including its "collective historical memory" in present-day "oppositional *thought*" in rock music (emphasis added).[25] Emotion should be as important an issue as express lyrics and ideas, instead, in describing the manufacture of meaning in popular song.

Scholars writing on popular music, habituated to intellectual reflection in tranquility, typically tend to emphasize content analysis and virtually ignore affective experience. (The one exception to this rule has been scholarship on the blues, although I suspect that's partly because foreswearing the usual efforts to elevate the intellectual status of a music was easier in writing on poor, uneducated rural blacks.) The general result is elitist quietism, a domestication of popular music by forcibly absorbing it into preferred critical approaches or theories, rather than accounting for popular music in ways relevant to its actual performance, production, and consumption. This academic imperiousness reaches its nadir in the egregious claims documented in Chapter 3, that rock and roll is identical with postmodernism and poststructuralism. But freelance intellectuals such as Lester Bangs, Robert Christgau, and Greil Marcus, as well as academics with original (if now secondary) lives as fans, like Simon Frith, have demonstrated that one can indeed write about the emotional component of music—that a critic so inclined can account dialectically for emotive as well as cognitive experience.

Since his earliest work, Marcus has been the critic most consistently attentive to the affective results of popular music. Concerning the relation between lyrical content and musical form (especially the grain or tone of the voice), he points out that to analyze "rock and roll strictly in terms of lyrics is the equivalent of raising a cultural theory based in Impressionism strictly in terms of Monet's occasions for painting (i.e., by discussing bridges, cathedrals, and ponds)." Criticizing the scholarly use of song lyrics to determine the banality or poetry of popular songs, Frith points out that "in songs, words are the sign of a voice," a voice, much as Bakhtin has it, "heard in someone's accent." As opposed to postmodern theorists of the purely embodied voice, Frith takes a dialectical view of meaning and sound: "Song words work as speech and speech acts, bearing meaning not just semantically, but also as structures of sound that are direct signs of emotion." Nonverbal devices such as "emphases, sighs, hesitations, [and] changes of tone" work to convey that emotional meaning.[26]

A fuller, dialectical description of popular music, accordingly, should first recognize the way emotional response includes cognition. Marcus originally made this point in *Rock and Roll Will Stand* (1969), finding that "the music is there, somehow, in the same place that the idea is, that somewhere the two have met." This widely shared, hence eminently social "style of feeling and responding [to] the totality of an experience . . . allows one to give mood and emotion the force of fact." (In this early piece, unfortunately, Marcus equates emotion with instinct.) Sound does not prevail over meaning, nor feeling over reason; form and content are one, as Bakhtin and Benjamin argue, in the sense that the emotion conveyed is meaningful in itself.

Like those earlier materialists, Marcus understands language as inseparable from its emotive context, in the social exchange between performer and listener. A song's metaphorical connotations lie not in its words alone: "More often it is that the music, or a phrase, or two words heard, jumping out as the rest are lost, seem to fit one's emotional perception of a situation, event, or idea. A pattern of notes or the way in which a few words happen to fit together hit a chord. . . . 'Message,' in music, isn't meaning alone." [27] This account of the relation of lyrics and performance echoes a well-known interview with Mick Jagger in *Rolling Stone,* cited elsewhere in *Rock and Roll Will Stand,* in which he attributes his notoriously indecipherable singing to a Fats Domino dictum, to the effect that " 'you should never sing the lyrics out very clearly.' " To the interviewer's observation that "You can really hear 'I got my thrill on Blueberry Hill,' " Jagger replies, "Exactly, but that'ₒ the only thing you can hear, just like you hear 'I can't get no satisfaction.' " [28] In the more recent *Lipstick Traces,* a history of the avant-garde culminating with punk, Marcus continues to work in this vein, casting the Sex Pistols' "Anarchy in the U.K." as a Dada sound poem with only a few comprehensible phrases. The song is nonetheless as replete with meaning as a more discursive critique of social life:

"Reduced to a venomous stew, . . . you heard not woe but glee.

> *Is this the em pee el ay*
> *Or is this the yew dee ay*
> *Or is this the eye rrrrrr ay*
> *I thought it was the yew kay*
> *Or just another country*
> *Another council tenancy!*

It was the sound of the city collapsing. In the measured, deliberate noise, . . . you could hear social facts begin to break up—when Johnny Rotten rolled his r's, it sounded as if his teeth had been ground down to points. This was a code that didn't have to be deciphered. . . . It *felt* like freedom" (emphasis added). [29]

Marcus's descriptions accord exactly with my own use of rock and roll: A few lyrics may come through, if only those that appear in the title; otherwise, whether listening to a song or remembering it, I go around either singing nonsense syllables approximating the vocal's tone and accent of certain phonemes or imitating instrumental passages, from guitar riffs to the basic rhythm of the drums, bass, or both. My years of intellectual work have not changed the fact that I often don't have much idea what I'm listening to, in terms of lyrics, although I know *perfectly* well in terms of fundamental emotive enunciations. This is not to say that lyrics don't matter. Some connection with them eventually becomes desirable not simply to deepen my connection with a song but especially to verify my judgment on the sentiments being expressed and to modify it if necessary—many wonderful rages in hip-hop and rock prove misogynist, for instance, on closer inspection. (This is not unlike the ideal process that

Fricker and Lyman describe, in which we work to articulate both the causes of our emotions and whether their expression has identified the right object.) After a while, whether through familiarity, lyric sheets accompanying a record, or a friend's transcriptions, I may learn a fair portion of the lyrics, but the greatest excitement and pleasure is always a song less fully registered. In extolling the Clash's "This Is England," a 1986 song "about life in a disintegrating world [in which] Joe Strummer could be singing about . . . anyplace where public policy has left a community to rot," Dave Marsh concludes that "I've heard it a hundred times, and I still don't know half the words—and that's the point." Even simply "Shooby shooby doo wah," Marcus pointed out in 1969, "heard in the right mood, has more meaning than a flat-out protest song ever does, because by definition when you listen to a protest song absolutely nothing is in doubt; the listener is in a box." [30] (Recall the critics in Chapter 4, in contrast, lamenting the inferiority of contemporary angry music to the noble protest songs of the 1960s.)

Most of the work on popular music coming out of my own field, literary studies, presents a sad contrast with this dialectical appreciation of the relation of sound and words. The literary are so out of it, in fact, that they may not seem worth lingering over. But the work described below, Aidan Day's *Jokerman* (1989), usefully illustrates a somewhat different problem than the contempt for emotion seen in earlier chapters. In this case, we find the ludicrous results of simply disregarding emotion altogether in music criticism in order to concentrate on lyrics as poetry. There is no recognition whatsoever of the irreducibility of language to its conceptual content alone, the same problem found in music journalism that declares Kurt Cobain's anger to be inarticulate because the lyrics are hard to understand, as well as in the scholarly collection *Embodied Voices*, almost entirely devoted to the thematic content of literary texts and lyrics. The relation of this disregard for emotion to romantic literary ideals, moreover, and their preference for the intellect (which aesthetes have long fraudulently cast as a concern for the "spirit") is nowhere more apparent than in writing on rock by literary scholars such as Day. The direct continuity of romanticism, modernism, and postmodernism is evident in his tendency to slip between those periods at a moment's notice.

A close reading of the lyrics of Bob Dylan, *Jokerman* is enthralled by "energies [outside the] control of the rational self" and "spaces beyond the limits of the social," expropriating rock into a mystified, autonomous high culture. The subject matter is "the processes of poetic creation," with Dylan's social and political commentary explicitly omitted, an asociality evident from the reading of the very first epigraph, which cites the song "I and I." Only much later does Day briefly acknowledge the source of the expression "I and I," the Rastafarian movement in Jamaica, practitioners of an idiosyncratic Christianity (well known through reggae music) with which Dylan apparently seeks to identify. At the beginning, however, Day seizes on the line to initiate a vaguely poststructuralist thesis on the "questions of identity" and "the many divisions of self" in Dylan's lyrics. The question "How does it feel / To be without a home?" (in "Like a Rolling Stone"), Day finds, is tantamount to his own question "And how does it feel to be without the reassurance of accepted ways of thinking about the self?"—a large leap in postmodern expropriation, although easy enough when the song is reduced to semantics. By the same illogic, Dylan's hope that "any day now / I shall be released" is "less a wish for release from any particular self than a generalized yearning for a suspension of the fractured, decentered self." [31] When Day does finally refer briefly to the Rastafarians, he limits the sense of "I and I" to an implied relation with God, omitting the much more social sense of the phrase explained by Dick Hebdige: The Rastas "refer to themselves as 'I and I' . . . to show that they are not alone: that God . . . is living within them. The phrase is also meant to express the Rastas' *feeling* of oneness—their sense of *solidarity* as a group" (emphasis added).[32] Focus on the intellect suppresses the social context that attention to feelings would entail.

The mystified romantic conception of the unique or autonomous artistic vision, combined with poststructuralist skepticism about subjectivity, also suggests the elitist continuities between modern and postmodern aesthetics. The modernist Mallarmé, the primary theorist of Symbolism, is cited on the mystery of poetry's silent music alongside the postmodern theorist Julia Kristeva, well known and often criticized for advocating the Symbolist subversion of rationality. Kristeva is a good example of the "baroque aestheticism" in French poststructuralist feminism, setting the body entirely against reason in *Revolution in Poetic Language* (1984), the work cited by Day. Yet Day himself, in his close readings, essentially practices an "ascetic" rationalism, and thus it seems highly inconsistent to invoke Kristeva and Mallarmé in the process.

Day's other very small, isolated references to contemporary theory—including the reduction of Bakhtin to content analysis—serve only to dress up what is, on the whole, old-fashioned close reading that quickly becomes unbearably minute and frequently verges on the inane. In "Visions of Johanna," as Day describes it,

> where stanzas one and three had nine lines and two and four ten lines, the fifth stanza has fourteen. The expansion allows for a pattern of seven rhyming lines beginning with line six. The rhymes of these seven lines . . . enact the sense of a violent disposal of constraint. . . . The whispering assonances, the haunting

incertitudes of the partial rhymes, the lassitude of the double and triple rhymes, the consonantal softness of the masculine rhymes, and the enervations of the inordinately extended lines, may . . . imply the entropy of a world succumbing to a power larger than itself.

More than the last clumsy effort to add some weight by invoking postmodern gloom, the instructive thing here is the meaninglessness of references to emotion in the midst of abstract technical description. One might compare this with another species of wrongheaded formalism, Wilfred Mellers's infamous musicological analysis of the Beatles: "A Hard Day's Night," as he described it, has a "plagal, 'flat' feeling, beginning with the dominant seventh of the subdominant. The tune itself is pentatonic until the chromatic extension in the final phrase," and so forth. In overanalyzing clearly throw-off lyrics, Day almost seems to satirize the habits of close reading in literary criticism. Only people who know nothing of contemporary culture need a guidebook to tell them that the Black English sense of "bad" and "nasty" signifies " 'good,' 'stylish,' or 'admirable.' " [33]

The slightness guaranteed by Day's total unconcern with the emotion of a performance, let alone any larger social context involving its reception, depressingly illustrates the traditional practices of the literary academy. The absurdity of hermetic textual analysis is highlighted when turned on a medium that is just that, a medium. Rock is more a context—an "open field for the most varied cultural activities"—than a text (which is just as true of literature). What "appears to be expressed in the lyrics," says Peter Wicke, "only form[s] the medium of which [the listeners] make *active* use. . . . Rock songs are not objects of contemplation, to be assessed according to how much hidden meaning they reveal in their innermost structures. . . . Seen in this light they are dreadfully banal." [34]

This is yet another recent academic discovery that freelance rock writer Robert Christgau made decades ago—writing on Dylan, in fact. In "Rock Lyrics Are Poetry (Maybe)" (1967), Christgau takes to task claims for Dylan as a poet, when his corpus doesn't "look so tasty on a paper plate," divorced from its performance: "Poems are read or said. Songs are sung. . . . Dylan's only [poetic] innovation is that he sings, a good way to control 'tone of voice,' but not enough to 'revolutionize modern poetry.' " [35] The obscurity and sheer profuseness of his lyrics—inviting any reading one wishes, as Day's *Jokerman* certainly illustrates—have more to do with claims for Dylan's stature as a poet. Close readings, therefore, continue to misapply the intellectual bias of high culture to mass culture: In essence, they assume that any positive claim for an artist must be a claim for intellectual complexity, requiring the examination of every nuance of his or her work *except* those involving mere emotion, presumably only a physical reflex. This is precisely where so much postmodern criticism merely represents a continuation of romanticism and modernism.

Although Day is aware of arguments against isolating lyrical content, he dismisses them. After one concessional paragraph describing Dylan's vocal style, Day declares that the "lyrics transgress any real distinction between a poetic richness of signification, a density of verbal meaning, on the one hand, and performance as song, on the other. [The semantic properties of] the words alone stand as significant texts, soliciting study in their own right." [36] The fact that Dylan has continually altered both his performance of signature songs and vocal style on new releases, however, would seem to indicate that it matters a good deal to him in its own right. The problem with ignoring his decisions in this regard was apparent, for example, in his appearance on the 1991 Grammy Awards show at the height of the Persian Gulf War, when for some reason he sang "Masters of War" in an incomprehensible mumble, defeating any purpose (although some who already knew the song professed to be enthralled).

At least Dylan didn't fully participate in the cowardly silence even of supposedly alternative and/or progressive rock performers during the Persian Gulf War. Later that same year, however, just when things couldn't have seemed worse, the picture changed completely with Nirvana's ascent. (My own favorite moment in 1991 was Uncle Tupelo's cover of Robyn Hitchcock's antiwar song "I Wanna Destroy You," with its evident reference to Bakunin's destructive urge regarding common sense.) But Nirvana's emergence, of course, only really indicated that many performers had continued to oppose prevailing tendencies like militarism. The late D. Boon of the Minutemen, in "The Price of Paradise," sang a cautionary tale about Vietnam when a U.S. invasion of Central America seemed imminent in the mid-1980s, lamenting "men who die very young / Afraid to see that their cause is unjust."

To contrast Boon with, say, Steven Tyler of Aerosmith, who actively cheered on the Gulf War, appears to continue to privilege "message" over music and emotion, however. The real political problem, Lipsitz points out in his Bakhtin essay, is not whether a song in and of itself "is oppositional or co-optive, but rather how it arbitrates tensions between opposition and co-optation at any given historical moment," in a specific social situation. [37] By this standard, I need at least to testify to how important Boon's song was to me, in the midst of post-Persian Gulf militarism, how often I still go around singing it, "singing" the crashing guitar in the chorus as much as the lyrics.

Although written in this spirit, I don't know that my next chapter does any better than other literary-based scholarship on rock and roll. But I'm going to try something different, at least, by following up on the suggestion of musicologists Susan McClary and Robert Walser that adequately addressing popular music "requires a greater willingness to . . . bring one's own experience as a human being to bear in unpacking musical gestures, to try to parallel in words something of how the music *feels*." [38]

In *Running with the Devil* (1993), unfortunately, Walser effectively abandons this project by echoing a familiar postmodern line on the adversarial relationship between the body and the mind. (McClary went on to peg Madonna and dance music to an antirational body). Rather than any of the scholarly work on emotion, Walser's account of that relation initially relies on Mark Johnson's *The Body in the Mind* (1987), a well-intentioned but strained philosophical account of the way our physical social experience generates prelinguistic connections or "image schemata" in our minds (note the visual terms that make it possible, we will see, to continue to consider the mind distinct from the tactile). These schematics are imaginatively translated into language as metaphor, in the sense that language involves relating one experience to another, or a categorizing of concepts and objects in the process of naming them. The meanings we make in this way are neither perfectly objective nor entirely arbitrary; they're shared, they're material, and thus they're real. I would add, however, that all this is essentially what goes on in emotion, the absence of which in Johnson's account seems fairly damningly oblivious to feminism. The crucial difference in acknowledging emotion is that the body and the mind are mutually interdependent therein, messily inseparable where Johnson has a fairly neatly apportioned theoretical schema. The dichotomy of body and mind, as a result, persists despite Johnson's labors to resolve it.

This failing is borne out by the ease with which Walser immediately contradicts Johnson by reducing the body to a matter solely of "mind," so to speak, in a passage echoing the Foucauldian denial that the body has a physical existence independent of discourse (which is the kind of thing I think Johnson meant to counteract). Like so many others offering footnotes to Foucault (see Chapter 5), Walser equates feelings with the body in a quite traditional fashion, with the difference that the body is deemed a mental construction, based entirely on discourse, so emotion winds up consigned to the mind:

> The body and the physical world cannot be experienced or thought outside of discourse. If musical gestures are experienced as physical or emotional gestures,

these experiences are dependent on the discursive operation of the concepts and metaphors that make all of these terms meaningful.[39]

So much for the feeling in a critic's own language paralleling the feeling in music—there are no actual tangible feelings that one could capture stylistically, just discursive concepts designating them.

Because feeling does exist beyond discursive constructions of it, I have tried to follow McClary and Walser's original suggestion in opening the next chapter: to register the frustration as well as anger but also enthusiasm and hope—that old dialectic between pessimism of the intellect and optimism of the will—that I feel myself and that I find resonant throughout Riot Grrrl music. But one thing must be acknowledged: There is only so much one can say about emotion when it comes to identifying it in a text. The main thrust of my book, for that reason, has been a defense of emotion rather than identifying the feelings in particular performances. The problem with talking at length about emotion in any one text is evident in Tricia Rose's *Black Noise*. Tim Brennan finds that Rose has "brilliantly grasped" the fact that "the emphasis on content in much popcult criticism needs to be rethought [since] the critic is superfluous" or unnecessary to the interpretation of lyrics, as I have pointed out in the case of Aidan Day's ludicrous book on Dylan. Analyzing a music like hip-hop "at the level of verbal meaning" can only make its contents "redundantly obvious." [40] But Brennan has in mind Rose's knowledge of technology, including drum machines and samplers. Yet in a chapter titled "Prophets of Rage," Rose resorts to the political contents of song lyrics to demonstrate the rage, enumerating the institutions that have been the objects of hip-hop wrath, such as the police.

I sympathize with this problem: Once one says a music is angry, there's not a lot of shading to add to description of the emotional performance—although I will describe an ambivalence between celebratory, outraged, and resigned feelings in a single Bikini Kill song. What I intend to do in the next chapter, therefore, is to lay out the complexity with which popular music is *received,* both emotionally and intellectually, rather than performed. Contrary to Fredric Jameson's assurance that the musical repetition in popular songs means that their reception is universally identical, I will indicate that the overlap between emotion and reason in encountering any song is quite complicated, even if the musical texts themselves aren't. (That ought to be a superfluous matter, too, except that postmodern exponents of modernist mass-culture theory, such as Jameson rehashing the Frankfurt School, continue to issue such sociologically uninformed, homogenizing judgments.) As George Lipsitz and Peter Wicke have stressed, popular music, like every other art form, is a medium whose meanings depend in large part on its uses—although always in a dialectic, as Bakhtin has it, with the intentions of the artist.

Given my interest in encouraging a better appreciation of the interplay between emotion and reason in the reception of popular music, I do not intend to do musicology in the next chapter. I don't find technical description of music all that revelatory, anyway; I only feel a compelling need to know the chords when I want to play along on my guitar, and they're usually easy enough to discover—rock and roll, after all, continues to be the same three chords over and over, or it wouldn't be rock and roll. (This observation is in no way a slight, when the point is that both the performance and the consumption of popular music involve unpredictable admixtures of emotional and intellectual experience, in which lies considerable complexity.) The rather dramatic claims that even the best musicologists sometimes make for the effect of chord progressions and musical modes, moreover, invariably seem inflated and unconvincing. Robert Walser does anticipate all these objections: "To argue that critical scrutiny of the details of rock music is inappropriate because people don't hear that way is like arguing that we can't analyze the syntax of language because people don't know that they're using gerunds and participles." [41] But gerunds and participles have never gotten anyone particularly excited, of course.

That trying to acknowledge feelings could be a radical proposition in the 1990s, for intellectuals at least, indicates how sorely and perpetually muddled the simple fact of human emotional experience has been in thinking about the arts that suppresses any feeling about them. (I've been told by an academic that the opening of the next chapter is "incoherent ranting.") The field of aesthetics has never bothered to adequately account for emotion, out of fear of anger and discontent, of course, as much as contempt. The appearance of that scholarly attitude as common wisdom seemingly everywhere, as rock journalism illustrates, has meant that emotion remains an object of derision, as the "feminine" excess of the passive, weak-minded mob devoted to purely physical pleasure. But there's always that perfectly astute fear in the derision, an actual recognition that emotion does indeed provide motivation and thus always poses a threat to authority. The nice thing about the situation, as a result, is that giving the slightest bit of serious attention to the actual nature and workings of emotion, which I hope my book provides enough information to do, has the potential to upset *everything*—not just the status quo in the arts but the *whole* status quo.

# CHAPTER 7

# The Riot Grrrls and Carnival

*Poetry happens to be wherever the stupidly*
*mocking smile of duck-faced man is not.*

—Lautréamont

I want to start with some good reasons why young women have seized on punk rock in the 1990s. I know I have to wear a drool cup for my bile: We live in a plutocracy so brazen that decent persons avert their eyes. You get as much health as you can pay for; you get as much "justice" as you can pay for; you get as much "democracy" as you can pay for in a world run by the wealthy and for the wealthy. That's always been true, but now, in making a point of letting everyone know it, this militant plutocracy has taken us back to the nineteenth century, social Darwinism, and the Gilded Age—it's no coincidence that we hear about Victorian "values" and orphanages for everyone outside the ruling class.

What *is* everybody else doing while money runs amok? Maybe postmodernism happened—everyone's given up because nothing can be said that anyone will hear unless it suits the corporate media, which are increasingly dominated

150

by a few giants created by mergers. Obviously, only dishonest people get to be on television, whereas anyone who makes discomforting feelings loud enough to briefly get heard faces co-option, ridicule, or the banishment of simply being ignored. Only the "angry white male" is in fashion, defending "property rights" against human rights. (Yet even the worst authoritarian types could only stand for so long to sit and listen to Rush Limbaugh rant all by himself night after night.)

It's so transparent, but it's also so muddy—it seems like there's nothing you can say that they can't pervert, can't turn into their own and silence you. It even makes you feel schizophrenic, like postmodernism says, but George Orwell pointed out well before postmoderns that political language doesn't seem to have much connection to material reality anymore. The worst is channeling all the wealth to a few "greedheads" on top and calling it a revolution. Corporations and the wealthy conduct open class warfare against the middle class, working people, and the poor, while politicians and pundits still denounce anyone who refers to social class, let alone class struggle, as a pinko, even an alien—the Cold War rages on in their minds, belying all their pronouncements about the eternal new world order of transnational capitalism, which continues to be dogged by Karl Marx wherever the number of people driven to desperation reaches critical mass, as in Mexico, or else we wouldn't be treated to so much good old-fashioned fascism.

The public/private schism is the really intense muddle, though. "Rights" are for private property, and public citizens are "special interests." Weird inversions result when public business goes on in private, as corporate lobbyists write the law, resulting in less public regulation of private business. At the same time, the government wants more power to regulate our private lives—having demanded "law and order," people have a thuggish police state ready to come after them for the slightest transgression. Meanwhile, in the mass media, other people's private lives are featured in the public eye.

All manner of schizophrenia flows from the basic division of virtuous private property and oppressive public interest (which used to be the "public good," but that's now an oxymoron). The much vaunted "consensus" means going along with whatever big business wants. Corporations deserve subsidies, but people on welfare need to get a job, say the politicians on page one, except we have to have millions unemployed, too, say the economists on the business page, or else competition for workers will unfortunately cause wages to rise, although competition in a free market is supposed to be good. As for who gets jobs, we have a "meritocracy" say the people who brought you Willie Horton ads, and "discrimination" is only suffered by white males, victims of a modest affirmative action that has supposedly eclipsed centuries of segregation and sexism. "Freedom," finally, refers only to business doing whatever it wants—in a competitive "free" market actually devoted to cooperative activities such as price-fixing, eliminating competition through mergers and monopolization, and reducing wages and benefits for employees through assaults on organized labor and the maintenance of a reserve army of unemployed workers. The special interests (formerly the people) outside the ruling class—especially the unruly poor—need less freedom, though, and more policing of their values, if not universal incarceration.

Observing that "public" is bad and police agencies run amok, "patriots" hate their government now—and for also being too "big." They're not far wrong, though: Multinational corporations—privately owned, so big but not bad—have made themselves virtually immune to law and regulation by buying the government and the system of "justice" and thus have been able to destroy opposition among working people, especially organized labor, another bad "big" institution. The angry white male does not generally exhibit "active racism and sexism," finds Fred Pfeil, but is better characterized by his antigovernment attitude, which has "something to do with gender and race" in its "rage at the breakdown of a profoundly undemocratic, patriarchal and racial hierarchy into which [white males] once believed they fitted organically, with their own zones of autonomy and deserved privilege, no matter how small." But white males continue to need, if also hate, "those tough-love local/transnational plants," and "anti-federalism" is the result.[1]

As Barbara Ehrenreich points out, the government is about the only agent of wealth that can be directly attacked:

> If you can't do anything about the size of your paycheck, . . . you may still be able to do something about the chunk that's withheld. You can make war against the government. And since the corporate elite will go along with you on this one (at least until the resulting anarchy gets in the way of profits) you might even win.

You can make war on the government, paradoxically, because its own massive military machine has trained millions to kill efficiently and ruthlessly once they get out and find little economic or educational opportunity, which the government might be providing if it weren't slashing all its functions *except* the military. "Still funded at Cold War levels," says Ehrenreich, the military "substitutes for college, teaching young recruits that there is at least one thing they can do well and be valued for"—killing.[2] And the purported government-haters among public officials (actually quite devoted to the two functions of government, corporate welfare and the military, involving massive redistributions of wealth to big business) are very concerned to keep lots of weapons freely available for the job.

We have a culture of violence thanks not solely to Hollywood but to a half-century of anticommunist militarism poisoning society at every level—the "buffed" U.S. male warrior in the movies is just a symptom of the disaster. The moral bankruptcy and social breakdown that result from living in a military state, however, is explained away by politicians and pundits as being the fault of unwed mothers. That's nothing, of course, compared to the real violence done to women every day. I'm not going to recite statistics on rape and domestic abuse, though, and all the other forms of violence everyone knows about but seems to consider just part of the scenery. Stalking women is a major sport; in the city I live in, some husband, ex-husband, or boyfriend kills his wife, ex-wife, or girlfriend just about every week. The routine is so dull it's middle of section B stuff.

The only thing I have to say about the stupid ways men take out their otherwise perfectly justified rage over their meaningless lives concerns why it's women that bear the brunt. Any sensate, honest male knows full well that supposedly wild-eyed radical feminists are absolutely right about our culture: Women are on constant display, everywhere, as semen receptacles. The "gaze," when it comes to women, is real; Riot Grrrls write BITCH, RAPE, SLUT and WHORE on their bodies because that's what a lot of men *already* see there. Beyond actual physical assault, though, as well as pornography and the whole sex industry, the problem is how "normal" guys have learned to look at women—as well as how *not* to hear them, a problem women in punk rock are obviously working on. (They're not preaching to the converted; even at shows by female-led punk bands, I've heard men in the presumably progressive audience enthuse about the performers' breasts.)

In referring to ordinary guys I'm not talking in the usual academic mode about some imaginary uneducated goons—I'm talking about myself. I can only claim that as much as I've been inundated for years by women offering me their bodies from a distance, there are still times I'm struck conscious again of how pornography has nothing on "mainstream" culture. I recall an issue of *Newsweek* that had a cover story on the sexual abuse of children, or maybe even child pornography, and in a different section happily featured a publicity photo of some 13-year-old actress (Drew Barrymore, I think) with her soaking-wet, skin-tight shirt and pants unbuttoned. In this respect, one of the finest moments in Riot Grrrl history occurred on the British talk-show *The Word,* when the group

Huggy Bear returned unexpectedly after its own performance to heckle host Terry Christian with audible cries of "Shame!" when he showed a film report on two topless models.

I was careful to say that women are always available *from a distance* because this is one reason why men take out their frustrations on women: Real-life women, try as many might, don't always live up to the promise of total satisfaction the culture invests in its images of femininity. Unlike the images one meets everywhere, actual women don't routinely offer to put out—so some men feel compelled to force them to do so, to make them conform to what anyone with eyes can see is their basic function. And if they do put out willingly, the bliss of a fully satisfying consumer's life revolving around a horde of commodities including cars, beer, cigarettes, and so on—as well as the woman—does not follow the way it does in the average advertisement, movie, or television program. Women are packaged with the good life: In real life, the woman can be gotten, but the good life is another matter, and women become convenient scapegoats. As throughout history before postmodern consumerism came along, women are closer at hand and usually weaker than other potential targets, so they're easier to take it out on—the abuse of women by men, especially, which goes on at every level of society, has always been a product of stupid laziness.

But right now things are particularly bad in a pathological culture of violence egged on by a cynical plutocracy—a combination that amounts to fascism. The only thing the developed nations lack is the systematic assassination of dissidents and slaughter of inconvenient powerless groups, but because those nations routinely sponsor such efforts in the rest of the world, it's hardly unthinkable—note all the right-wing rhetoric about "eliminating" even hapless, unthreatening liberals. (Limbaugh would save one for a museum.)

When you add to this ugliness the fact that any words you could use to condemn it have already been taken and twisted, the only thing left for any sensible person to do is *scream,* which is exactly what a lot of young people are doing. They're not worrying about a "message," which fascists like Gingrich and Limbaugh, given the absence of anyone in the government or news media who will contradict them, would just spin into a soundbite. Pure screaming is what grunge, hip-hop, metal, punk, and Riot Grrrls have in common—not scream therapy, either, for the point isn't letting it out and feeling better (or a catharsis) but enlisting other screamers—and they're doing it in the public eye, which the authorities hate. "Screaming," says Kim Gordon of Sonic Youth, "is a kind of vehicle for expressing yourself in ways society doesn't let you." [3]

Writing on the Riot Grrrl subculture, Joanne Gottlieb and Gayle Wald toy with reducing the scream to dead-end postmodern terms of "jouissance" and "a radically polysemous nonverbal articulation," but they resist discounting the emotion involved: "Far from being a fluid signifier, screams are also emotional ejaculations bearing specific associations with highly charged events—like rape, orgasm, or childbirth." Because those events are "associated with femininity at its most vulnerable, the scream in its punk context can effect a shocking juxtaposition of sex and rage," going well beyond the evident assertion of a "form of expression both denied to women in public (screaming is unladylike) and devalued in private (women are so emotional)." [4] (Gottlieb and Wald contrast quite starkly with Joy Press and Simon Reynolds's postmodern celebration of the bliss of the mother's womb, which leads them to a quick dismissal of the Riot Grrrls in *The Sex Revolts*.) The expression of "collective outrage at abuse," I would add, is attributed by Donna Gaines to the whole "fucked generation"—male and female alike—in the obituary for Kurt Cobain that she wrote for *Rolling Stone*.

Most young people wouldn't provide such a full account of why they're screaming, but that doesn't mean they couldn't—that they haven't absorbed, at some level, plenty of good reasons for screaming. And many of them are trying like mad to dredge up those reasons out of the swamp of incoherence the culture's inundated them with. Cacophony in music, by their own account, is an attempt to get a grip on the way the whole culture sounds—and there's nothing (like postmodernism's beloved "power") that guarantees they won't do so. Much of the music is merchandised by multinational corporations, of course, but that's the saving grace of selfishness—it's blind to where self-interest really lies, which is always in the common good. That's a disaster when the CEOs set people against each other, through their political henchmen and pundits, and foul the air and water, as if they don't eventually live with the consequences, too. But sometimes, like when the robber barons think they're just exploiting vulgar tastes in marketing angry music, their blindness leads them to inadvertently serve the common good, or at least to let others do so. (Then the demagoguing politicians step in.) And the many petit entrepreneurs involved in music are definitely out to cause trouble—more so, even, than many of their own bands. Even if angry music were only a caricature of truly deviant, subversive impulses, which it's not, the response to it is never predictable. There could be a backlash or even an upheaval of the genuine feelings supposedly being prostituted: "There is always the chance that the promise of revolution on a billboard will be taken literally in the streets." [5]

I don't think we have to fall back on last-gap ironies like this, however, although I'm compelled to reiterate it because so many complacent postmodernists will insist despite all the evidence to the contrary that commercial "incorporation" is universally damaging. Just because "a particular form [is] marketed for profit," says Rita Felski, in arguing specifically for feminist forms in mass culture, "we may not automatically conclude that it is irredeemably compromised and cannot constitute a legitimate medium of oppositional cultural activity." Feminist theorists need to pay "serious attention . . . to the political potential of more popular forms such as . . . rock music." [6]

The new wave of young women making rock music in the 1990s, whether on independent or corporate labels, has similarly had no truck with postmodern notions that popular music, given its commerciality, can only be subversive by being "deadpan, indifferent, depersonalized, [and] effaced, . . . effectively cancel[ing] the possibility of traditional audience identification." [7] The new female rockers have tried like hell, instead, to open up a new way of living for hordes of young women—basically the refusal to be a victim of gendering that feminists have long sought, but breaking with the elders' intellectual-literary bent by making self-creation a more exciting and attractive matter than studiously absorbing feminist tracts or spinning out *écriture féminine* for literary theorists. Instead, groups like Bikini Kill, says Sandy Carter, defy "traditional roles and images open to women while simultaneously slashing through doctrinaire notions of feminism." The members of the British group Huggy Bear "see Riot Grrrl as connecting theory with action, connecting feminism with nothing less than the urge to live. . . . The music, the literature, the hanging out—all reveal this relentless urge, the speed and seriousness of this impulsion. A call to any girl open to it." [8]

At first, though, the Riot Grrrl movement existed primarily "in the minds of a handful of boho progeny with access to copy machines and feminist reading lists," such as Kathleen Hanna writing in *Jigsaw* (which was founded by Bikini Kill drummer Tobi Vail), and Allison Wolfe and Molly Neuman of Bratmobile, publishers of *Girl Germs*.[9] (Organized groups such as Riot Grrrl NYC emerged about two years after the public attention the first wave received in 1991.) Riot Grrrl feminism is hardly a single platform, but "a crazy salad that mixes rhetoric from 1960s-style women's liberation, green politics, vegetarianism, Susan Faludi's *Backlash*, Naomi Wolf's *Beauty Myth* and other disparate sources." [10] The result is exemplified by Bikini Kill's "florid, pen-pal rhetoric, . . . an essential emotional and intellectual process primarily because it's so much *fun*: Revolution as everyday play; girls getting off on rock gestures and nonsense without ever *considering* boy consent." [11]

Musicians and audience have together overcome a problem the authors of *Emotion and Gender* recollect in their girlhoods: "There are very few examples where we as girls played to an audience of peers. . . . There was a collectivity of action in many of the young men's [activities] that was almost completely absent from the women's." We can see the significance, then, of women in rock music creating a "feminist public sphere" much like that advocated by Felski in her defense of feminists working through both the mass media and independent popular forms (like the fanzine): "*Internally*, it generates a gender-specific identity grounded in a consciousness of community and solidarity among women; *externally*, it seeks to convince society as a whole of the validity of feminist claims, challenging existing structures of authority." [12]

Kathleen Hanna describes just such a public sphere in the Riot Grrrl movement, which at a time "when *Time* or *Newsweek* said feminism was dead, around 1989, [told] girls who are not involved in tight feminist communities" that the possibility "*does* exist" and needs to keep being created. She feels that she achieved her original goal because "feminism really *is* cool now," and Andrea Juno likewise finds that the recent changes women have brought about in rock and roll "reflect the thriving and flowering of feminism, despite the perpetual media-pronounced deaths and backlashes" (and the death of rock has been refuted, as well, in the process). But as Candice Pedersen of K Records points out, Riot Grrrl continues to be important for its original function, as well, in simply providing young women "with a network that prevents them from thinking they're insane." The level of organization in the Riot Grrrl subculture is unusual in youth culture, in fact, belying all the "serious" politicos (such as Tom Frank and Adolph Reed) castigating the whole idea of popular cultural pastimes having political results. The subculture extends beyond the making of music and the creation of expressive subcultural styles, Gottlieb and Wald emphasize, "into the realms of political strategizing and continually re-rehearsed self-definition through fanzine publication." Ann Powers, a member of Strong Women in Music (or SWIM), notes that the new wave of women in rock has also affected the production end of the music business in the United States, with "women getting more involved at all levels," an essential development if the new prominence of women is to have a lasting impact. [13]

The music that young women have recently found most useful to forming an audience of other young women is punk rock, of course: The Riot Grrrl "movement is above all a triumph of punk." The Riot Grrrls and virtually every other new rock band featuring women

> say they owe their existence to punk's do-it-yourself ethic: if you have something to say, pick up a guitar, write a song and say it. "There's no way any of this could have happened if it wasn't for punk rock," says Molly Neuman, Bratmobile's 21-year-old drummer. [14]

Perhaps the best known of female rock critics (if one excludes Patti Smith for being better known as a performer), Ellen Willis, had written in 1977 "that she preferred the Sex Pistols to the women's music genre because 'music that boldly and aggressively laid out what the singer wanted, loved, hated . . . challenged me to do the same. [E]ven when the content was antiwoman, . . . the form encouraged my struggle for liberation.' " [15]

As Simon Frith and Angela McRobbie also noted at the time, in the 1978 essay "Rock and Sexuality," women in popular music before punk tended to take the role of the "singer/songwriter/folkie lady—long-haired, pure-voiced, self-accompanied on acoustic guitar"—and thus "reinforced in rock the qualities traditionally linked with female singers, sensitivity, passivity, and sweetness." Exceptions like Janis Joplin and Grace Slick found it necessary to "become 'one of the boys.' " (Whether "tomboyism" is actually a bad thing, we will see, is a hotly debated issue among present-day female rockers). Punk, given its do-it-yourself amateurism rejecting musical virtuosity, and especially its antiromance stance, allowed "female voices to be heard that are not often allowed expression on record, stage, or radio—shrill, assertive, impure" voices of "strident insistency" like those of the Pretenders' Chrissie Hynde (who worked in Malcolm McLaren's Sex shop, after which the Sex Pistols were named), Pauline Murray of Penetration, Siouxsee Sue of the Banshees, Poly Styrene of X-Ray Spex, and groups like the Raincoats and the Slits.[16] The Riot Grrrls are not simply a second coming of female punk, though, but "a new moment in this history," Gottlieb and Wald believe, moving well beyond the first wave of iconoclasts "playing back images of women" by adding "a deep sense of abuse and a stronger critique of patriarchy."

The hiatus between the trailblazers of the 1970s and the emergence of the female punk bands in 1991 accords with the submergence of punk, in popular attention, in the decade before Nirvana. But Gottlieb and Wald note that the successor to punk in the United States, hardcore music of the 1980s, was "aggressively masculinist" and often "resorted to blatant misogyny," to some extent disenfranchising women interested in punk music. (I would object that Exene Cervenka of X, who came out of the hardcore scene in Los Angeles, goes unmentioned in the article.) Gottlieb and Wald conclude nonetheless that the "potent combination" of anger and "frank expressions of sexuality" in punk has served to open "a fertile space both for women's feminist interventions and the politicization of sexuality and female identity." They also note an "incremental, progressive change" in the 1980s in the increasing number of female instrumentalists participating relatively equitably with males, such as Georgia Hubley of Yo La Tengo, as well as the godmother of Riot Grrrls, Kim Gordon.[17] (All the biggest bands in Austin, Texas, in the mid-1980s, such as Glass Eye, Grains of Faith, and the Reivers, seemed each to be made up of two men and two women.)

By the 1990s, says Carola Dibbell,

what had changed was not so much the issues, but who cared about them. In the 1970s a critical fringe had contemplated gender in punk, in the 1980s an academically hip media had debated Madonna's sexuality, but by the 1990s riot grrrls had helped make feminist issues, if not cool, at least impossible to ignore.[18]

I think it's safe to say as well that the fact it took more than a decade for female punk performers to coalesce into a broad-based phenomenon also indicates the continuing difficulty young women face in breaking with conventional expectations of femininity—which makes the breakthrough of female punks in the 1990s all the more exciting.

The results of women making punk rock are hardly appealing only to other women either. Greil Marcus, for example, agrees with female critics that the general effect has been a resuscitation of rock and roll by "the most vital and the most open punk music . . . heard in years." Few rockers "play music that genuinely challenges the dominant mind set of the pop audience," says Sandy Carter, and the "clearest and freshest exceptions to the rule are coming from rock women." Thus their "arrival signals serious change in the landscape," according to Ann Powers, offering "a different vision to fans: that of a woman setting a spark to herself." The enormous possibilities opened up by more than half of humanity finally making space for itself in rock music—hardly a small minority creating a fad—makes the "subtext . . . almost always the joy and liberation found in a woman's own act of expression." Andrea Juno likewise asserts that no one could be better suited to take over the image of rock and roll outlaw from exhausted "geriatric 'Rock Gods' " than women being "bold, brash, and loud, all the things they were taught not to be." The sheer exhilaration created by punk women leads Elizabeth Wurtzel (author of *Prozac Nation*) to say simply that "Women playing hard-and-fast rock music do bring something to the style that is different from—and often, I think, better than—what the men, who have been doing it forever bring," without feeling compelled to specify what that "something" is.[19]

Revolution girl-style is quite thrilling not just for critics but for many males in the audience, too; I have become a compulsive buyer of punk (or quasi-punk) music by women. The rock audience in general, says Carter, "seems increasingly willing to accept the fact that women can create hard, exciting guitar [and vocal] sounds on [a] par with their male peers."[20] Female performers are just more interesting, their discoveries more relevant, in my own case, to my desire to

discover similarly pissed-off people with new ways of speaking and singing—
and in the best cases, with a sense of humor about themselves. As my last chapter
argues, men and women are not all that dissimilar in their anger nor in the
possibilities their voices hold. This is especially true for younger persons: One
of the few instances in postmodern theory of any belief in new progressive social
forces derives from feminist psychoanalytic work on incomplete "Oedipaliza-
tion"—or an incomplete entry into patriarchy and masculinity (see Chapter
3)—which finds that "the contemporary boy [is] in [a] developmental position
that looks much like that traditionally characteristic of little girls." [21]

In light of the broad appeal of the new wave of women in rock, it's
understandable that the Riot Grrrl label is actually seen by many female
musicians as a way of pigeonholing them as a novelty or a specialty item or,
when they succeed on a larger level, incorporating them as a fad. (Thus I've
mostly been using terms like "women making punk rock"; Andrea Juno's title
*Angry Women in Rock* is another suitably broad rubic.) With increasing attention
from establishment media and the music press, in fact, adherents of the Riot
Grrrl movement launched a nationwide media blackout in late 1992. Bikini Kill
even felt compelled to disavow the Riot Grrrl label: In the liner notes to *The
C.D. Version of the First Two Records,* Bikini Kill insists that it is not "the
definitive 'riot girl band,' [nor] in any way 'leaders of' or authorities on the 'Riot
Grrrl' movement. . . . Tho we totally respect those who still feel that label is
important and meaningful to them, we have never used that term to describe
ourselves *as a band.*" Bikini Kill does add, however, that its members "subscribe
to a variety of different aesthetics, strategies, and beliefs, both political and
punk-wise, some of which are probably considered 'riot girl.' " Because the term
"Riot Grrrl" doesn't give total offense, I've used it freely throughout my book.
But in doing so I risk appearing to incorporate the subject into "the male-defined
spaces of academia and academic discourse," another form of "recuperation"
that has met with resistance by Riot Grrrls. (I trust that my account of the Riot
Grrrls, set in the larger context of validating anger and given my excitement at
their music, doesn't seem like "exploitation, trivialization, and tourism.") From
their point of view, report Gottlieb and Wald, even "left or feminist" intellectual
work has a "cultural centrality" that threatens to appropriate the ability of the
Riot Grrrls to speak for themselves "as a marginal group."

But in resisting an "undifferentiated 'mainstream,' " Gottlieb and Wald
argue, "Riot Grrrl risks setting itself up in opposition to the status quo" with the
same "elitism [as] independent music generally." As in the aesthetic tradition
running from romanticism to postmodernism, rejecting the popular may simply
serve to "preclude the possibility of having a broad cultural or political impact."

Resisting popularity also seems belated in this case, for the mass-circulation magazine *Sassy* has already been instrumental in popularizing the Riot Grrrl movement. *Sassy*, moreover, treated it with "respect and even commitment," hardly diluting Riot Grrrl ideology, another good reason to question postmodern notions about the complete ideological incorporation of deviant subcultures by commercial popularity: "The media, beyond its function to control and contain this phenomenon, may also have helped to perpetuate" and encourage it in a relatively positive fashion.[22] This is not unprecedented, either; in *Pop Practices/ Subcultural Articulations* (1994), Van Cagle documents how Andy Warhol and camp sensibility were transmitted by the mass media (unwittingly in this case) to gender-bending rockers such as David Bowie and their followers in the glam subculture—an important precursor to Riot Grrrl work on gender, in fact, argue Gottlieb and Wald. Kathleen Hanna confirms the potential usefulness of the media in her account of lying in an early interview about Riot Grrrl chapters having cropped up in several cities and finding a year later that young women in those cities had gone looking for the groups, couldn't find them, and decided to create their own. ("It's *totally* Situationist," she concludes.)[23]

The 1992 media blackout also risks endorsing the perception that feminine agency in popular music can never overcome co-optation, which in the hands of male critics becomes a source of ridicule (see Jon Pareles in Chapter 4). Women are assumed, not without reason, to have little choice in the matter of selling out because they have long been commodities, or linked to commodities in advertising, and thus have little or no distance from commercial culture to relinquish. The problem with acceding too easily to the view that women are deeply embedded in the production of mass culture can be seen in its most extreme form: the misogyny with which elitist critics, such as Theodor Adorno bewailing castration by jazz, have traditionally cast the supposedly pacifying effect of mass culture as the threat of feminization.

Even from a less extreme perspective, the best that can presumably be said of a commercial success such as Madonna is simply that she has been "in charge" of her own selling-out process. These terms have been used to describe male performers, too, especially the early Rolling Stones and the Sex Pistols. But there has always been a sense that these male exemplars combined an exposé of selling out with an undiminished, blisteringly caustic outrage. Madonna, in contrast, can only manipulate conventional expectations of feminine sexuality to little or no subversive end, leaving a large part of the audience completely oblivious to any feminist component in her work.

Many female performers understandably resist consignment to this fate by disavowing Madonna. Chrissie Hynde wonders "why people pay such tribute" to Madonna for having "kicked open doors," when at best "she was a great disco queen." Although Courtney Love is often described as building on Madonna's legacy of overt sexuality (a legacy Gottlieb and Wald read into the Riot Grrrl movement as well), Love pointedly distances herself in observing that Madonna's dance music "has always sucked." Liz Phair, on the other hand—whom Hynde does consider important—cites Madonna as a precursor, and I know from personal experience that many Riot Grrrl followers despise Phair for capitalizing, however ironically, on physical attractiveness. Phair wonders, as a result, how "you get away with this kind of thing," if "you vote *for* sex and yet *against* sexism." [24] The thought has undoubtedly crossed Madonna's mind, too, but I find Phair's parody of the Rolling Stones on *Exile in Guyville* more compelling than Madonna's incessant mining of whatever's cutting edge in black culture, which bell hooks execrates in *Black Looks* (1992).

As the example of Liz Phair indicates, there might be some ground in between Madonna's overexposure (in more than one sense) and a media blackout. Rather than resisting commercial incorporation so strenuously, could women not highlight it, just as men have done, while remaining rebel rock—the classic punk formula? Kathleen Hanna endorses the original "press block" as necessary to getting the Riot Grrrl movement off the ground with some authentic roots, but she also resists a permanent adherence to the romantic rejection of commerce: "Getting trapped in little circles of shame and blame isn't going . . . to make corporations or co-optation go away." (Valerie Agnew of 7 Year Bitch criticizes another self-defeating exclusionary practice, the refusal of some women at Riot Grrrl shows to give fanzines to men, which just "takes you back ten steps.")[25]

The primary problem in discussing the Riot Grrrl movement, finally, is simply that it doesn't encompass the music of the wide range of groups and individuals that can be roughly lumped together as women playing punk rock, angry women in rock, or whatever. "When it comes to women in music," says Wurtzel, "one size certainly does not fit all." The diversity of the musicians whom I've actually heard and could have examined indicates that "generalizations about them [are] difficult if not ridiculous," as Ann Powers puts it[26]:

| | |
|---|---|
| Babes in Toyland | Joan Jett |
| Belly | L7 |
| Bikini Kill | Lunachicks |
| Bratmobile | Mecca Normal |
| Breeders | Liz Phair |
| Concrete Blonde | Pork |

| | |
|---|---|
| Elastica | Red Aunts |
| Fluffy | Scrawl |
| Kim Gordon | 7 Year Bitch |
| P. J. Harvey | Siren |
| Juliana Hatfield | Slant 6 |
| Heavenly | Sleater-Kinney |
| Heavens to Betsy | Team Dresch |
| Hole | Throwing Muses |
| Huggy Bear | Veruca Salt |

I spent a lot of time listening continuously to everything by all of them, which was a bad idea, in part because I wound up preferring the poppier ones for being easier to take in large doses than the straightforwardly angry, screaming ones.

I think that the single best song *about* anger may nonetheless really be Veruca Salt's MTV hit "Seether," sung by Nina Gordon and Louise Post (also the guitarists), who have nice high-pitched "feminine" voices, setting up a jarring chasm of a contradiction with their account of the monster "at the center of it all," their seething anger, which they just can't seem to "cram back" in their mouths. Derided as pop, rip-offs of the Breeders and others, the "lovely daughters" in Veruca Salt are the most subversive *and* the most enjoyable to listen to of the whole lot—by my standards. Among the new wave of women in rock, moreover, Gordon and Post are virtually unique in openly declaring themselves feminists: "I hope the term 'post-feminism' will become obsolete when people start recognizing that there is nothing 'post' about feminism," says Post.[27] I agree with music critics, though, that the most significant performer in the long run is likely to be P. J. Harvey, whose invocation of the whole of popular music's history on *To Bring You My Love* does suggest a genius at work. Harvey's voice bends gender (as well as race), though—a British woman in her early 20s singing, at times, like Howling Wolf—and thus Courtney Love of Hole "may be the first [female rock performer] to demand the audience's total immersion in a woman's world."[28]

This devotion to the "total" world of women has led Love to attack "fascistic" musicians and critics who draw lines between female performers (although Love later mocked Riot Grrrls as "estrogen lemmings").[29] She is particularly incensed by accusations of "assimilationism," a term used by Kathleen Hanna to criticize tomboy groups like L7 who are "trying to just fit in" with male musicians.[30] (I think L7 deserves more credit than this, too; its best-known song, "Pretend We're Dead," rewrites *Society of the Spectacle* as a catchy pop song—no mean feat.) Love may be sensitive on this account because she, too, invites the assimilationist charge, if for a different reason: her professed desire to demonstrate to young women that expressing virulent anger does not preclude being conventionally attractive, even sexy if not oversexed—that being a feminist doesn't mean one couldn't make it as a woman. Hanna is no absolutist, though, having worked with Joan Jett, who is often mentioned in the same breath with L7. I should note that I'm reading political differences out of more publicized personal ones: Hanna and Love came to blows at a Lollapalooza show in 1995 after Hanna reportedly antagonized Love with cracks about her fitness to raise her daughter by the late Kurt Cobain. Hanna knew Cobain before Nirvana became famous—her graffiti, in most accounts, having supplied him with the title of his breakthrough single "Smells Like Teen Spirit"—and the hostility between her and Love apparently stems from that earlier relationship.

With respect to the politics of music, Love's argument for inclusiveness has been strongly seconded by Evelyn McDonnell: To dismiss "L7 for simply doing what boys do [is] an underestimation of tomboyism woefully au courant among cultural feminists. The point of . . . 'female machisma' is not simply to emulate and assimilate, but to invade men's exclusive realms of privilege and freedom." [31] Besides, as Rita Felski points out, there has really never been any form of expression, including musical genres, that can be said to be distinctly gendered, or inherently masculine or feminine. Rather than worrying about such classification, we should recognize an important achievement on the part of all the female performers listed above: For women to play and sing through the same forms dominated by men is inherently a form of resistance, refusing to accept the definition of woman as the male's subordinate "Other." This is true in terms not only of the voice, Gottlieb and Wald note, but also of the guitar: "something potentially radical happens when women appropriate [an] instrument . . . tirelessly resurrected [as] signifying male power and virtuosity, the legitimate expression of phallic sexuality, perversity (Jimi Hendrix), and violence (Pete Townshend)." [32]

If women making music derived from punk do have something in common, for all their diversity, my listening to them en masse was a big mistake nonetheless. The problem was not just that the more strident performers wear thin, though, but also that I was lining them up and knocking them down in just the way Georgia Christgau describes as typical of male rock critics:

> The way men are men and men are critics is that they're really into the stats. [T]hey know the facts about the band, and they know their discographies, and they know everything everybody else has written about somebody. I think

especially the more academic ones have a host of comparisons they can make between artists. I feel like all of that's very male. It's a competitive, aggressive way to look at an individual artist.

Will Straw adds that "connoisseurship"—establishing masculine authority by "tracking down old albums, learning genealogical links between bands, and so on"—remains prevalent even in alternative rock, supposedly more receptive to female musicians.[33] But I have to object that I have known at least a few women who were widely considered archival resources on alternative and other musical genres, and especially that my female students find the whole argument inexplicable—if they like a band, they find out more about it. To argue that women are not aficionados, worse still, replicates the self-defeating if well-intentioned essentialism that portrays women as intuitive, nonintellectual, and devoid of any concern with mastery of knowledge. But I suspect, finally, that the dramatic changes in the participation of women in rock, following the Riot Grrrl breakthrough, have already rendered the issue moot for a new generation of young women.

Christgau is right, however, in the respect that a comprehensive comparative survey, academic or otherwise, is a deadening way to go at popular music—I didn't enjoy the music much when I listened to it in long, compulsory sittings. Thus I actually felt relief rather than shame in considering her own approach: "I consciously try not to compare artists to other artists. I just try to describe what it is that I see and feel and think that the artist is trying to say to me as a member of the audience." [34] A "new feminist music criticism" in academia, as well, wishes to shift attention from musical description to "the perspective of the listener/fan [who] actively engages in the construction of the meaning of a vocal performance." [35] Emboldened by this development, and especially by Christgau's disgust at comparison-and-contrast games, I'm not going to issue half-assed personal judgments on the whole array of angry girl bands nor recapitulate journalistic overviews. Considering how widely known women playing punk have become, as evidenced by the attention of *The New Yorker* (Wurtzel), the *New York Times* (Powers), and other periodicals, no one needs another gloss by me anyway.

Instead, I'm only going to deal with a single song by Bikini Kill, "Carnival," the subject with which I began my book. The appeal of "Carnival" is obvious enough: it blasts along at a speed dance-music fans (who live for bpms, or beats per minute) would be hard-pressed to keep up with, as drummer Tobi Vail repeatedly forces the tempo with double-time and rolls. Like all great punk songs, "Carnival" attacks the viscera through a roller coaster ride, up and down, between two chords (if a different pair in the chorus than in the verses). In keeping with the two-chord minimalism, guitarist Billy Karren, the token boy, plays a hilarious two-note guitar solo. The song only lasts less than a minute and a half before collapsing in an exhausted heap; no one could possibly sustain the energy, musician or audience. Hanna's vocal is simultaneously blasé and cele- bratory (as ambiguous as the song's content, we'll see) and supplies a rhythmic counterpoint—a melody, even—over the band's unvaried thrashing.

Most angry girl bands are in fact "pop rock," or melodic; Bikini Kill "rarely *just* 'rock.' " [36] The sound may be harsh, but female punks are not averse to caring about songwriting and finding hooks. This is not to suggest they're compromised in any way; the frequent combination of "pop" vocal stylings from girl groups of the 1960s with punk arrangements, for example, is intended to set up the same contradictions between prettiness and hardness found in "Seether." It doesn't hurt the simultaneously catchy and abrasive effect of "Carnival," either, that Kathleen Hanna accidentally has a perfect nonvirtuoso voice of yowling authenticity, which has made her stand out in the same unpredictable, unlikely way that Poly Styrene did in 1977. When Hanna sings "When you get right down to the heart of the matter" in "This Is Not a Test," I believe that's what's happening. Marcus could once say of Bikini Kill, as a result, that "this stuff is so primitive and so raw and so direct that you could almost imagine that this is where punk began, and the Sex Pistols heard this stuff and made something a little more shapely out of it." [37] But judging from the attention to melody and hooks on *Reject All American* (1996)—pop qualities embraced by Sleater- Kinney, as well, on *Call the Doctor* (1996)—Bikini Kill has apparently under- taken just such a remodeling in an effort to enlarge its audience.

That's all by way of "musicology" that I intend to offer, for the reasons spelled out at the end of the previous chapter. As to what "Carnival" is *about,* after the preceding chapter I'm obviously loath to dwell on lyrical content. So it should be understood throughout what follows that the meaning—or different meanings—that make the song great art lie in the intersection of the lyrics with the emotional and musical performance. (That harmony of form and content is something of a classical ideal but includes an avant-garde emphasis that the expressive discoveries in the form or technique matter most, if one is going to make people sit up and take notice of what one has to say.) Rather than immediately peeling away the lyrics, moreover, I'd rather explain the song by telling a story about what happened when I played "Carnival" at an academic colloquium.

Like all great rock songs, according to Fats Domino's theory of mumbling and transmitters of it such as Mick Jagger and Greil Marcus, "Carnival" provides only a few intelligible lyrics, just enough to give the listener a vague start on figuring out what's going on. Hanna makes a point of doing this, in fact, in a spoken introduction over just a drumbeat, in which she describes the "seedy underbelly" of the carnival, "the part that only the kids know about," where 16-year-old girls give "head to carnies for free rides and hits of pot." As the song revs up, the last intelligible bit after this fairly horrific picture of vulgarity and abuse immediately complicates matters: Hanna doesn't decry the scenario, as one might expect, but instead declares "I wanna go to the carnival," too, as if she wants in on the action.

The move, at first listen, invites the response it got as soon as the panel I was on had finished. A female graduate student from the English department simply said "I find that song very disturbing." The words are engraved on my brain because they put me seriously on the spot, although they shouldn't have: "Carnival" was disturbing to her, I am quite certain, because she assumed Hanna eagerly wanted to be defiled by carnies. The assumption, in other words, is that performers of popular music, unlike the literary, are to be taken absolutely literally because they are incapable of complexity, ambiguity, parody, and other traditional shibboleths of literary criticism.

I couldn't say any of this, in part, admittedly, because it didn't all occur to me right away, but also because I was stunned and embarrassed by the clear implication that I was insensitively and uncritically, even vicariously exulting in a song that glorifies the sexual abuse and self-degradation of adolescent females. I suspect the motive was a reflexive fault-finding with men not uncommon among academic feminists—not that I blame them, but if the further inference was that I had no business discussing Riot Grrrls in the first place, I would have to object that identity politics doesn't work with regard to tastes in popular music. What I wish I'd said about "Carnival" itself is that it is, in fact, about as ambiguous a work of art as William Empson (author of the classic *Seven Types of Ambiguity*) could hope for.

I want to dwell on that ambiguity, on the possible explanations for why a tale of degradation leads to celebration, desire, and a little ennui as well, because we wind up with an appreciation of the significance not just of angry girl bands but of the best popular music in any genre. In dwelling on the possibilities in understanding "Carnival," mind you, I am not arguing for the complexity of the song itself, or that it rewards intense inspection and interpretation just like a literary text. The reasons for the meanings I make of it are not hard to detect, for one thing. If I elaborate them at some length, the point is to demonstrate that the real complexity of simple popular songs lies in the meanings and uses people can make of them, with myself as illustration. As Georgia Christgau would have it, I'm going to stick to my own impression of what the artists are trying to get me to see and feel and think; I'm sure it's not completely idiosyncratic, and hopefully it will add at least a little to the experience of other listeners, as useful criticism has always done.

I don't want to seem oblivious to the sociological question of how Bikini Kill is understood by a variety of members of its audience, however, because some cases may indeed offer reasons to be "disturbed." As I was writing this, a female undergraduate complained about young women she knows who sleep around indiscriminately while professing to be followers of Bikini Kill and Hole and thus to exercise a new, radical self-assertion. I don't mean to deny this possibility; sexual freedom as advocated by 1960s-style feminism is certainly expressed by some angry young female performers such as Courtney Love, though more in her self-presentation than in her songs, like "Asking For It," which hardly suggest that sex is always good. But if the Riot Grrrls are understood by some young women, apparently, to offer a glamorous rationale for being used quite traditionally by young men, we have a situation that does resemble Foucault's "repressive hypothesis," or the mistake of equating the unleashing of sexuality with social liberation, when one may only wind up subjected all the more. This is the age of AIDS, moreover, and one may wind up dead, as well.

For me, at any rate, there are at least three ways to take "Carnival," if one pays any attention at all to the song itself and knows something about Bikini Kill's general approach. The most direct understanding would likely be that "Carnival" confronts us with sexual abuse. Making listeners face unpleasant realities about sex and violence is a staple of Riot Grrrl subject matter, part of the whole confrontational approach including Hanna scrawling SLUT on her belly (more specifically a parody of Madonna's "Boy Toy" phase). Considering that Hanna has worked in battered women's shelters, was raped (by her own account in an interview with Andrea Juno), may have been a victim of parental abuse (but "that's for *me* to know," she tells Juno), and objects to songs based on those experiences being "framed as part of a victim or a freak show," [38] she would hardly mindlessly glory in wantonness, as the graduate student at the colloquium was disturbed to discern.

"Carnival" certainly seems to establish some linkage between its spoken introduction and the song, if one cheats and consults the lyric sheet: Hanna sings repeatedly about the carnival costing $16, through a sort of numerology, apparently, echoing the opening invocation of 16-year-old girls who can't afford rides. If she does take the role of willing participant, though, at first glance a puzzling and even shocking move, Hanna accomplishes more than just putting the subject matter all the more directly in our faces; above all, she refuses to condemn other women, eschewing the lofty, judgmental view of a detached observer. In the fanzine *Jigsaw,* Hanna expresses admiration even for the "big haired makeup girl," more than likely the kind in "Carnival" who wears plastic boots "that go way up to there," especially when she performs an act of solidarity like alerting others as to which men are date rapists.[39]

Hanna may even be playing an edgy game by championing "sluts" for doing what they want—the gusto of the performance has something to do with being bad, although definitely not everything. (Having worked as a stripper, Hanna particularly wants "other women who work in the sex industry to remember that we can be . . . writers, musicians, [or] artists" as well.[40]) I say "edgy" particularly because such celebration invites opportunistic listeners to find justification for careless sex. (For all their personal and political differences, she and Courtney Love resemble each other in this respect—as their pairing by some promiscuous teenage girls seems to indicate—although Hanna certainly doesn't make sexual voraciousness such a central part of her persona.) The Bikini Kill anthem "Rebel Girl," for example (rerecorded with Joan Jett for added punch), concerns a woman whom everyone says is a slut, but when she talks, Hanna hears the revolution, and even in the sluttish way she walks "there's revolution" in her hips—which Hanna can taste in her kiss as well, tossing bisexuality into the whole confrontational stew. "Carnival," though, in its lyrics, expresses little if any sense of rebelliousness; the sometimes jaded tone of the vocal, accordingly, may indicate a certain abjectness to the whole business.

Either in addition to or instead of a celebration of wanton women, "Carnival" might also be taken at a second, larger level as a parody. The target of the parody is not only conventional notions about sluts but also the whole process of gendering, or constructing femininity. This "parodic use and abuse of mass-culture representations of women subvert[s] them by excess, irony, and fragmented recontextualization," says Linda Hutcheon (whose work on parody predates Judith Butler's better known *Gender Trouble,* which is less interested in political coherence). But if a song like "Carnival" may be ironic about its fragmentary subject matter, that doesn't mean it's endorsing postmodern theory, which takes irony as a simple destabilizing of meaning through the tactic of being in two places at once. Irony in this sense lies not just in the difference between what one says and what one means but also in the difference between the external world from which one draws one's subjects and the internal world of art in which they're recontextualized—and typically demoted, as in romanticism and modernism, beneath freeplay with form. That is not the only possibility for irony, however: "It is interesting," Hutcheon finds, "that few commentators on postmodernism actually use the word 'parody' " as well, which suggests that they can't allow that irony sometimes has definite political results.

Parody may work through irony, but in reproducing (or imitating) common sense about a group like women, it proposes an alternative view that one is supposed to prefer to what's being parodied rather than just remaining suspended between the two. That distinct alternative is an exposé of "the *politics* of representation [and] the entire representational process." When one of my students says the cacophony of angry music captures the way the whole culture sounds to him, he has just this sweeping sort of parody in mind. In waking us up more specifically to the artificiality and falsehood of stereotypes about different groups, Nirvana's *Nevermind,* starting with the album title itself, is a parody of conventional wisdom about the apathy and passivity of postmodern youths, including such views among young people themselves. Even gangsta rap does something very similar to grunge and the Riot Grrrls: The face it presents to white audiences, at least, seems to parody the hysterical mainstream images of urban black youths that substitute for any concern for their deprivation—they're presumably only depraved, instead. That gangsta-rap performers sometimes feel compelled to live out their subject matter suggests that even artists, let alone the uninitiated, don't always get the point. (Tupac Shakur died after being shot just as I was completing this book, although the violence around him had come to have less to do with his "Thug Life" than with the rivalry between the hip-hop business empires on the east and west coasts.)

Such misunderstandings occur because parody, by imitating conventional representations, is partially complicit with them and is only going to reinforce such images for many people. But Hutcheon makes an exception for feminist art that parodies conventions of femininity because it is "not content with exposition" but has the ultimate purpose of "real social change" always in sight. This political intent distinguishes feminist parody from postmodernism, which "has not theorized agency" (but only what prevents it, power), and thus must be resisted. "While feminists may use postmodern parodic strategies, . . . they never suffer from [a] confusion of political agenda" [41] in which the complicity obscures the critique, as detractors claim about postmodernism's poster girl, Madonna, whom Andrea Juno calls "mainstream and synthesized." [42] The best feminist artists are fully aware at all times that they are parodying conventions of female representation and the processes by which various media propagate them. (Whether the audience gets the joke, of course, is always a sticking point.)

Hutcheon's distinction of feminist work from other forms of postmodern parody may seem somewhat arbitrary, but her claim that feminists are more lucid in their politics holds up in the case of the Riot Grrrls. Simply "reclaiming the word 'girl' " in the first place, Gottlieb and Wald point out, "and reinvesting it with new meaning within their own feminist punk vernacular has proved one of the most salient aspects of the riot grrrl revolution." They describe that "recuperation of patriarchal language"—of the diminution of women in the word *girl*—as parody with serious connotations, including "a nostalgia for . . . close relationships between girls prior to the intrusion of heterosexual romance." Above all, though, "the riot grrrls, in rewriting 'girl' as 'grrrl,' also incorporate anger, defiance, and rebellion into their self-definition." [43]

Writing in *Jigsaw* in spring 1991, when "Carnival" was being recorded, Hanna expresses a consciousness of working against precisely the stereotyping, or "cardboard cutouts," generated by the entire representational process. At first she sounds postmodern, contrasting the real "world of constant flux" with the artificiality of "some forever identity." But what she actually means is that "Jigsaw Youth" first have to break with learned identities like gender, the "boxes and labels" targeted by feminist parody, and then they can put together the puzzle pieces of a more authentic, although never static identity out of the "fucked-up culture" of parents and "TV people," the real chaos. "It seems like it will never come together," she says, "but it can and it does and it will," a distinctly *anti*-postmodern sentiment. [44]

One commentator on Bikini Kill, Charles Aaron, finds that "they sneer, you know, *compassionately,* and spit in the pale, male face of the Generation X cliché, possessed by a radical desire to 'do' something." [45] Placing the word *do* in quotation marks may be intended as a form of condescension akin to the theory of *ressentiment*—an insinuation that Bikini Kill is confined to passion, unable to act on its anger. Whatever Aaron's intent, he captures precisely the point of Bikini Kill, that anger and the passion for change are powerful forces in themselves. Hanna, for example, sums up her whole project in simple terms of feelings: "I am not afraid to say things matter to me." She chides cliques driven instead by a hipness, mythologized by Douglas Coupland in *Generation X,* that tries "to dictate . . . what is and what isn't cool or revolutionary or resistance," a fallacy characteristic of postmodern disdain for angry, defiant music. "Just because someone is not resisting in the same way you are"—because he or she values feelings over your ideology, for instance—"does not mean they are not resisting," a point lost on intellectuals. "Resistance is everywhere," Hanna believes; "it always has been and always will be [among] Jigsaw Youth, listening, strategizing, tolerating, screaming, confronting, fearless." [46]

This impassioned advocacy, including but going well beyond the element of parody, is the last and most profound sense in which I understand "Carnival." The song's greatest resonance for me has everything to do with the music and virtually nothing to do with the words except for the title, the sort of keyword that Mick Jagger and Greil Marcus theorize about. I take "Carnival" most fundamentally to be a complete reversal of the dire, depressive effect of the opening subject matter, in a celebration of young women liberating themselves not only from abuse but in a much larger respect, summed up in the use of "carnival" as a metaphor for the whole breakthrough of the Riot Grrrls and angry girl bands.

Most of the original Riot Grrrls were college students, and I have a sneaking suspicion someone in Bikini Kill knows about Mikhail Bakhtin, one reason I've been invoking his work throughout my book. (After I'd finished, in fact, one of my female undergraduates noticed the Bikini Kill/Bakhtin connection without any prompting from me.) What I haven't taken up until now is his concept of *carnival,* which a number of academics, such as Natalie Davis, Teresa Ebert, Nancy Fraser, Mary Russo, and Robert Stam, find promising for feminism, like Bakhtin's general materialism, or his argument (like Hanna) that a social contest is always occurring in the emotional inflection of language. Bakhtin refers to a "material *bodily* principle" (emphasis added), in his description of carnival as "grotesque realism," but he has feelings in mind as much as the body, specifically an antiauthoritarian attitude.[47] As in feminist philosophy, his bodies are the meeting point of affect and intellect—expressive, intelligent bodies capable of challenging authority, unlike the mute, dominated bodies described in postmodern theory.

As Stam sums it up, carnival "is more than a party or a festival; it is the oppositional culture of the oppressed, a countermodel of cultural production and desire" like the feminist public sphere created by the Riot Grrrls, in which "all that is marginalized and excluded . . . takes over the center." Especially by advancing the unruly or disorderly woman, says Davis, the function of carnival in early modern Europe was "first, to widen behavioral options for women, . . . and second, to sanction riot and political disobedience for both men and women in a society that allowed the lower orders few formal means of protest"—a description obviously meant to pertain to the present.[48]

Bakhtin most extensively develops his concept of carnival in *Rabelais and His World,* which was written in the 1930s but unpublished until 1965 (and fairly quickly translated into English in 1968). Taken at face value, the book concerns the High Middle Ages; it couldn't be published for three decades, however, because the book is an allegory repudiating not only the insipid version of folk culture that Stalin's minions encouraged, reducing the folk to the decorative arts, but also the general authoritarianism of Stalinism.

Bakhtin's description of carnivals in medieval marketplaces clearly has something larger in mind: "During carnival there is a temporary suspension of all hierarchic distinctions and barriers among men"—and women, we obviously need to add—and of the "prohibitions of usual life." The result of this "world upside down" is a "new type of communication [that] creates new forms of speech or a new meaning given to the old forms"—like rock and roll—"impossible in ordinary life." The context of the "marketplace" clearly suggests work in contemporary mass culture; an opponent of modernist literary elitism (as evidenced by his attack on Russian Formalism), Bakhtin is well aware that references by aesthetes to their loathing of the market, commerce, and so on, always connoted mass culture. In the process of assaulting decorum, carnival is very specifically an assertion of the powers of mass culture against the contempt of official culture, not only high culture but also the mass media, which constantly insist on their own banality. The poet's pose of superiority is attacked by mixing up the sacred and the profane—making a montage out of them, in other words, along lines similar to those laid out by Walter Benjamin—as in the Riot Grrrls' combination of feminist intellectual work and rock and roll. Carnival works with mass culture, instead, to challenge its admittedly largely oppressive contents with "dynamic expression . . . opposed to all that was ready-made and completed"—such as identity, as Hanna describes it—and "to all pretense at immutability," or the usual instruction in the mass media, emotional as well as ideological, that the status quo is forever, whether Stalinism or capitalism.

As one might expect, academic postmodernists have a simplistic, knee-jerk response to any optimistic reference to carnival: It's all "authorized transgression," or part of the closed circuit organized by power, whether in the medieval period or the present. Bakhtin himself, supposedly, inadvertently demonstrates this in depicting the medieval carnival as a permitted release of energy. In fact, he takes pains to resist such a view, contrasting carnival with officially sanctioned feasts that "did not lead people out of the existing world order" but "asserted all that was stable, unchanging, perennial," precisely what carnival opposes.[49] The unleashing of energy in carnival, moreover, had a long preexistence that the diminished official festivals of the Middle Ages could never suppress. If carnival has at times been a tool of the powerful, says Stam, used only to "channel energies that might otherwise fuel popular revolt, it has just as often been the case that carnival has been the object of official repression," out of fear of the dangers it poses.[50]

In contrasting carnival and official feasts, to read this matter into the present, Bakhtin in essence distinguishes good and bad outcomes in mass culture, like his contemporaries in the 1930s, Walter Benjamin and Bertolt Brecht. The mass media, Stam points out, do offer ersatz, "weak or truncated forms of carnival" that trivialize its "utopian promise," such as patriotic celebrations, icon-worshipping rock shows, and "festive soft-drink commercials."[51] But that is hardly the whole story, and it takes a willfully ignorant postmodern theorist to insist that only a negative outcome is possible. Umberto Eco, for example, echoes Derrida, Foucault, Lyotard, and others in declaring that "the law" is always "overwhelmingly present at the moment of its violation" in carnival.[52] Carnivalesque attacks on authority, through mass-culture forms like rock music, presumably only serve to drain away rebellious energies. This postmodern view, as always, is nothing more than the hoary elitism of Nietzsche, belittling the disenchanted for not immediately having a revolution. Bakhtin's theory of carnival, though, actually owes a good deal to Nietzsche's description of Dionysian festivity in *The Birth of Tragedy* (1872). Both contrast "a stifling official culture with a vital unofficial one" based in collective folk rites of physical exuberance, Stam points out. The crucial difference is that Bakhtin is a populist, preferring the masses to the "finer sensibilities" of "higher souls" that Nietzsche opposes to the "herd." [53]

Bakhtin's inversion of Nietzsche, in this respect, is much like Benjamin's recasting of *ressentiment* as a virtue. And, also much like Benjamin, Bakhtin proposes this populism to the avant-garde, or movements trying to integrate art and everyday life: Carnival is similarly defined as "the borderline between art and life," or "life itself, but shaped according to a certain pattern of play," namely that found in the best of mass culture and its popular audience. Bakhtin opposes the "aesthetics of the beautiful" of romanticism and modernism, again like Benjamin, for leading to "a private 'chamber' character," or veneration of the isolated artist in the garret. Romanticism "cut down" grotesque realism and its parody of official culture to "cold irony"—and here we find the roots of postmodernism (see Chapter 3 on Franco Moretti). Bakhtin actually draws a contrast between the "Romantic tradition," including modernism, and the "realist grotesque" art of none other than Bertolt Brecht, who was busy at the time incorporating popular music and other "bad new" forms into the theater, an approach Bakhtin commends as reflecting "the direct influence of carnival forms."

The bad new forms of speech that empower "the people" in carnival, Bakhtin specifies, are comic compositions, specifically parodies, combined with "various genres of billingsgate," or "curses, oaths," and other "abusive language" directed at people with power. This is a matter of collective activity, of individuals celebrating their unification through a regenerated social identity and purpose. Marketplace speech permits "no distance between those who come in contact with each other," liberating them "from norms of etiquette and decency," a formulation clearly pertinent to women. People are thereby "reborn for new, purely [and truly] human relations," [54] for a new life, even, much as

Bikini Kill once wrote in a fanzine that "this world doesn't teach us how to be truly cool to each other, and so we have to teach each other." [55]

The two essential forms of speech in carnival, parody and billingsgate, are of course abundantly apparent in Bikini Kill's own "Carnival." The song's parody of conventional representations of women, in particular, is exactly what Stam's contemporary rewriting of Bakhtin advocates: "By appropriating an existing discourse for its own ends, parody . . . assumes the force of the dominant discourse only to deploy that force, through a kind of artistic jujitsu, *against* domination." [56] Complicity in the form of parody, in other words, turns into critique, into the negation of conformist common sense.

Bakhtin's work on parody is most extensive in essays written at the same time as *Rabelais and His World* and collected in *The Dialogic Imagination* (trans. 1981). The clown and the fool, in carnival, "struggle against conventions, and against the inadequacy of all available life-slots to fit an authentic human being"—against the cardboard cutouts of static identity attacked by Kathleen Hanna. When an artist like Hanna dons the "mask" of the clown, and she's certainly clownish in "Carnival" in tempting us to think that she exults in abuse and vulgarity, she acquires the ability "to rip off [other] masks, . . . to rage at others," and "to betray to the public a personal life." Bakhtin's work, in other words, contains very nearly the whole Riot Grrl catalog: the exposé (or *parody*) of the whole process of feminine representation, the cultivation of the energy of anger (or *billingsgate*), and the revelation of personal experience according to the feminist commonplace that the personal is the political.

In ensuring that "no language could claim to be an authentic, incontestable face," the clown's parody is "aimed sharply and polemically against the official languages of its given time." [57] This antiauthoritarian emphasis in parody, in *Rabelais and His World,* leads directly on to the outright terms of billingsgate, or curses and oaths against authority. The combination of comic parody and angry billingsgate, moreover, is explicitly linked to negation. In a description of carnival laughter, stressing that billingsgate speech must have the clown's sense of humor about itself, we find a fundamental anarchism, which I want to take up in part because literary scholars argue endlessly and unhelpfully about whether Bakhtin's a Marxist, a good Orthodox Christian, and so forth.

His anarchism is apparent in his description of the "ambivalence" that results from the mixture of billingsgate speech, not in itself obscene, with "profanities and oaths." In the marketplace and its carnival atmosphere, obscenity "acquired the nature of laughter and became ambivalent." What Bakhtin actually means is that it became dialectical, and the dialectic he has in mind is Michael Bakunin's famous line that the destructive passion is the creative passion, which he derived from Georg Hegel's theory of negation and extended to include common sense about feelings as well as ideology. In the combination of anger and laughter, in Bakhtin's further derivation from Bakunin, "the element of negation" has a positive, regenerative outcome; the "degradation" of profane billingsgate, in "contact with earth," simultaneously brings "forth something more and better. [I]t has not only a *destructive negative* aspect, but also a regenerating one" (emphasis added). Something better—terms ridiculed by postmodernism, in fact, since at least Donald Barthelme's novel *Snow White* (1967)—appears when "primitive verbal functions" infused by "a general tone of laughter" (also scoffed at by postmodernism, as affect without meaning) become "sparks of the carnival bonfire which renews the world," or the social community.[58] The dialectic between anger and laughter, and its positive, regenerative outcome, is precisely what critics infected by cynical postmodernism are unable to comprehend. An article about the "bratty" punk group Green Day, for example, observes that music critics "still puzzle over the band's importance, citing joie de vivre as its only tenuous hold on the popular imagination." [59] Bakhtin's account of carnival laughter ought to make us skeptical of a perspective that appends the reductive terms *only* and *tenuous* to joie de vivre.

"Modern indecent abuse and cursing," unfortunately—and this remains true—"have retained dead and purely negative remnants of the grotesque concept of the body," Bakhtin notes. What we lack in particular is an "important trait of the people's festive laughter: that it is also directed at those who laugh." Bakhtin's description of the "satirist whose laughter is [only] negative, plac[ing] himself above the object of his mockery" seems to anticipate Rush Limbaugh, whose "humor" consists entirely of ridiculing people he believes inferior to himself and enlisting no one other than white males in his mean-spirited divisiveness. A properly "ambivalent" or dialectical laughter, aimed destructively at those with power and trying creatively to heal divisions between those without it, "expresses the point of view of the whole world," offering a source of social renewal and counteracting "cosmic fear" (like that many consider characteristic of postmodernity).[60]

As a renewal simply of belief, carnival, finally, is "not actually directed against institutions," Renate Lachemann points out, "but rather against the loss of utopian potential brought about by dogma and authority." The dogma, the counseling of resignation by authority, is assailed and "dispersed through ridicule and laughter," the dialectic of negation and regeneration. The postmodern accusation that carnival is only authorized transgression, in other words, is moot; the point isn't to escape from or overthrow the organization of power immediately. Even the best of contemporary carnival "ultimately leaves everything as it was before" as far as social institutions go. The music of Green Day and others such as the Riot Grrrls may indeed have only a tenuous (or transient) impact, but that expression of carnival energy nonetheless "offers a permanent alternative to official culture," a lasting, "irrepressible, unsilenceable" example of the possibility of refusing to express oneself only in permitted ways.[61]

At this point we've returned to where I began my book: negation in the tradition of anarchism and the avant-garde, a quest simply to hold open the possibility of refusing to go along with the status quo. Just as Bakhtin describes it, negation actually has a positive, regenerating result, in creating a sense of solidarity and sustenance for everyone angry at the authoritarian conformity that allows the misery of so many to go unchallenged. That anger should include laughter at its own excess not simply because it's the authoritarian who takes himself entirely seriously but also because the prospect of changing the world, however dim it may be, ought to promise pleasure. As Lachemann emphasizes, though, a revolution doesn't have to occur for carnival to be successful. People just have to come together—including at a distance that may even be mass mediated—and rediscover the possibility of refusal, precisely the effect of movements related to popular music like the Riot Grrrls. Much of the angry music at present belongs to the anarchist avant-garde tradition, but the angry girl bands are most exciting because women have hardly even begun to expand on that tradition.

Taken as a metaphor—in terms of the energy of its performance as much as the title's connotations—Bikini Kill's "Carnival" celebrates that beginning. As Kurt Cobain once said, the future of rock belongs to women. And with "women entering as a steady and unstoppable force" into popular music, says Andrea Juno, "they can't help but change the [whole] status quo in as yet unknown ways." [62]

Avant-gardes of this sort persist in the arts because elitist contempt for emotion and popular culture has changed not one iota since the eighteenth century; the anarchist political component of the avant-garde persists, obviously, because authoritarianism continues to run rampant. I also began the book with fairly positive reference to the eighteenth-century Enlightenment, though, and in closing want to draw a distinction in its legacy along these artistic and political lines. We *don't* need the tradition in aesthetics, beginning two centuries ago, of valuing intellectual depth over emotion, an elitist, sexist separation of feelings and reason (affect and ideology, etc.). In politics, on the other hand, we continue to need the Enlightenment belief that we will work things out reasonably, the possibility despaired at by postmodernism, and foreclosed by its complete rejection of the Enlightenment. We shouldn't repudiate Enlightenment optimism—

after all, the first theorist of anarchism, William Godwin, lived in the eighteenth century. George Woodcock, in the survey *Anarchism* (1962), even calls him a "man of reason," a creature of his age, and the best of anarchists, in Godwin's wake, have never rejected social organization along rational lines. Their point, instead, has been that negation in thought and expression, in art and in popular life—a continual questioning of the common wisdom—should be a buttress ensuring that social institutions necessary for the common good remain genuinely democratic.

Rather than repudiating the Enlightenment, the best forms of contemporary anarchism improve on it by insisting on integrating feelings into our understanding of the way reason operates. In *Demanding the Impossible: A History of Anarchism* (1992) Peter Marshall observes that "the continued appeal of anarchism can probably be attributed to its enduring affinity with *both* the rational and emotional impulses lying deep within us. It is an attitude, a way of life as well as a social philosophy." [63] The Situationist International, for example, perhaps the best known of anarchist avant-garde movements, called for "the most thoroughgoing fusion of reason and passion." [64]

To take feelings seriously is fundamental to correcting the problem that has tainted the Enlightenment: the long-standing hypocrisy of excluding so many from sharing in its purportedly universal ideals. The original Enlightenment and its successors justified the exclusion of women and racial minorities, from both politics and the arts, by identifying them with emotionality (or nature, the body, etc.), and white males with reason (or culture, intellect, etc.). To consider emotion and reason interdependent, instead, as the mutual products of social interaction, therefore implies that *everyone* will be included in our attempt to make "something better," to use the phrase scoffed at by postmodernists. We need to believe in the possibility of something better, and have a little faith ("unreasonable" as that sounds) in the energy of our anger at the injustices of the militant plutocracy in which we live. Otherwise, we surrender to the vision of chaos and fragmentation promoted by the multinationals and abetted by the postmodernists.

By way of suggesting what paradigm might replace postmodernism, I want to return to Raymond Williams's observation that the term *postmodern* leaves us stuck in the "post," or at the end of development, belatedly "after" the achievements of modernism (as if modernism was all that happened in the first half of the twentieth century). By the logic Williams criticizes, whatever epochs we perceive after postmodernism can only be labeled by appending more "posts" ad infinitum, beginning with post-postmodernism (a coinage, to reiterate, that I have employed only as an expedient for the moment). If enough people were to decide to escape this trap and replace the postmodern with something better, therefore, the new paradigm should be named with extraordinary care. I wish I could conclude, in the words of the Velvet Underground, that discarding the postmodern would be "the beginning / Of our New Age," but as we've seen, a particularly loopy, regressive version of postmodernism beat me to it. I don't have a suggestion for a label that I can see being either immune to attack or especially catchy and inspirational, and I'm also reluctant to offer one because it would require projecting the course of future events.

A very provisional rubric, befitting my conclusion, would be something like "New Enlightenment"—open to everyone, to every cultural form, and to the undivided experience of the body and mind, nature and culture. I'm not the first person to conclude with this possibility: Patrick Brantlinger, in *Crusoe's Footprints* (1990), and Terry Eagleton, in *The Ideology of the Aesthetic* (1990), both conclude by suggesting a fusion of Jürgen Habermas's and Raymond Williams's theories of communication that aim for the full realization of the Enlightenment project. It is understandably suspect that white males advocate such a position, although as I've pointed out along the way, many feminists as well as national liberation movements around the world continue to feel a need for ideals of freedom, justice, and truth. Advancing a "new, improved" version of anything also invites suspicion because it seems to reproduce the spurious claims of the commodity world treated (however incorrectly) as synonymous with a bleak postmodernity. But no sensible person would argue that anything progressive is going to come from forgetting or rejecting the past or by cultivating into schizophrenia the difficulties of identity and the general historical amnesia at present, as some postmodern theorists advocate. A renaissance is a rebirth, not an event based on completely new resources; the original Renaissance essentially began with a recycling of classical antiquity. So I'll go ahead and say it: Let's have a New Enlightenment—this time with feeling(s).

# Notes

## Introduction

1. Nancy Hartstock, "Foucault on Power: A Theory for Women?" in *Feminism/Postmodernism,* ed. Linda J. Nicholson (New York: Routledge, 1990), 158.

2. Immanuel Kant, *Critique of Judgment,* 1790, trans. J. H. Bernard (New York: Hafner, 1951), 58, 146.

3. Andrew Goodwin, "Popular Music and Postmodern Theory," *Cultural Studies* 5 (1991): 186.

4. Peter Stearns, *American Cool: Constructing a Twentieth-Century Emotional Style* (New York: New York University Press, 1994), 7.

5. PMRC, in Lawrence Grossberg, *We Gotta Get Out of This Place: Popular Conservatism and Postmodern Culture* (New York: Routledge, 1992), 6.

6. Andrea Juno and V. Vale, eds., *Angry Women* (San Francisco: Re/Search, 1991), 5.

7. Stuart Hall, *The Hard Road to Renewal: Thatcherism and the Crisis of the Left* (New York: Verso, 1988), 216-218.

8. Adolph Reed, Jr., "Martyrs and False Prophets," *Progressive,* October 1995, 18, and "Posing as Politics: Youth Culture: Left Behind?" *Village Voice,* 5 December 1995, 20.

9. Simon Frith, *Sound Effects: Youth, Leisure, and the Politics of Rock 'n' Roll* (New York: Pantheon, 1981), 201; Henry A. Giroux, "Beating Up on Kids," *Z Magazine,* July/August 1996, 14-15; Donna Gaines, in *Microphone Fiends: Youth Music and Youth Culture,* ed. Andrew Ross and Tricia Rose (New York: Routledge, 1994), 7; Donna Gaines, "Border Crossing in the U.S.A.," in *Microphone Fiends,* ed. Ross and Rose, 228.

10. Tom Frank, "Scholar's Soft Sell: Cultural Studies' Field Trip to the Mall," *Voice Literary Supplement,* November 1995, 29.

180

11. Jim McGuigan, *Cultural Populism* (New York: Routledge, 1992), 90-91; Herbert I. Schiller, *Culture Inc.: The Corporate Takeover of Public Expression* (New York: Oxford University Press, 1989), 153, 156.

12. Raymond Williams, *The Long Revolution* (Hammondsworth: Penguin, 1965), 63; Dick Hebdige, *Hiding in the Light* (New York: Routledge, 1988), 48.

13. Andrea Juno, *Angry Women in Rock: Volume One* (New York: Juno Books, 1996), 5.

14. Ellen Willis, "When Bad Things Happen to Good Brains," *Village Voice,* 13 June 1995, 8.

15. Michael Bérubé, "Bite Size Theory: Popularizing Academic Criticism," *Social Text* 36 (1993): 95.

16. Peter Lyman, "The Politics of Anger: On Silence, Ressentiment, and Political Speech," *Socialist Review* 11 (1980): 62.

17. June Crawford et al., eds., *Emotion and Gender: Constructing Meaning From Memory* (Newbury Park, CA: Sage, 1992), 183.

18. Catherine A. Lutz, "Engendered Emotion: Gender, Power, and the Rhetoric of Emotional Control in American Discourse," in *Language and the Politics of Emotion,* ed. Lila Abu-Lughod and Catherine A. Lutz (New York: Cambridge University Press, 1990), 81.

19. Valerie Agnew, in Juno, *Angry Women in Rock,* 109.

20. Simon Frith, "Britbeat: I Am What I Am," *Village Voice,* 3 August 1993, 82.

21. Greil Marcus, *Ranters and Crowd Pleasers: Punk in Pop Music* (New York: Doubleday, 1992), 337; Gina Birch, in Amy Raphael, *Grrrls: Viva Rock Divas* (New York: St. Martin's, 1995), 105-106.

22. Hebdige, *Hiding in the Light,* 221.

23. Dennis Cooper, "Grain of the Voice," *Spin,* June 1994, 37.

24. Marcus, *Ranters and Crowd Pleasers,* 350.

25. Simon Frith and Jon Savage, "Pearls and Swine: The Intellectuals and the Media," *New Left Review* 198 (1993): 115.

26. Steve Redhead, *The End-of-the-Century Party: Youth and Pop Towards 2000* (Manchester: Manchester University Press, 1990), 7; Dominic Strinati, *An Introduction to Theories of Popular Culture* (New York: Routledge, 1995), 43.

27. Angela McRobbie, "Shut Up and Dance: Youth Culture and Changing Modes of Femininity," *Cultural Studies* 7 (1993): 408, 422.

28. Mikal Gilmore, "The Road from Nowhere," *Rolling Stone,* 2 June 1994, 46.

29. John Cook, "Dead Again," *New York Press,* 17-23 July 1996, 32.

30. Frith and Savage, "Pearls and Swine," 116.

31. Eric Weisbard, "Revolutionary Debris," *Spin,* June 1994, 40; Kathleen Hanna, in Juno, *Angry Women in Rock,* 87, 93.

32. Dana Polan, "Postmodernism and Cultural Analysis Today," in *Postmodernism and Its Discontents,* ed. E. Ann Kaplan (New York: Verso, 1988), 49; John Clarke, *New Times and Old Enemies: Essays on Cultural Studies and America* (New York: HarperCollins, 1991), 22.

33. Bérubé, "Bite Size Theory," 87-88.

# Chapter 1

1. I came up with this typology of postmodernism on my own some time ago, but I've borrowed some terms from a similar scheme in J. G. Merquior, "Spider and Bee: Towards a Critique of the Postmodern Ideology," in *Postmodernism: ICA Documents,* ed. Lisa Appignanesi (London: Free Association, 1989).

2. Angela McRobbie, "New Times in Cultural Studies," *New Formations* 13 (1991): 5.

3. Sara Cohen, "Ethnography and Popular Music Studies," *Popular Music* 12 (1993): 127; Holly Kruse, "Subcultural Identity in Alternative Music Culture," *Popular Music* 12 (1993): 39.

4. Bruce Robbins, "*Social Text* and Reality," *In These Times*, 8 July 1996, 29.

5. Nina Gordon, in Raphael, *Grrrls*, 87.

6. Rob Wilkie, "Postmodernism as Usual: 'Theory' in the American Academy Today," review of *Theory as Resistance*, by Mas'ud Zavarzadeh and Donald Morton, *Journal of Postmodern Culture* (electronic), 5 (1995): 5.995.

7. Clarke, *New Times and Old Enemies*, 25.

8. Alan Sokal, "Transgressing the Boundaries: Toward a Transformative Hermeneutics of Quantum Gravity," *Social Text* 14 (1996): 217.

9. Hebdige, *Hiding in the Light* (see introd., n. 12), 201; Chantal Mouffe, "Hegemony and New Political Subjects: Toward a New Concept of Democracy," in *Marxism and the Interpretation of Culture*, ed. Lawrence Grossberg and Cary Nelson (Urbana: University of Illinois Press, 1988), 90; Judith Butler, in Alan D. Schrift, "Reconfiguring the Subject as a Process of Self: Following Foucault's Nietzschean Trajectory to Butler, Laclau/Mouffe, and Beyond," *New Formations* 25 (1995): 36.

10. Cohen, "Ethnography and Popular Music Studies," 132; Kwame Anthony Appiah, "Is the Post- in Postmodernism the Post- in Postcolonial?" *Critical Inquiry* 17 (1991): 353.

11. Michel Foucault, *Discipline and Punish: The Birth of the Prison* (New York: Vintage, 1979), 202, 217.

12. Schrift, "Reconfiguring the Subject," 32, 34; Kate Soper, "Forget Foucault?" *New Formations* 25 (1995): 25, 27.

13. Butler, in Schrift, "Reconfiguring the Subject," 37; Steven Connor, *Postmodernist Culture: An Introduction to Theories of the Contemporary* (Oxford: Blackwell, 1990), 234.

14. Hartstock, "Foucault on Power" (see introd., n. 1), 163-164; Dick Hebdige, "The Impossible Object: Towards a Sociology of the Sublime," *New Formations* 1 (1987): 70.

15. Sadie Plant, *The Most Radical Gesture: The Situationist International in a Postmodern Age* (New York: Routledge, 1992), 118-119; Jacques Derrida, in Alex Callinicos, *Against Postmodernism: A Marxist Critique* (Cambridge: Polity, 1989), 78; Jacques Derrida, "Structure, Sign, and Play in the Discourse of the Human Sciences," in *The Structuralist Controversy: The Languages of Criticism and the Sciences of Man*, ed. Richard Mackey and Eugenio Donato (Baltimore: Johns Hopkins University Press, 1972), 250; Jean-François Lyotard, in Plant, *The Most Radical Gesture*, 115.

16. Lyman, "The Politics of Anger" (see introd., n. 16), 61.

17. Jon Schiller, in Fred Pfeil, "Postmodernism as 'Structure of Feeling,'" in *Marxism and the Interpretation of Culture*, ed. Grossberg and Nelson, 389; Donna Haraway, "A Manifesto for Cyborgs: Science, Technology, and Socialist Feminism in the 1980s," in *Coming to Terms: Feminism, Theory, Politics*, ed. Elizabeth Weed (New York: Routledge, 1989), 181-182.

18. Leslie Savan, "Niked Lunch: Ads from the Underground," *Village Voice*, 6 September 1994, 51.

19. Plant, *The Most Radical Gesture*, 111; Michel Foucault, in Callinicos, *Against Postmodernism*, 82 (see also 71, 165-171); Laura Kipnis, "Feminism: The Political Conscience of Postmodernism?" in *Universal Abandon? The Politics of Postmodernism*, ed. Andrew Ross (Minneapolis: University of Minnesota Press, 1988), 162.

20. Kipnis, "Feminism," 151, 156.

21. John McGowan, *Postmodernism and Its Critics* (Ithaca: Cornell University Press, 1991), 68; Ernesto Laclau and Chantal Mouffe, in Kipnis, "Feminism," 151.

22. McGowan, *Postmodernism and Its Critics*, 69, 144; Ian Hunter, "Setting Limits to Culture," *New Formations* 4 (1988): 103-123, and "Aesthetics and Cultural Studies," in *Cultural Studies*,

ed. Lawrence Grossberg, Cary Nelson, and Paula Treichler (New York: Routledge, 1992); Soper, "Forget Foucault?" 24.

23. Kipnis, "Feminism," 150.

24. Editorial, *In These Times,* 8 July 1996, 5.

25. Strinati, *Introduction to Theories of Popular Culture* (see introd., n. 26), 45, 48.

26. John M. Ellis, *Against Deconstruction* (Princeton: Princeton University Press, 1989), 151; Paul De Man, *Blindness and Insight: Essays in the Rhetoric of Contemporary Criticism* (Minneapolis: University of Minnesota Press, 1983), 214.

27. Andrew Goodwin, "Sample and Hold: Pop Music in the Digital Age of Reproduction," in *On Record: Rock, Pop, and the Written Word,* ed. Simon Frith and Andrew Goodwin (New York: Pantheon, 1990), 272.

28. David Simpson, *The Academic Postmodern and the Rule of Literature: A Report on Half-Knowledge* (Chicago: University of Chicago Press, 1995), 2-3, 14.

## Chapter 2

1. George Lipsitz, *Time Passages: Collective Memory and American Popular Culture* (Minneapolis: University of Minnesota Press, 1990), xvi.

2. Linda Hutcheon, *The Politics of Postmodernism* (New York: Routledge, 1989), 1-2, 4; Greil Marcus, *Lipstick Traces: A Secret History of the Twentieth Century* (Cambridge: Harvard University Press, 1989), 239.

3. Fredric Jameson, "Marxism and Postmodernism," *New Left Review* 176 (1989): 32.

4. Strinati, *Introduction to Theories of Popular Culture* (see introd. n. 26), 33.

5. Fredric Jameson, "Postmodernism, or the Cultural Logic of Late Capitalism," *New Left Review* 146 (1984): 56; David Lowery, "Shock Steps between Klein and His Ads," *Austin American-Statesman,* 31 August 1995, sec. A, p. 21.

6. Fredric Jameson, *Marxism and Form: Twentieth-Century Dialectical Theories of Literature* (Princeton: Princeton University Press, 1971), 105.

7. Michel de Certeau, *The Practice of Everyday Life,* trans. Steven Rendall (Berkeley: University of California Press, 1984), 1, 29; Jean Baudrillard, *In the Shadow of the Silent Majorities or, the End of the Social and Other Essays,* trans. Paul Foss, John Johnston, and Paul Patton (New York: Semiotext[e], 1983), 28, 33, 43.

8. Jean Baudrillard, *Simulations* (New York: Semiotext[e], 1983), 138, 148.

9. Redhead, *End-of-the-Century Party* (see introd., n. 26), 44, 46; Simon Frith, "Trash Across the Water," *New York Rocker,* September 1981, 8.

10. Hanna, in Juno, *Angry Women in Rock* (see introd., n. 19), 103.

11. Johan Fornäs, "Listen to Your Voice! Authenticity and Reflexivity in Rock, Rap and Techno Music," *New Formations* 24 (1994): 160-161.

12. Fredric Jameson, "Postmodernism and Consumer Society," in *The Anti-Aesthetic: Essays on Postmodern Culture,* ed. Hal Foster (Port Townsend, WA: Bay Press, 1983), 124, and "Postmodernism, or the Cultural Logic," 87.

13. Howard Hampton, "Dueling Cadavers: Fredric Jameson Buries Modernism, the Mekons Dig Up the Bones," *LA Weekly* 9-15 August 1991, 44; Jameson, "Postmodernism, or the Cultural Logic," 56.

14. Savan, "Niked Lunch," 50-51, and "Own Your Own Mind," *Village Voice,* 13 June 1995, 46.

15. McRobbie, "Shut Up and Dance" (see introd., n. 27), 412.

16. Candice Pedersen, in Juno, *Angry Women in Rock,* 180.

17. Juno, *Angry Women in Rock,* 5.

18. Tom Frank, "Rebel, Rebel," *In These Times,* 14 November 1994, 39, and "Scholar's Soft Sell" (see introd., n. 10), 29; Andrew Goodwin, *Dancing in the Distraction Factory: Music Television and Popular Culture* (Minneapolis: University of Minnesota Press, 1992), 148.

19. Jameson, "Postmodernism and Consumer Society," 124, and "Postmodernism, or the Cultural Logic," 56 (on the Frankfurt School, see "Reification and Utopia in Mass Culture," *Social Text* 1 [1979]: 132-148); Raymond Williams, *The Politics of Modernism: Against the New Conformists* (New York: Routledge, 1989), 35.

20. Bertolt Brecht, *Brecht on Theatre: The Development of an Aesthetic,* trans. John Willett (New York: Hill & Wang, 1964), 101, 162.

21. Max Horkheimer and Theodor Adorno, *Dialectic of Enlightenment,* 1944, trans. John Cumming (New York: Continuum, 1987), 144, 164.

22. Theodor Adorno, "On Popular Music," *Studies in Philosophy and Social Science* 9 (1941): 40-42.

23. Herbert Marcuse, *One-Dimensional Man* (Boston: Beacon, 1964), 61.

24. Kant, *Critique of Judgment* (see introd., n. 2), 148.

25. William Wordsworth, in Martha Woodmansee, *The Author, Art, and the Market: Rereading the History of Aesthetics* (New York: Columbia University Press, 1994), 114-115; Sarah Webster Goodwin, "Wordsworth and Romantic Voice: The Poet's Song and the Prostitute's Cry," in *Embodied Voices: Representing Female Vocality in Western Culture,* ed. Leslie C. Dunn and Nancy A. Jones (Cambridge: Cambridge University Press, 1994), 66-67.

26. Stéphane Mallarmé, "Poetry as Incantation" and "Art as Aristocratic Mystery," in *The Modern Tradition,* ed. Richard Ellmann and Charles Feidelson (New York: Oxford University Press, 1965), 111, 206.

27. Patrick Brantlinger, *Bread and Circuses: Theories of Mass Culture as Social Decay* (Ithaca: Cornell University Press, 1983), 71.

28. Friedrich Nietzsche, "The Death of God and the Antichrist," in *The Modern Tradition,* ed. Ellmann and Feidelson, 909.

29. Friedrich Nietzsche, *On the Genealogy of Morality,* 1887, trans. Carol Diethe (Cambridge: Cambridge University Press, 1994), 21-22, 29-30, 52, 96, 99.

30. Max Scheler, *Ressentiment,* 1915, trans. William W. Holdheim (New York: Free Press, 1961), 76; Nietzsche, *Genealogy of Morality,* 99.

31. Lutz, "Engendered Emotion" (see introd., n. 18), 70; Elizabeth V. Spelman, "Anger and Insubordination," in *Women, Knowledge, and Reality: Explorations in Feminist Philosophy,* ed. Ann Garry and Marilyn Pearsall (Boston: Unwin Hyman, 1989), 267.

32. Adolph Reed, Jr., "Looking Backward," review of *The Bell Curve,* by Richard J. Herrnstein and Charles Murray, *Nation,* 28 November 1994, 654.

33. Nietzsche, *Genealogy of Morality,* 28-30.

34. Gilles Deleuze and Felix Guattari, *Anti-Oedipus,* trans. Robert Hurley, Mark Seem, and Helen R. Lane (Minneapolis: University of Minnesota Press, 1983), 215; Michael André Bernstein, "The Poetics of *Ressentiment,*" in *Rethinking Bakhtin: Extensions and Challenges,* ed. Gary Saul Morson and Caryl Emerson (Evanston: Northwestern University Press, 1989), 201.

35. Gilles Deleuze, *Nietzsche and Philosophy,* 1962, trans. Hugh Tomlinson (New York: Columbia University Press, 1983), 111; Jon Pareles, "Now Is the Summer of Our Discontent," *New York Times,* 25 August 1991, sec. H, p. 20, sec.H, p. 22; Sarah Ferguson, "The Comfort of Being Sad: Kurt Cobain and the Politics of Damage," *Utne Reader,* July/August 1994, 61.

36. Cornel West, "Marxist Theory and the Specificity of Afro-American Oppression," in *Marxism and the Interpretation of Culture,* ed. Nelson and Grossberg, 28, "Ethics and Action in Fredric Jameson's Marxist Hermeneutics," in *Postmodernism and Politics,* ed. Jonathan Arac

(Minneapolis: University of Minnesota Press, 1986), 135, and "Rap it Up," *Voice Literary Supplement,* October 1991, 21; Adorno, "On Popular Music," 42, 44.

37. Adorno, "On Popular Music," 44.

38. Nietzsche, *Genealogy of Morality,* 28-29. On Nietzsche's voluntarism, see Kenneth Asher, "Deconstruction's Use and Abuse of Nietzsche," *Telos* 62 (1984-85):169-78.

39. Michel Foucault, in Schrift, "Reconfiguring the Subject" (see chap. 1, n. 12), 29.

40. Schrift, "Reconfiguring the Subject," 31, 36.

41. Lawrence Grossberg et al., *It's a Sin: Essays on Postmodernism, Politics, and Culture* (Sydney: Power, 1988), 39-43. Cf. Grossberg, *We Gotta Get Out* (see introd., n. 5), 223.

42. Grossberg, *We Gotta Get Out,* 80-81, 83-86.

43. Lawrence Grossberg, "Is There Rock after Punk?" *Critical Studies in Mass Communication* 3 (1986): 54-55.

44. Lawrence Grossberg, "Pedagogy in the Present: Politics, Postmodernity, and the Popular," in *Popular Culture: Schooling and Everyday Life,* ed. Henry A. Giroux and Roger I. Simon (Granby, MA: Bergin and Garvey, 1989), 96.

45. Grossberg, *We Gotta Get Out,* 283.

46. Grossberg, *It's a Sin,* 47, 60.

47. Grossberg, *We Gotta Get Out,* 9, 127, 145, 156, 179, 210, 258, 289.

48. Grossberg, *It's a Sin,* 39.

49. Bernstein, "The Poetics of *Ressentiment,*" 212-213.

50. Grossberg, *We Gotta Get Out,* 198, 265.


# Chapter 3

1. Barry Shank, *Dissonant Identities: The Rock 'n' Roll Scene in Austin, Texas* (Hanover: Wesleyan University Press, 1994), 69, 133-34.

2. Pfeil, "Postmodernism" (see chap. 1, n. 17), 396, 403. See also Fred Pfeil, *Another Tale to Tell: Politics and Narrative in Postmodern Culture* (New York: Verso, 1990).

3. Douglas Coupland, *Generation X: Tales for an Accelerated Culture* (New York: St. Martin's, 1991), 5, 7-8, 13, 59.

4. Pfeil, "Postmodernism," 396.

5. Frank, "Rebel" (see chap. 2, n. 18), 39.

6. Pfeil, "Postmodernism," 399.

7. Anthony DeCurtis, "Introduction: The Sanctioned Power of Rock and Roll," *South Atlantic Quarterly* 90 (1991), 641, and "Kurt Cobain 1967-1994," *Rolling Stone,* 2 June 1994, 34.

8. Daniel Harris, "Make My Rainy Day," *Nation,* 8 June 1992, 792-793; Mark Dery, "Signposts on the Road to Nowhere: Laurie Anderson's Crisis of Meaning," *South Atlantic Quarterly* 90 (1991), 785.

9. Paul Smith, "Playing for England," *South Atlantic Quarterly* 90 (1991), 751.

10. David Shumway, "Rock and Roll as a Cultural Practice," *South Atlantic Quarterly* 90 (1991), 765, 768.

11. Michael Jarrett, "Concerning the Progress of Rock and Roll," *South Atlantic Quarterly* 90 (1991), 814-815.

12. Shumway, "Rock and Roll as a Cultural Practice," 767.

13. Fornäs, "Listen to Your Voice!" (see chap. 2, n. 11), 155, 168-169, 172; Keith Negus, *Producing Pop: Culture and Conflict in the Popular Music Industry* (New York: Edward Arnold, 1992), 62.

14. Stephen Lee, "Re-examining the Concept of the Independent Record Company: The Case of Wax Trax! Records," *Popular Music* 14 (1995), 13-15, 17, 26, 29; Kruse, "Subcultural Identity" (see chap. 1, n. 3), 38.

15. Negus, *Producing Pop,* 15-17.

16. Simon Reynolds, *Blissed Out: The Raptures of Rock* (London: Serpent's Tail, 1990), 101-14.

17. Shumway, "Rock and Roll as a Cultural Practice," 754, 768; Robert Ray, "Tracking," *South Atlantic Quarterly* 90 (1991), 777.

18. Guy Debord, *Comments on the Society of the Spectacle* (New York: Verso, 1988), 6.

19. Jameson, "Reification and Utopia" (see chap. 2, n. 19), 137-138, 140.

20. Horkheimer and Adorno, *Dialectic of Enlightenment* (see chap. 2, n. 21), 143; Elayne Rapping, "TV Guides," *Voice Literary Supplement,* December 1990, 17.

21. Simon Frith, "The Adman's Loop," *Village Voice,* 17 May 1988, 79.

22. Antonio Gramsci, *Selections from the Prison Notebooks,* ed. and trans. Quintin Hoare and Geoffrey Nowell Smith (New York: International Publishers, 1971), 418.

23. Grossberg, *We Gotta Get Out,* 234.

24. Pagan Kennedy, "Generation Gaffe," review of *American Psycho,* by Bret Easton Ellis, *Nation,* 1 April 1991, 427.

25. Grossberg, *We Gotta Get Out* (see introd., n. 5), 215.

26. Bret Easton Ellis, in Grossberg, *We Gotta Get Out,* 186.

27. Jason Cohen and Michael Krugman, *Generation Ecch!* (New York: Fireside, 1994), 11.

28. Grossberg, *We Gotta Get Out,* 168.

29. Redhead, *End-of-the-Century Party* (see introd., n. 26), 41-42, 44, 75-76, 78, 84, 89, 94-95, 103, 105-106.

30. Simon Frith, *Music for Pleasure* (New York: Routledge, 1988), 1, 5-6.

31. Frith and Savage, "Pearls and Swine" (see introd., n. 25), 116.

32. Simon Frith, "Video Pop: Picking Up the Pieces," *Facing the Music,* ed. Simon Frith (New York: Pantheon, 1988), 129-130.

33. Goodwin, "Popular Music" (see introd., n. 3), 176; Tim Brennan, "Off the Gangsta Tip: A Rap Appreciation, or Forgetting about Los Angeles," *Critical Inquiry* 20 (1994): 676.

34. Goodwin, "Popular Music," 176-77, 179-181.

35. Goodwin, "Popular Music," 178, 182. See Jameson, "Reification and Utopia," 140.

36. Brecht, *Brecht on Theatre* (see chap. 2, n. 20), 109-110.

37. Goodwin, *Dancing* (see chap. 2, n. 18), 6, 8-9, 181-182, 187.

38. Franco Moretti, in Goodwin, *Dancing,* 165-166.

39. Houston Baker, *Black Studies, Rap, and the Academy* (Chicago: University of Chicago Press, 1993), 81-82.

## Chapter 4

1. Rachel Felder, *Manic Pop Thrill* (Hopewell, NJ: Ecco Press, 1993), 2, 6.

2. Dave Marsh and Phyllis Pollack, "Wanted for Attitude," *Village Voice,* 10 October 1989, 33-37; Jerry Adler et al., "The Rap Attitude," *Newsweek,* 12 March 1990, 59.

3. Pareles, "Now Is the Summer" (see chap. 2, n. 35), 20, 22, and "The Angry Young Woman," *New York Times,* 28 January 1996, sec. H, p. 24.

4. John Leland, "Welcome to the Jungle," *Newsweek,* 23 September 1991, 52-53.

5. John Leland, "Searching for Nirvana II," *Newsweek,* 30 March 1992, 63. See Pleasant Gehman, "Artist of the Year: Nirvana," *Spin,* December 1992, 53.

6. Karen Schoemer, "A Band That Deals in Apathy," *New York Times,* 27 September 1991, sec. C, p. 30; Michael Lev, "Is Hit Album a Fluke or a Marketing Coup?" *New York Times,* 13 January 1992, sec. D, p. 1. See also Peter Watrous, "Nirvana's 'Nevermind' Is No. 1," *New York Times,* 8 January 1992, sec. C, p. 13; Karen Schoemer, "The Art Behind Nirvana's Ascent to the Top," *New York Times,* 26 January 1992, sec. H, p. 26.

7. Reynolds, *Blissed Out* (see chap. 3, n. 16), 147.

8. Tom Carson, "What We Do Is Secret: Your Guide to the Post-Whatever," *Village Voice Rock & Roll Quarterly,* Fall 1988, 21.

9. Evelyn McDonnell, "Rebel Music," review of *The Sex Revolts: Gender, Rebellion, and Rock 'n' Roll,* by Joy Press and Simon Reynolds, *Village Voice,* 18 July 1995, 67; Kim Gordon, in Kim France, "Angry Young Women," *Utne Reader,* September/October 1992, 24.

10. Reynolds, *Blissed Out,* 135.

11. Simon Reynolds, in Redhead, *End-of-the-Century Party* (see introd., n. 26), 81.

12. David Stubbs, "Fear of the Future," *Zoot-Suits and Second-Hand Dresses: An Anthology of Fashion and Music,* ed. Angela McRobbie (Boston: Unwin Hyman, 1989), 275.

13. Reynolds, *Blissed Out,* 12, 105-106, 112, 114-116, 168.

14. Simon Reynolds, "Boredom + Claustrophobia + Sex = Punk Nirvana," *New York Times,* 24 November 1991, sec. H, p. 34.

15. *Option,* in Dick Dahl, "Is It Only Rock 'n' Roll?," *Utne Reader,* May/June 1992, 43.

16. Reynolds, "Boredom," 34; Neil Strauss, "Has Success Spoiled Green Day?" *New York Times,* 5 February 1995, sec. H, p. 32.

17. Jeff Giles, "You Call This Nirvana?," *Newsweek,* 17 May 1993, 69-70. On the rumors surrounding the production of *In Utero,* see Fred Goodman, "Nirvana to 'Newsweek': Drop Dead," *Rolling Stone,* 24 June 1993, 21; Darcey Steinke, "Smashing Their Heads on the Punk Rock," *Spin,* October 1993, 48.

18. Lisa McLaughlin et al., "Never Mind," *Time,* 18 April 1994, 72.

19. Bobby S. Fred, "How the Game Works," *Maximum Rock 'n' Roll* 133 (1994).

20. Lauren Spencer, "Heaven Can't Wait," *Spin,* January 1992, 32, 34.

21. Jon Pareles, "Nirvana, the Band That Hates to Be Loved," *New York Times,* 14 November 1993, sec. H, p. 32.

22. Nathaniel Wice, "How Nirvana Made It," *Spin,* April 1992, 58.

23. Gina Arnold, "Into the Black," *Spin,* June 1994, 34, 37; on the Sex Pistols, see 40.

24. Steinke, "Smashing Their Heads," 42; Howard Hampton, review of *In Utero,* by Nirvana, *Spin,* October 1993, 99. See also Jonathan Poneman, "Family Values," *Spin,* December 1992, 44-50; Gehman, "Artist of the Year: Nirvana," 51-53.

25. Chris Mundy, "Nirvana," *Rolling Stone,* 23 January 1992, 39-41; Reynolds, "Boredom," 34.

26. Michael Azerrad, "Nirvana: Inside the Heart and Mind of Kurt Cobain," *Rolling Stone,* 16 April 1992, 38-39, 97.

27. Donna Gaines, "Suicidal Tendencies: Kurt Did Not Die for You," *Rolling Stone,* 2 June 1994, 60-61.

28. Dahl, "Is It Only Rock 'n' Roll?" (see chap. 4, n. 15), 42-43.

29. Lorraine Ali, "Kurt Cobain Screamed Out Our Angst," *New York Times,* 17 April 1994, sec. H, p. 28; McLaughlin et al., "Never Mind," 72.

30. Ferguson, "The Comfort of Being Sad" (see chap. 2, n. 35), 62.

31. See Mark Kendall Anderson, "More Than a Trace of Lipstick," *Houston Press,* 19 August 1993, 73.

32. Ferguson, "The Comfort of Being Sad," 60-62; Kurt Cobain, in Pareles, "Nirvana," sec. H, p. 32.

33. Michael Ventura, "The Age of Endarkment: Listening to the Psychic Cacophony of Adolescence," *Utne Reader,* July/August 1994, 65-66.

34. Robert Hilburn, "Year in Rock Proves What a Jungle It Is Out There for Youth," *Austin American-Statesman,* 27 December 1994 (from *Los Angeles Times*), sec. E, p. 7. See Simon Frith, "We Win Again," *Village Voice,* 29 December 1987, 83.

35. Chuck Eddy, review of *Bikini Kill, Rolling Stone,* 4 February 1993, 68.

36. Simon Reynolds, "Belting Out That Most Unfeminine Emotion," *New York Times,* 9 February 1992, sec. H, p. 27; Leland, "Searching for Nirvana II," 63; Simon Reynolds, "Ethereal Girls," *Spin,* April 1992, 57. Nine months after Reynolds's first *Times* article on women in rock, when the explosion of Riot Grrrl groups like Bikini Kill, Bratmobile, and Heavens to Betsy quickly overran Reynolds's slight expectations, the *Times* had to play catch-up with a more positive article, though the writer was only allowed to perform a fairly simple survey. See Ann Japenga, "Punk's Girl Groups Are Putting the Self Back in Self-Esteem," *New York Times,* 15 Nov. 1992, sec. H, p. 30.

37. Tricia Rose, *Black Noise: Rap Music and Black Culture in Contemporary America* (Hanover: Wesleyan University Press, 1994), 134; Brennan, "Off the Gangsta Tip" (see chap. 3, n. 33), 670.

38. Stephen Holden, "How Pop Music Lost the Melody," *New York Times,* 3 July 1994, sec. H, p. 1, sec. H, p. 24.

## Chapter 5

1. Lyman, "The Politics of Anger" (see introd., n. 16), 61.

2. Lutz, "Engendered Emotion" (see introd., n. 18), 78, 80; Peter Middleton, *The Inward Gaze: Masculinity and Subjectivity in Modern Culture* (New York: Routledge, 1992), 179; Crawford et al., *Emotion and Gender* (see introd., n. 17), 21.

3. Willard Gaylin, *The Rage Within: Anger in Modern Life* (New York: Simon & Schuster, 1984), 55.

4. Antonio R. Damasio, *Descartes' Error: Emotion, Reason, and the Human Brain* (New York: Grosset/Putnam, 1994), xii, xiv, xvi; Gaylin, *The Rage Within,* 50.

5. Middleton, *The Inward Gaze,* 181.

6. Carol Tavris, *Anger: The Misunderstood Emotion* (New York: Touchstone, 1989), 264, 271-272.

7. Norbert Elias, "On Human Beings and Their Emotions: A Process-Sociological Essay," in *The Body: Social Process and Cultural Theory,* ed. Mike Featherstone et al. (Newbury Park, CA: Sage, 1991), 124. See also Cas Wouters, "On Status Competition and Emotion Management: The Study of Emotions as a New Field," *Theory, Culture & Society* 9 (1992), 229-252.

8. Stearns, *American Cool* (see introd., n. 4), 267, 272, 280-281, 287.

9. Lila Abu-Lughod and Catherine A. Lutz, "Introduction: Emotion, Discourse, and the Politics of Everyday Life" (see introd., n 18), *Language and the Politics of Emotion,* ed. Abu-Lughod and Lutz, 6, 9, 14-15; Lutz, "Engendered Emotion," 72, 77, 87.

10. Anne Cvetkovich, *Mixed Feelings: Feminism, Mass Culture, and Victorian Sensationalism* (New Brunswick, NJ: Rutgers University Press, 1992), 1-2, 28, 39.

11. Carol Z. and Peter Stearns, *Anger: The Struggle for Emotional Control in America's History* (Chicago: University of Chicago Press, 1986), 226; Stearns, *American Cool,* 3.

12. Sebastian Timpanaro, *On Materialism* (London: New Left Books, 1970), 50; Stearns, *Anger,* 5, 7.

13. Soper, "Forget Foucault?" (see chap. 1, n. 12), 27.

14. Susan Bordo, in Soper, "Forget Foucault?" 22.

15. Terry Eagleton, "It is not quite true that I have a body, and not quite true that I am one either," *London Review of Books*, 27 May 1993, 7-8.

16. Adalaide Morris, "The Body Politic: Body, Language, and Power," *College English* 52 (1990), 571-573; Soper, "Forget Foucault?" 23-24.

17. Scott Lash, "Genealogy and the Body: Foucault/Deleuze/Nietzsche," in *The Body: Social Process and Cultural Theory*, ed. Featherstone et al., 259; Sally Banes, *Writing Dancing in the Age of Postmodernism* (Hanover: Wesleyan University Press, 1994), 46-47.

18. Ronald de Sousa, in Middleton, *The Inward Gaze*, 189.

19. Stearns, *Anger*, 6.

20. Middleton, *The Inward Gaze*, 179-180.

21. Elaine Showalter, *A Literature of Their Own: British Women Novelists from Brontë to Lessing* (Princeton: Princeton University Press, 1977), 35; Patricia Meyer Spacks, *The Female Imagination* (New York: Alfred A. Knopf, 1975), 30, 321.

22. Toril Moi, *Sexual/Textual Politics: Feminist Literary Theory* (New York: Routledge, 1985), 8, 40, 62-63.

23. Jane Flax, "Postmodernism and Gender Relations in Feminist Theory," *Signs* 12 (1987), 632; Kipnis, "Feminism" (see chap. 1, n. 19), 154, 164.

24. Flax, "Postmodernism and Gender," 632.

25. Olivia Frey, "Beyond Literary Darwinism: Women's Voices and Critical Discourse," *College English* 52 (1990), 507. See Jane Tompkins, "Me and My Shadow," *New Literary History* 19 (1987), 169-178.

26. Jane Tompkins, "A Short Course in Post-Structuralism," *College English* 50 (1988), 737, 740.

27. Julia LeSage, "Women's Rage," in *Marxism and the Interpretation of Culture*, ed. Nelson and Grossberg, 421-422.

28. Alison M. Jaggar, "Love and Knowledge: Emotion in Feminist Epistemology," in *Gender/Body/Knowledge: Feminist Reconstructions of Being and Knowing*, ed. Alison M. Jaggar and Susan Bordo (New Brunswick, NJ: Rutgers University Press, 1989), 159-161.

29. Spelman, "Anger and Insubordination" (see chap. 2, n. 31), 267.

30. Lyman, "The Politics of Anger," 59, 66.

31. Morwenna Griffiths, "Feminism, Feelings, and Philosophy," in *Feminist Perspectives in Philosophy*, ed. Morwenna Griffiths and Margaret Whitford (Bloomington: Indiana University Press, 1988), 132-133.

32. Spelman, "Anger and Insubordination," 263-264, 270-271.

33. Miranda Fricker, "Reason and Emotion," *Radical Philosophy* 57 (1991), 17-18.

34. Lyman, "The Politics of Anger," 66-67, 69-71.

35. Fricker, "Reason and Emotion," 19; Naomi Scheman, "Anger and the Politics of Naming," in *Women and Language in Literature and Society*, ed. Sally McConnell-Ginet et al. (New York: Praeger, 1980), 176, 180; Lyman, "The Politics of Anger," 68.

36. Terry Eagleton, *The Ideology of the Aesthetic* (Cambridge, MA: Blackwell, 1990), 207.

37. Middleton, *The Inward Gaze*, 167.

38. Griffiths, "Feminism, Feelings, and Philosophy," 140, 146; Middleton, *The Inward Gaze*, 211; Crawford et al., *Emotion and Gender* (see introd., n. 17), 115.

# Chapter 6

1. Terry Lovell, in Graeme Turner, *British Cultural Studies: An Introduction* (Boston: Unwin Hyman, 1990), 222.

2. Christopher Norris, *Deconstruction: Theory and Practice* (New York: Routledge, 1982), 28-29.

3. Deleuze and Guattari, *Anti-Oedipus* (see chap. 2, n. 34), 203, 205; Deleuze and Guattari, in Grossberg, *We Gotta Get Out* (see introd., n. 5), 154.

4. de Certeau, *Practice of Everyday Life* (see chap. 2, n. 7), 132, 163-164; Theodor Adorno, in Barbara Engh, "Adorno and the Sirens: Tele-phonographic Bodies," in *Embodied Voices,* ed. Dunn and Jones (see chap. 2, n. 25), 128.

5. Kaja Silverman, *The Acoustic Mirror: The Female Voice in Psychoanalysis and the Cinema* (Bloomington: Indiana University Press, 1988), 43-44.

6. Susan McClary, *Feminine Endings: Music, Gender and Sexuality* (Minneapolis: University of Minnesota Press, 1991), 153; Barbara Bradby, "Sampling Sexuality: Gender, Technology, and the Body in Dance Music," *Popular Music* 23 (1993), 157.

7. Rita Felski, *Beyond Feminist Aesthetics: Feminist Literature and Social Change* (Cambridge, MA: Harvard University Press, 1989), 156; Lawrence Grossberg, in Philip Tagg, "From Refrain to Rave: The Decline of Figure and the Rise of Ground," *Popular Music* 13 (1994), 211; Tagg, "From Refrain to Rave," 212.

8. Silverman, *The Acoustic Mirror,* 79-80.

9. Leslie C. Dunn and Nancy A. Jones, eds., *Embodied Voices,* 1-2, 9. See 4, 53-55, 128 for prominent references to Silverman, Barthes, and Kristeva.

10. Fornäs, "Listen to Your Voice!" (see chap. 2, n. 11), 171-172; Crawford et al., *Emotion and Gender* (see introd., n. 17), 122.

11. Richard Johnson, "What Is Cultural Studies Anyway?," *Social Text* 16 (1986/1987), 63, 69.

12. Peter Middleton, "Vanishing Affects: The Disappearance of Emotion from Postmodernist Theory and Practice," *New Formations* 12 (1990), 133.

13. V. N. Volosinov, *Marxism and the Philosophy of Language,* trans. Ladislav Matekja and I. R. Titunik (Cambridge, MA: Harvard University Press, 1986), 103-104; Mikhail Bakhtin, *The Dialogic Imagination,* ed. and trans. Caryl Emerson and Michael Holquist (Austin: University of Texas Press, 1981), 163, 259, 263, 273.

14. Walter Benjamin, *The Origin of German Tragic Drama,* trans. John Osborne (London: Verso, 1985), 233-234.

15. Raymond Williams, *Marxism and Literature* (New York: Oxford University Press, 1977), 132-133, 154, 156, and *Politics of Modernism* (see chap. 2, n. 19), 74-75; Terry Eagleton, *Walter Benjamin or Towards a Revolutionary Literary Criticism* (London: New Left Books, 1981), 124.

16. Bérubé, "Bite Size Theory" (see introd., n. 15), 89.

17. Williams, *Marxism and Literature,* 125.

18. Brecht, *Brecht on Theatre* (see chap. 2, n. 20), 101; Williams, *Marxism and Literature,* 132-133.

19. Flax, "Postmodernism and Gender," 632, 637.

20. Crawford et al., *Emotion and Gender* (see introd., n. 17), 181.

21. Dunn and Jones, eds., *Embodied Voices,* 2-3.

22. Simon Frith, "High Signs," *Village Voice,* 7 June 1994, 80.

23. Karen Offen, "Defining Feminism: A Comparative Historical Approach," *Signs* 14 (1988), 152.

24. Henry A. Giroux and Roger I. Simon, "Popular Culture as a Pedagogy of Pleasure and Meaning," in *Popular Culture: Schooling and Everyday Life,* ed. Giroux and Simon (see chap. 2, n. 44), 17.

25. Lipsitz, *Time Passages* (see chap. 1, n. 2), 132.

26. Greil Marcus, "Critical Response," *Critical Studies in Mass Communication* 3 (1986), 79; Frith, *Music for Pleasure* (see chap. 3, n. 30), 120.

27. Greil Marcus, "Who Put the Bomp in the Bomp De-Bomp De-Bomp?," in *Rock and Roll Will Stand,* ed. Greil Marcus (Boston: Beacon, 1969), 20-21.

28. Jonathan Cott and Sue Clark, "Mick Jagger," in *The Rolling Stone Interviews* (New York: Paperback Library, 1971), 163.

29. Marcus, *Lipstick Traces* (see chap. 2, n. 2), 7-8.

30. Dave Marsh, review of "This is England," by the Clash, *Nation,* 27 December 1986/3 January 1987, 747; Greil Marcus, "A Singer and a Rock and Roll Band," in *Rock and Roll Will Stand,* ed. Marcus, 93.

31. Aidan Day, *Jokerman: Reading the Lyrics of Bob Dylan* (Cambridge, MA: Blackwell, 1989), 1-2, 6, 9, 26, 51, 110.

32. Hebdige, *Hiding in the Light* (see introd., n. 12), 54.

33. Day, *Jokerman,* 95, 121, 123; Wilfrid Mellers, "New Music in a New World," in *The Age of Rock: Sounds of the American Cultural Revolution,* ed. Jonathan Eisen (New York: Vintage, 1969), 182-183.

34. Peter Wicke, *Rock Music: Culture, Aesthetics and Sociology,* trans. Rachel Fogg (New York: Cambridge University Press, 1990), ix, 25-26, 181.

35. Robert Christgau, "Rock Lyrics Are Poetry (Maybe)," in *The Age of Rock,* ed. Eisen, 233-234.

36. Day, *Jokerman,* 2-3, 5.

37. Lipsitz, *Time Passages,* 102.

38. Susan McClary and Robert Walser, "Start Making Sense! Musicology Wrestles with Rock," in *On Record,* ed. Frith and Goodwin (see chap. 1, n. 27), 288-289.

39. Robert Walser, *Running with the Devil: Power, Gender, and Madness in Heavy Metal Music* (Hanover: Wesleyan University Press, 1993), 31-32.

40. Brennan, "Off the Gangsta Tip" (see chap. 3, n. 33), 672-673.

41. Walser, *Running with the Devil,* 30.

# Chapter 7

1. Fred Pfeil, "Sympathy for the Devils: Notes on Some White Guys in the Ridiculous Class War," *New Left Review* 213 (1995), 122-123.

2. Barbara Ehrenreich, "Playing Rambo," *Z Magazine,* July/August 1995, 7-8.

3. Gordon, in France, "Angry Young Women" (see chap. 4, n. 9), 24.

4. Joanne Gottlieb and Gayle Wald, "Smells Like Teen Spirit: Riot Grrrls, Revolution and Women in Independent Rock," in *Microphone Fiends,* ed. Ross and Rose (see introd., n. 9), 261-262.

5. Plant, *The Most Radical Gesture* (see chap. 1, n. 15), 85.

6. Felski, *Beyond Feminist Aesthetics* (see chap. 6, n. 7), 174, 181.

7. Pfeil, "Postmodernism" (see chap. 1, n. 17), 384.

8. Sandy Carter, "Courtney Love & Liz Phair," *Z Magazine,* Nov. 1994, 68; Huggy Bear, in Raphael, *Grrrls* (see introd., n. 21), 150.

9. Charles Aaron, "A Riot of the Mind," *Village Voice,* 2 February 1993, 63.

10. Dana Nasrallah, "Teenage Riot," *Spin,* November 1992, 81.

11. Aaron, "A Riot of the Mind," 63.

12. Crawford et al., *Emotion and Gender* (see introd., n. 17), 189; Felski, *Beyond Feminist Aesthetics,* 168.

13. Hanna, in Juno, *Angry Women in Rock* (see introd., n. 19), 89, 101; Juno, *Angry Women in Rock,* 5; Pedersen, in Juno, *Angry Women in Rock,* 177; Gottlieb and Wald, "Smells Like Teen Spirit," 253; Ann Powers, in Raphael, *Grrrls,* xxxiii.

14. Japenga, "Punk's Girl Groups" (see chap. 4, n. 36), sec. H, p. 30.

15. Ellen Willis, in Evelyn McDonnell, "The Feminine Critique: The Secret History of Women and Rock Journalism," *Village Voice Rock & Roll Quarterly,* Fall 1992, 8.

16. Simon Frith and Angela McRobbie, "Rock and Sexuality," in *On Record,* ed. Frith and Goodwin (see chap. 1, n. 27), 377, 384.

17. Gottlieb and Wald, "Smells Like Teen Spirit," 252-253, 225-256, 268.

18. Carola Dibbell, "Better with Age," review of The Raincoats, *Looking in the Shadows, Village Voice,* 21 May 1996, 52.

19. Marcus, in Anderson, "More Than a Trace of Lipstick" (see chap. 4, n. 31), 73; Carter, "Courtney Love & Liz Phair," 68; Ann Powers, "When Women Venture Forth," *New York Times,* 9 October 1994, sec. H, p. 32; Juno, *Angry Women in Rock,* 4; Elizabeth Wurtzel, "Girl Trouble," *New Yorker,* 29 June 1992, 70.

20. Sandy Carter, "Women, Guitars, and Rebellion," *Z Magazine,* May 1993, 52.

21. Stephanie Engels, in Pfeil, "Postmodernism," 396.

22. Gottlieb and Wald, "Smells Like Teen Spirit," 265, 270-271.

23. Hanna, in Juno, *Angry Women in Rock,* 99-100.

24. Chrissie Hynde, in Juno, *Angry Women in Rock,* 199; Courtney Love, in Raphael, *Grrrls,* 14; Liz Phair, in Raphael, *Grrrls,* 225.

25. Hanna, in Juno, *Angry Women in Rock,* 86, 99; Agnew, in Juno, *Angry Women in Rock,* 108.

26. Wurtzel, "Girl Trouble," 63; Powers, "When Women Venture Forth," sec. H, p. 32.

27. Louise Post, in Raphael, *Grrrls,* 94.

28. Powers, "When Women Venture Forth," sec. H, p. 39.

29. Courtney Love, in Kim France, "Grrrls at War," *Rolling Stone,* 8-22 July 1993, 24; Love, in Raphael, *Grrrls,* 12.

30. Kathleen Hanna, in Wurtzel, "Girl Trouble," 70.

31. McDonnell, "Rebel Music" (see chap. 4, n. 9), 68.

32. Gottlieb and Wald, "Smells Like Teen Spirit," 257-258.

33. Georgia Christgau, in McDonnell, "The Feminine Critique," 9; Will Straw, in Bradby, "Sampling Sexuality" (see chap. 6, n. 6), 162.

34. Christgau, in McDonnell, "The Feminine Critique," 9.

35. Dunn and Jones, eds., *Embodied Voices* (see chap. 6, n. 9), 5.

36. Aaron, "A Riot of the Mind," 66.

37. Marcus, in Anderson, "More Than a Trace of Lipstick," 73.

38. Hanna quoted in Juno, *Angry Women in Rock,* 85, 89-90.

39. Kathleen Hanna, "Jigsaw Youth," *Jigsaw* Spring 1991, in Liner Notes, *The C.D. Version of the First Two Records,* Kill Rock Stars KRS/204.

40. Hanna, in Juno, *Angry Women in Rock,* 96.

41. Hutcheon, *The Politics of Postmodernism* (see chap. 2, n. 2), 93-95, 152-54, 168.

42. Juno, *Angry Women in Rock,* 200.

43. Gottlieb and Wald, "Smells Like Teen Spirit," 266.

44. Hanna, "Jigsaw Youth," CD version.

45. Aaron, "A Riot of the Mind," 66.

46. Hanna, "Jigsaw Youth," CD version.

47. Mikhail Bakhtin, *Rabelais and His World,* trans. Hélène Iswolsky (Bloomington: Indiana University Press, 1984), 19.

48. Robert Stam, *Subversive Pleasures: Bakhtin, Cultural Criticism, and Film* (Baltimore: Johns Hopkins University Press, 1989), 86, 95; Natalie Davis, in Mary Russo, "Female Grotesques," *Feminist Studies/Critical Studies,* ed. Teresa de Lauretis (Bloomington: Indiana University Press, 1986), 215.

49. Bakhtin, *Rabelais and His World,* 9,11, 15-16.

50. Stam, *Subversive Pleasures,* 92.

51. Robert Stam, "Mikhail Bakhtin and Left Cultural Critique," in *Postmodernism and Its Discontents,* ed. Kaplan (see introd., n. 32), 137.

52. Umberto Eco, in Stam, *Subversive Pleasures,* 91.

53. Stam, *Subversive Pleasures,* 89-90.

54. Bakhtin, *Rabelais and His World,* 5, 10, 27, 37-38, 46.

55. Bikini Kill, in Japenga, "Punk's Girl Groups," sec. H, p. 30.

56. Stam, "Mikhail Bakhtin and Left Cultural Critique," 139.

57. Mikhail Bakhtin, *Dialogic Imagination* (see chap. 6, n. 13), 163, 273.

58. Bakhtin, *Rabelais and His World,* 17, 21, 23.

59. Gina Arnold, "Making Green Day," *Reverb,* 8-14 December 1995, 4.

60. Bakhtin, *Rabelais and His World,* 12, 28.

61. Renate Lachemann, "Bakhtin and Carnival: Culture as Counter-Culture," *Cultural Critique* 11 (1988/89), 125, 130.

62. Juno, *Angry Women in Rock,* 5.

63. Peter Marshall, *Demanding the Impossible: A History of Anarchism* (London: HarperCollins, 1992), xv.

64. Raoul Vaneigem, *The Revolution of Everyday Life,* trans. Donald Nicholson-Smith (London: Left Bank Books/Rebel Press, 1983), 183.

# Index

# About the Author

Neil Nehring is Associate Professor of English at the University of Texas at Austin, where he has taught since 1986. His first book, *Flowers in the Dustbin: Culture, Anarchy, and Postwar England* was published in 1993 by the University of Michigan Press. He has published articles on the avant-garde, cultural studies, popular music, and twentieth-century English literature and popular culture in journals such as *American Literary History, Australian Journal of Communication, Discourse, LIT,* and *PMLA.*

Printed in the United Kingdom
by Lightning Source UK Ltd.
102747UKS00002B/91-96